THE PEOPLE'S VOICE

THE
PEOPLE'S VOICE

The Orator in American Society

BARNET BASKERVILLE

THE UNIVERSITY PRESS OF KENTUCKY

LIBRARY OF CONGRESS CATALOGING IN PUBLICATION DATA

Baskerville, Barnet.
   The people's voice.

   Includes bibliographical references and index.
   1. Oratory — United States — History. I. Title.
PN4055.U5B33   815'.01   79-4001
ISBN 0-8131-1385-7

Scholarly publisher for the Commonwealth,
serving Berea College, Centre College of Kentucky,
Eastern Kentucky University, The Filson Club,
Georgetown College, Kentucky Historical Society,
Kentucky State University, Morehead State University,
Murray State University, Northern Kentucky University,
Transylvania University, University of Kentucky,
University of Louisville, and Western Kentucky University.

Editorial and Sales Offices: Lexington, Kentucky 40506

For Laura and Bob,
and especially for Jo

CONTENTS

Some observations on a form of effort which has absorbed a good deal of the talent of the nation, seem properly to belong to an account of its intellectual life.

JAMES BRYCE, "American Oratory,"
in *The American Commonwealth*

INTRODUCTION

To be a perfect and consummate orator is to possess
the highest faculty given to men.
SENATOR GEORGE F. HOAR

Whin a man has something to say an' don't know how
to say it, he says it pretty well. Whin he has something to say, an knows how to say it, he makes a
gr-reat speech. But whin he has nawthin' to say, an'
has a lot iv wur-ruds that come with a black coat, he's
an orator.
"Mr. Dooley" (FINLEY PETER DUNNE)

The words *oratory* and *eloquence* are not frequently on the tongues
of contemporary Americans. For some the terms have an
amusingly archaic sound, like *methinks* or *eftsoons*. In our time one
seldom accuses a politician of oratory without humorous or derogatory intent; a public man, finding himself referred to in the
newspapers as an "orator," is probably justified in regarding the
characterization as pejorative. When Senator Margaret Chase
Smith spoke out courageously against abuse of congressional im-
munity during the McCarthy era, she began her now famous "Declaration of Conscience" with these words: "I speak as simply as
possible because the issue is too great to be obscured by eloquence."[1] No one mistook her meaning. The subject, she was saying, is too serious for wordy obfuscation.

A century earlier, Senator Smith's statement would have puzzled an American political audience. Then eloquence was a quality
universally admired and zealously coveted. Speakers might fall
short in practice, but the ideal was always there — beckoning with
rich personal satisfactions and public rewards. American journals
published with remarkable frequency articles entitled simply
"Oratory" or "Eloquence." In 1851, just one hundred years before
Senator Smith's steadfast refusal to resort to eloquence, a popular
journal declared that "eloquence . . . is beyond all question the

greatest exertion of the human mind. It requires for its conception a combination of the most exalted faculties; for its execution, a union of the most extraordinary powers."[2] At about the same time America's distinguished man of letters Ralph Waldo Emerson, who earlier had written of his "passionate love for the strains of eloquence," was delighting audiences with his lecture on "Eloquence," which he defined as "the power to translate a truth into language perfectly intelligible to the person to whom you speak" — a conception in striking contrast to that implied by Senator Smith.

What may appear to be a mere change in usage actually suggests a significant change in attitude. The current widespread distrust of the political speaker, the frequently expressed contempt for "mere rhetoric," may cause us to forget that throughout the greater part of our history as a nation the orator was chief among American folk heroes. In the late eighteenth and nineteenth centuries our countrymen engaged in spirited discussions of what was the most eloquent speech ever given and who was the greatest orator of this or some other nation in much the same way as twentieth-century Americans argue about the most skillfully executed double play, the most exciting runback of a kickoff, or whether Joe Louis could have knocked out Muhammad Ali. Oratory was an integral part of all great celebrations. The arrival of a great orator in town was a splendid occasion, and his speech the subject of comment for days afterward. Debates among congressional giants packed the galleries of Senate and House, and legends clustered about the chief participants. And after the Civil War, although contemporary orators were seldom lionized in the same way, writers and speakers repeated and supplemented the old legends, recollected with pride the heroes of a former day, and confidently predicted the imminence of another golden age.

It has frequently been asserted that Americans have traditionally displayed a keen appetite for oratory. Wendell Phillips contended that as soon as a Yankee baby could sit up in his cradle, he called the nursery to order and proceeded to address the house. "If there ever was a country where eloquence was a power," Emerson exclaimed in one of his lectures on the subject, "it is the United States." "The American people have always been ardent admirers of genuinely great oratory," said Warren C. Shaw in introducing his *History of American Oratory* in 1928. The theme is reiterated endlessly by essayists, biographers, historians, and especially by anthologists of speeches, who predictably introduce their collections with such statements as: "The love of oratory is inherent in Americans," or "In no other country have orators and oratory played so conspicuous a part in shaping public affairs, as in America."

It is this latter theme, the part played by oratory in shaping public affairs, that has occupied greatest attention in the past. The error of many enthusiastic commentators on oratory has been that they have dwelt unduly upon the influence of the orator, picturing him as a cosmic traffic cop, standing at the crossroads of history, directing the flow of events. Historians, often aware of more potent influences, have sometimes tended to underplay the role of rhetoric in public affairs. Striking evidence of the influence of individual orators can undoubtedly be found; Hitler, Mussolini, Churchill, and Roosevelt are perhaps the most obvious recent examples. But the study of oratory is more than a study of influence. The orator is at once engine and mirror; not only can he provide the impetus toward what he feels should be, he can also reflect (often unconsciously) what is. Since his success at persuasion depends in part upon an accurate assessment of existing states of mind, he gives expression directly or indirectly to ideas and attitudes prevalent at the time.

The conception of speeches as vehicles of ideas current in society is of course not a new one. Subjects repeatedly taken to the public platform and discussed in the public forum are presumably matters of interest to both speaker and audience; hence biographers and historians have long regarded speeches as indexes to the mind of the audience as well as of the speaker. A history of the Civil War period without reference to the speeches of Abraham Lincoln is as inconceivable as an account of America's late nineteenth-century adventure in imperialism which ignores the speeches of Albert J. Beveridge, William Jennings Bryan, and Theodore Roosevelt. Indeed, speeches (and pamphlets, their written equivalents) are the chief sources of insight into certain periods of the American past. John Adams's familiar words, spoken in 1816, "I would have these orations collected and printed in volumes, and then write the history of the last forty-five years in commentaries upon them," may have overstated the case, but a modern American historian, Daniel Boorstin, has observed, "We can find few nations whose oratory can bring the student so close to their history." In the spirit of John Adams, Boorstin suggests that it would be possible to compile a complete American history which would present "the substance of what is now taught in our public school courses in history" through a series of well-chosen public speeches.[3]

The present volume advances the thesis that societal values and attitudes are reflected not only in what the speaker says but also in how he says it — not only in the ideas and arguments to be found in speeches of the past but in the methods and practices of representative speakers and in the role and status accorded speakers by the listening public. As public tastes and public needs change, so do speaking practices — types of appeal, verbal style, modes of delivery. I propose here to examine the connections, the reciprocal relationships, between the emphases, enthusiasms, preoccupations of a given age and the nature of the speaking heard from the public platform. My principal concern is not with the appraisal of individual orators, but with the orator and his art, and with audiences and eras as determinants of the orator's role. When individual speakers are mentioned, as they frequently are, it is to illustrate a generalization. To the disappointed reader who finds here no mention of his favorite American orators, it must be pointed out that my purpose is not to review all the speakers and speeches of a given period, but to delineate central tendencies, to illustrate chief distinguishing characteristics.

This book is not a history of oratory, a systematic chronicle of speakers and speeches. Rather, it is an inquiry into American attitudes toward orators and oratory and the reflection of these attitudes in speaking practices. Attention will sometimes be focused more upon the audience than upon the speaker or his message. What was the nature and importance of oratory as perceived by audiences and by the speakers themselves? What kinds or qualities of oratory were dominant at a given time? What role did the speaker play; what public position did he occupy? What has been the public image of the orator during the two centuries of our history as a nation, and what can an examination of this image tell us about the people who created it? That it has been a continually changing image is obvious. Not only have speakers been variously regarded during different eras, but they have been subject to dramatically different evaluations by different elements in the population during the same historical period. I shall propose possible reasons for these differing appraisals and perceptions.

William E. Gladstone, the British orator-statesman, expressed the intimate relationship between speechmaking and society in this way:

> [The work of the orator] from its very inception, is inextricably mixed up with practice. It is cast in the mould offered to him by the mind of his hearers. It is an influence principally received from his audience (so to speak) in vapour, which he pours back upon them in a flood. The sympathy and concurrence of his time is with his own mind joint parent of his work. He cannot follow nor frame ideals; *his choice is to be what his age will have him, what it requires in order to be moved by him, or else not to be at all.*[4]

Gladstone goes too far; the orator both follows and frames ideals. But he must always be a product of his times, creature as well as shaper of the circumstances in which he is placed. Cognizant of what his age would have him be, he must accommodate to (while attempting to influence) the tastes, values, and expectations of those to whom he speaks.

In tracing the changing public image of the orator, therefore, I shall comment upon changes in society. Since speech practices have their roots in social needs and expectations, judgments about practices — and ultimately practice itself — change as society and social institutions change. Where a certain kind of oratory is valued, it will flourish; when it ceases to be valued, it will change or cease to exist. The value we assign to an activity is likely to determine the quantity and quality of the product.

A word about terminology. Since *orator* and *oratory* are commonly encountered in the early literature under examination, I shall use them, as they were then used, without the embellishment of quotation marks and without derogatory intent. Later, I shall call attention to a tendency to distinguish between oratory and public speaking. Then the term *oratory* was used to designate a particular kind of public discourse. To some it became an opprobrious term referring to speech characterized by labored periods, gaudy verbal embellishments, and ostentatious histrionic display. To others, it meant speaking of genuine distinction and literary artistry which, alas, was beyond the reach of the mere "public speaker" who, like many of his auditors, lacked the imagination and cultivation to achieve or even to appreciate great art. The terms *eloquence* and *oratory* are frequently used interchangeably; for example, an article on "Oratory" is later reprinted in an anthology of speeches under the title "Eloquence." Nevertheless, *eloquence* is more properly regarded as a quality of speaking or writing — a quality that defies precise definition and is more readily recognized than described. Rhetorician George Campbell stressed appropriateness to purpose and situation ("Eloquence is the art by which a discourse is adapted to its end"). Others emphasize felicity of expression or "literary" quality; to Governor John P. Altgeld "literary excellence is the very breath of eloquence." The most common conception of eloquence seems to be that of a judicious mixture of reason and emotion — "impassioned reasoning" or "logic on fire." *Eloquence,* like *oratory,* is employed as a term of derision as well as of praise.

Finally, I shall not take all oratory (or public speaking) as my province; some limitation is necessary. Henry Jephson, in his important work *The Platform: Its Rise and Progress,*[5] suggests some serviceable boundaries: "Every political speech at a public meeting, excluding those from the Pulpit, and those in Courts of Justice, comes within the meaning of 'the Platform.' " This work (with the single exception of my discussion of the Revolutionary period) will follow Jephson in excluding specific consideration of pulpit and courtroom speaking, but its scope will not be restricted to political speaking alone.

&1&
THE REVOLUTIONARY PERIOD
The Orator as Hero

> Our epoch of revolutionary strife was a strife of
> ideas: a long warfare of political logic; a succession of
> annual campaigns in which the marshalling of argu-
> ments not only preceded the marshalling of armies,
> but often exceeded them in impression upon the
> final result.
>
> MOSES COIT TYLER

> Then patriotism is eloquent; then self-devotion is
> eloquent. The clear conception, outrunning the de-
> ductions of logic, the high purpose, the firm resolve,
> the dauntless spirit, speaking on the tongue, beaming
> from the eye, informing every feature, and urging
> the whole man onward, right onward to his object,
> — this, this is eloquence; or rather it is something
> greater and higher than all eloquence, it is action,
> noble, sublime, god-like action.
>
> DANIEL WEBSTER

The opening chapter of most chronicles of American oratory is
traditionally devoted to the orators of the American Revolution.
Of this band of spokesmen against British tyranny (actual or anticipated) only a few names survive in the memory of their countrymen: Patrick Henry, certainly; James Otis, Samuel and John
Adams, probably; and John Hancock — though remembered
perhaps more for his signature than his eloquence. But a host of
others, once-celebrated orators such as Josiah Quincy, Joseph Warren, Richard Henry Lee, William Henry Drayton, John Rutledge,
Jonathan Mayhew, Charles Chauncy, Samuel Cooper, Jacob Duché
— if recognized at all, evoke only the vaguest of associations.

The speeches have proved even more ephemeral than the
speakers. No stenographer took down the hundreds of spirited
addresses delivered to Boston town meetings by Samuel Adams
and his colleagues. No adequate record remains of the debates in
the Continental Congress preceding the adoption of the Declaration of Independence. And the most famous revolutionary speech

of all, Henry's "Call to Arms," preserved in dozens of anthologies and declaimed by generations of schoolboys, had to be reconstructed nearly half a century after the event by a man who had never heard Patrick Henry speak.

Indeed, one of the most remarkable things about revolutionary speakers and speeches is how very little we really know about them. Indicative of the paucity of extant materials is the fact that Rufus Choate's famous oration, "The Eloquence of Revolutionary Periods," while dwelling at length upon the oratory of Greece, Rome, and Ireland, makes only passing reference to the American Revolution. Speaking of the congressional debate on independence, he says: "Of that series of spoken eloquence all is perished; not one reported sentence has come down to us." When early in the nineteenth-century Hezekiah Niles committed himself to the task of collecting revolutionary speeches and papers, he immediately regretted his decision. "The patriots of the revolution," he discovered, "did not make speeches to be unattended by their brethren in Congress and fill up the columns of newspapers. They only spoke when they had something to say, and preferred *acting* to *talking* — very unlike the legislators of the present time." After examining a cartload of books, turning thousands of pages without profit, he concluded: "Of this I am satisfied, that very few of the 'soul-stirring' speeches of the revolutionary period remain to warm the hearts of a grateful posterity; they were pronounced to be *heard,* not *published.*"[1]

Still, we are not completely without clues to the nature and importance of revolutionary speaking. From letters, diaries, and memoirs of the participants, from eulogies, early efforts at biography, and popular anecdotes of forensic triumphs, we can learn something of the role played by the speaker, as well as of the tastes, expectations, and responses of those who listened.

We know, in the first place, that Niles was right when he said that these speeches were pronounced to be heard, not published. These speakers were intent not upon creating great literature for posterity but upon changing minds, intensifying attitudes and opinions, arousing men to action. Aesthetics, conscious artistry, were subordinated to energy and intensity of feeling. Daniel Webster, in his eulogy on Adams and Jefferson, captured the spirit of the time. The eloquence of Mr. Adams, he said, "was bold, manly and energetic; and such the crisis required." "When public bodies are to be addressed on momentous occasions, when great interests are at stake and strong passions excited," Webster asserted, "clearness, force, and earnestness are the qualities which produce conviction." Perhaps of no other time in our history could Webster's famous words be more accurately spoken: "True eloquence . . . does not consist in speech. It cannot be brought from far. Labor and learning may toil for it, but they will toil in vain. . . . It must exist in the man, in the subject, and in the occasion." In our revolutionary period extraordinary men achieved eloquence by dealing in very practical ways with vital subjects on momentous occasions.

It has been observed that all modes of expression, written and spoken, tended to be "rhetorical" in nature in that they sought to work definite persuasive effects, sought not primarily to delight but to motivate. A polemic spirit pervaded the literature of the day. It is perceived not only in speeches and political pamphets where it might be expected but also in letters, in the poetry and prose of such writers as Francis Hopkinson, John Trumbull, and Philip Freneau, in political and military songs, and even in drama. Moses Coit Tyler describes the literature of the American Revolution as "a literature of strife" — combative, argumentative, appealing, retaliatory. More than most revolutionary periods, he believes, "our epoch of revolutionary strife was a strife of ideas: a long warfare of political logic; a succession of annual campaigns in which the marshalling of arguments not only preceded the marshalling of armies, but often exceeded them in impression upon the final result."[2]

It is quite clear that Americans at the time were conscious of being involved in a battle of ideas and principles in which writers and speakers confronted the forces of tyranny and oppression. The imagery of warfare became common long before Patrick Henry forsook the figure of speech and issued his literal "Call to Arms" from the old church in Richmond, Virginia. John Dickinson, author of the celebrated "Letters from a Farmer in Pennsylvania," in a letter written to Samuel Adams in 1773 referred to himself as "a man pressed into the service of my country by a sense of duty to her" and said he meant to maintain his post only "till a better soldier could come completely armed to defend it."[3] When Elias Magoon wrote his book on *Orators of the American Revolution,* he titled his opening chapter "The Battlefields of Early American

Eloquence." He wrote not of the battlefields of Lexington, Bunker Hill, or Yorktown, but of the places where "Otis, Henry and Adams struggled on the rostrum, and pleaded with a price set upon their heads, while they cleared a space for the sunshine and growth of enlarged liberty." His catalog included the Liberty Tree in Boston, rallying point for the Sons of Liberty, to whose trunk were tacked anonymous calls to resist and from whose branches effigies of the enemy were suspended; the old Boston State House, where "unrighteous taxation was combatted and true ground won"; Faneuil Hall, "Cradle of Liberty," where battle strategy was hatched; Hanover County courthouse, where Patrick Henry vanquished the Parsons; the Virginia House of Burgesses, from which was launched a campaign against the Stamp Act; the Richmond church which rang with the cry of "liberty or death." And "the most glorious battle-field of all," Independence Hall in Philadelphia, headquarters of the Congress of 1776, which Magoon thought more evocative of significant sentiments than the plains of Marathon. "Collisions with a mightier foe, and deeds of daring put forth for richer conquests, took place there, than when heroic Greeks grappled with the Persian host."

Thus the orator of the revolutionary period was perceived as a soldier of liberty. In this era of vast energy and activity, eloquence was bold, fervent, activist. Orators, no less than soldiers in the field, were heroes, splendid inspiring figures. The emphasis was on action; these men were fighting battles, challenging an enemy, winning victories. To participants, witnesses, and recorders of these scenes the later distinction between the vigorous man of action and the impotent man of words — he who spoke because incompetent to act — was not frequently made. The speaker was an actor. Webster put it forcefully in his eulogy of Adams and Jefferson: In times of crisis, when the firm resolve, the dauntless spirit speaks on the tongue, beams from the eye, urging the whole man forward, eloquence at its finest is "ACTION — NOBLE, SUBLIME, GODLIKE ACTION."

Given the tumultuous tenor of the times, it is not strange that so few of the words spoken were recorded. What we know of the orators of that day we learn primarily through contemporary accounts of the effects they wrought upon listeners, rather than of the words they spoke. These accounts, though in many cases romanticized and exaggerated, reveal, as well as the techniques of the speaker, the susceptibility of audiences to certain kinds of appeals, the aspects of oratory which were most admired, and hence most worth reporting.

The three most famous orators of the American Revolution, Samuel Adams, James Otis, and Patrick Henry, are known to us chiefly through reports of the effects they had on their contemporaries. Of the speeches of Samuel Adams only fragments remain. We know he was an effective agitator, one of the most powerful leaders in Boston. His kinsman John Adams says he made a strong impression on his auditors. But he left no model speeches for subsequent admiration and declamation. We must rely for the most part on the testimony of his auditors and on such brief items as this one from a South Carolina newspaper in September 1776: "A very artful speech made at Philadelphia by Samuel Adams (who is esteemed by all as one of the most subtle men in the Congress) to a very numerous body of the citizens, militia, &c., has almost irritated them to madness against Great Britain, and made them resolve to conquer or die in the cause they have espoused."[4]

The case of James Otis, whose fame as an orator rests largely upon his speech against the Writs of Assistance in 1761, is similar. The extant version of this speech, which occupied more than four hours in delivery, was reconstructed from a few pages of notes taken by John Adams. Adams recalled in later years that "Otis was a flame of fire," that he "hurried everything away before him," that he rendered his audience "ready to take up arms against Writs of Assistance." There seems no doubt that Otis elicited wild enthusiasm when he spoke, but his reputation for eloquence is sustained by tradition rather than by a precise record of his utterance.

From the most famous orator of the three, Patrick Henry, we have not a single speech manuscript. We are told that with terrible invective he chilled the blood of those in attendance at the trial of the Parsons, that the jury was stampeded into a verdict after a moment's deliberation, and that he was borne from the courtroom on the shoulders of an enthusiastic multitude. There are stories of his electrifying eloquence in introducing the Stamp Act resolutions and tales of his delighting, cajoling, and dominating juries in innumerable court trials. But except for the reconstructed "Liberty or Death" speech and incomplete records of the Virginia ratifying convention in 1788, we are ignorant of the composition of the speeches by which he achieved these remarkable effects.

It is indisputable that the claim of these men to be ranked with the great orators rests largely on tradition, but this is not to say that the tradition is wholly without foundation. We need not believe, for example, that Henry cried out to the Virginia House of Burgesses in 1765, "If this be treason, make the most of it" (a subsequently discovered eyewitness report indicates that he was much more conciliatory in his remarks), or that in a single speech he swayed the jury in the Hanover County courthouse to vote against damages for the Reverend James Maury (they were probably sympathetic to the speaker's point of view from the start), to accept the reports of the wondrous effects of these speeches upon those who heard them and upon subsequent events. The results of Henry's Stamp Act resolutions are generally conceded to have been far-reaching throughout the Colonies, and the same French traveler whose eyewitness account of the events of May 30, 1765, tempered William Wirt's romantic version of the "Treason" speech acknowledged that there was much praise of "the Noble Patriot Mr. henery" and that "the whole Inhabitants say publiqly that if the least injury was offered to him they'd stand by him to the last drop of their blood."[5] Nor was such admiration limited to the impressionable multitude. Thomas Jefferson, who was present during the Stamp Act speech, pronounced Henry's talents as a public orator "such as I have never heard from any other man" and said that on this occasion "He appeared to me to speak as Homer wrote." George Mason, a judicious observer, thought Henry in 1774 "by far the most powerful speaker I have ever heard." And Silas Deane of Connecticut, in a letter to his wife from the first Continental Congress, called him "the completest speaker I ever heard . . . . I can give you no idea of the music of his voice, or the high-wrought yet natural elegance of his style and manner."

Reports of this nature are too numerous to be dismissed. They serve as convincing testimonials to the power of orators and at the same time as indexes to public taste. Evidence abounds of a widespread sensitivity to spine-tingling appeals from the platform. Audiences of the day responded to the oratory of personal ascendancy; they thrilled to the personal triumphs of the hero who spoke in words of fire. Reminiscences of those who took the trouble to commit them to paper emphasize the dramatic aspects of delivery and visible reactions of auditors. Moments of crisis apparently seldom failed to bring forward men of talent who could satisfy the popular appetite for eloquent speech.

There are, however, two important exceptions to our generalization regarding the paucity of authentic manuscripts. Two genres of revolutionary oratory were carefully recorded and preserved: the annual orations commemorating the Boston Massacre and the signing of the Declaration of Independence, and the political sermons of the patriot clergy.

The tragic altercation between British troops and citizens of Boston took place March 5, 1770. When a lone sentry was taunted and pelted with rocks and snowballs, a squad of soldiers under a Captain Preston was sent to his aid. Under circumstances that have never become completely clear, the soldiers, goaded beyond endurance, fired into the mob, killing or fatally wounding five men. A subsequent trial, in which the soldiers were courageously defended by two patriot lawyers, John Adams and Josiah Quincy, resulted in acquittal on the charge of murder. But the potentialities for effective propaganda were quickly seized upon by such firebrands as Samuel Adams and Joseph Warren; the affair became known as "the bloody massacre," and arrangements were made to commemorate the occasion with an annual oration designed to remind Americans of "the danger of standing armies stationed in populous cities in time of peace." For many years thereafter these annual celebrations served their intended purpose of exacerbating animosity toward Great Britain. As David Ramsay put it, they fueled the fire of liberty and "kept it burning with an incessant flame." In 1783 commemoration of the Boston Massacre was superseded by a celebration on July fourth of the declaration of national independence, and the tradition of an annual oration was continued unbroken.

One indication of the importance attributed to these orations is the fact that each was published in pamphlet form and given wide circulation. John Adams reported that they were read by nearly everyone who could read — "and scarcely ever with dry eyes." Moreover, they were zealously preserved through reprinting by those conscious of their historical significance and today remain among the few authentic records of revolutionary speechmaking. In 1785 all Boston Massacre orations from 1771 to 1783 were republished in book form by Peter Edes, a Boston printer. In a preface addressed "to the Inhabitants of the Town of Boston," Edes, observing that many of the original pamphlets were no longer available, presented his collection as an answer to contemporary criticism that Americans had been careless about preserving records of the period. "Many of these Orations," he stated, "have been considered as the sentiments of this metropolis, from time to time, touching the revolution, and as our earliest public invectives against oppression."[6] Also included in this volume is a eulogy by Perez Morton of Boston Massacre orator Joseph Warren, slain at Bunker Hill, and a poem on the massacre by James Allen, reprinted here "to convince the British that true classical English poetry may be produced in other parts of the world, as well as in their own little island."

Peter Edes's little volume is found today only in rare book collections, but his foresight in preserving these speeches made it possible for Hezekiah Niles to reprint the entire collection in his *Principles and Acts of the Revolution in America*, published in 1822. Subsequent anthologists and biographers have drawn upon Niles for examples of revolutionary eloquence. Elias Magoon, seeking representative passages to illustrate his sketches of Warren and Hancock in *Orators of the American Revolution* (1848), found himself limited to a few excerpts from their March 5 orations. The complete texts of the Warren and Hancock addresses are reproduced in Frank Moore's *American Eloquence* (1857) as the sole examples of the speaking of these men. In 1852 James Spear Loring provided a valuable supplement to collections of the speeches themselves in his *Hundred Boston Orators*, a series of biographical sketches of publicly appointed orators from 1770 to 1852. The list includes, in addition to the Boston Massacre orators from 1771 to 1783, a host of Fourth of July orators and eulogists over a period of eighty years.

Toward the end of the nineteenth century, Henry Hardwicke, a New York lawyer, wrote a *History of Oratory and Orators* "from the earliest dawn of Grecian civilization down to the present day." The staggering scope of this enterprise permitted Hardwicke to devote only a few pages to oratory of the American Revolution. But before a brief discussion of Henry and Otis, he presented excerpts from the Boston Massacre orations of Warren and Hancock "in order to exhibit the style of oratory prevalent in those days." Hardwicke in making use of materials most easily available was, of course, making a virtue of necessity, for it is unlikely that the style prevalent in those days is actually exhibited in such passages as this: "Let this sad tale of death never be told without a tear; let not the heaving bosom cease to burn with a manly indignation at the relation of it through the long tracts of future time. . . . Dark and designing knaves, murderers, parricides! How dare you tread upon the earth which has drunk the blood of slaughtered innocence, shed by your hands? How dare you breathe that air which wafted to the ear of heaven the groans of those who fell a sacrifice to your accursed ambition?" Surely it was not with such stilted sentences that Samuel Adams moved a Boston town meeting to action. Certainly neither a Henry, an Otis, a Quincy, nor a Lee ever established a reputation for blood-chilling eloquence with effusions like these.

Indeed, the modern reader finds it incredible that the Boston Massacre orations should have had the effects attributed to them. There is to us something artificial and contrived in the act of assembling once a year to rekindle old hatreds. We are wearied by the speakers' repeated professions of unworthiness and inability to perform their assigned task and by their tedious excursions into history, ancient and modern. And when they reach the point in their remarks where they must depict "that unequaled scene of horror," the bloody details of "that distressful night," they seem to vie with one another in tearing a passion to tatters. There is, it is true, at least one suggestion that even at the time the judicious were inclined occasionally to grieve. Of Warren's oration on March 5, 1775, in which he conjured up the vision of a return to the horrid scene, and cautioned infant babes to take heed, "lest, whilst your streaming eyes are fixed on the ghastly corpse, your feet slide on the stones bespattered with your father's brains," it was reported that "he was applauded by the mob, but groaned at by the people of understanding." Still, this report appeared in *Rivington's Gazette* a Tory journal; most accounts of these occasions have quite a different tone. Even the decorous John Adams, who successfully defended the accused British soldiers and who often expressed disapproval of oratorical excess, seems to have approved of these annual orations. After hearing Hancock in 1774 he wrote in his diary: "An elegant, a pathetic, a spirited performance. A vast crowd, rainy eyes, &c. The composition, the pronunciation, the action, all exceeded the expectations of everybody. They exceeded even mine, which were very considerable."[7]

Years later, in an often quoted letter to Jedediah Morse, he reflected upon these orations and the incident which they commemorated. He regarded the battle of King Street, on the fifth of March 1770, as important as the battle of Lexington or Bunker Hill. Of the orations he observed: "There are few men of consequence among us who did not commence their career by an oration on the 5th of March." Of the forty-five orations delivered since 1771, he said he had read as many as he had seen. Noting a change in theme from "standing armies" to "feelings which produced the revolution," he expressed dissatisfaction with certain of the later variety: "Young gentlemen of genius describing scenes they never saw, and descanting on feelings they never felt, and which great pains had been taken that they never should feel." He thought them "infinitely more indicative of the feelings of the moment, than of the feelings that produced the revolution." It was in this context that Adams made his famous comment that were he fifty years younger, and had he nothing better to do, he would have these orations collected and write the history of the last forty-five years in commentaries upon them.[8]

Grateful though we must be to Peter Edes and Hezekiah Niles for saving these authentic revolutionary documents from oblivion, we are left with the conviction that (with one possible exception yet to be discussed) the greatest oratory of the time perished after utterance and must forever be known to us at second hand through the subjective reactions of those who felt its power. If the texts of Boston Massacre orations appear not to sustain a tradition of heroic orators with the power to make the blood run cold and the hair to stand on end, we shall do well to recall that these were ceremonial addresses presented to audiences already convinced. Their primary function was ritualistic rather than persuasive. If they were received with enthusiastic applause and "rainy eyes," as we have reason to believe they were, a partial explanation may be found in an observation made by John Adams in another connection. After hearing himself described on completion of a minor court case as "equal to the greatest orator that ever spoke in Greece or Rome," Adams confided to his diary: "What an advantage it is to have the passions, prejudices, and interests of the whole audience in a man's favor! These will convert plain common sense into profound wisdom, nay, wretched doggerel into sublime heroics."[9]

If the orations delivered annually on the fifth of March have about them something of the smell of the lamp, one genre of revolutionary oratory of which numerous examples remain is alive with the argumentative, combative spirit of the times. Unquestionably the political sermons of the patriot clergy of New England constitute the richest source for documenting the speaking of the period. These were set speeches, carefully prepared to deal with issues of the moment, and usually delivered from manuscript. Hundreds of these sermons were printed in pamphlet form at public expense and widely distributed, some going through several printings. They may be reread today as orginally printed or as collected in such volumes as J. W. Thornton's *The Pulpit of the American Revolution* (1860) and Frank Moore's *The Patriot Preachers of the American Revolution* (1862).

It is understandable that the clergy should have been the leading purveyors of the spoken word in the intense propaganda battle which preceded armed conflict. Since church was the most potent social institution in eighteenth-century America, the pulpit was at the center of colonial life as the chief source of information, instruction, and inspiration. The preacher was a leader in the community, respected and revered. A religious people acknowledged his role as interpreter of the will of God. His utterances carried divine authority, whether he spoke of sacred or secular matters — and the two were much more closely allied than they are today. John Quincy Adams later emphasized this closeness of religion to politics when he asserted that "the highest glory of the American Revolution was this: it connected in one indissoluble bond, the principles of civil government with the principles of Christianity." The role of the preacher and his potential for reinforcing a secular message by divine sanction were never more convincingly described than by a Loyalist, Judge Daniel Leonard, who wrote with some bitterness in 1774 of "our dissenting ministers": "When the clergy engage in a political warfare, religion becomes a most powerful engine, either to support or overthrow the state. What effect must it have had upon the audience, to hear the same sentiments and principles, which they had before read in a newspaper, delivered on Sundays from the sacred desk, with a religious awe, and the most solemn appeals to Heaven, from lips, which they had been taught from their cradles to believe could utter nothing but eternal truths!"[10]

But their influence was not limited to "Sundays from the sacred desk"; the revolutionary clergy had manifold opportunities for persuasion during the week, some afforded by firmly established institutions reaching back to the early seventeenth century, others improvised for the purpose of enunciating revolutionary principles. For more than a hundred years clergymen had been expected, in addition to preaching two sermons on Sunday, to deliver a Thursday lecture, a spring election sermon, annual Fast and Thanksgiving Day sermons, as well as sermons at public hangings. From the early 1770s to the end of the war, various governing bodies such as the Virginia House of Burgesses, the Massachusetts Congress, and the Continental Congress made it a practice to set aside special days of thanksgiving and prayer which provided further opportunities for politico-religious sermons declaring the right of resistance to unauthorized power. That the British understood the purpose and the effectiveness of such occasions is evidenced by the opposition of General Gage on one occasion to a day of fasting and prayer on the ground that "the request was only to give an opportunity for sedition to flow from the pulpit." After the convening of the Continental Congress, the Provincial Congress of Massachusetts urged the clergy to advise strict obedience to its directives and to "make the question of the rights of the colonies and the oppressive conduct of the mother country a topic of the pulpit on week days."[11]

As Daniel Leonard observed, these pronouncements on a variety of occasions by the patriot clergy owed much of their persuasiveness to the fact that they seemed to bestow divine approval upon sentiments read in the newspapers and heard at town meetings. Much was being spoken and written on the subject of "natural law" and "natural rights." To the clergy, natural law was part of God's law; certain rights had been bestowed by God and were not to be given up. God ruled men by a kind of "divine constitution," a fundamental law that even governments and kings were obliged to obey. Against this touchstone the laws and acts of men might be measured. If found to violate the fundamental law, they could be declared, as it were, "unconstitutional" and disregarded — since it was a Christian duty to resist the exertion of unlawful power. This line of reasoning impelled the Reverend John Cleaveland to brand British General Gage "a wicked Rebel," since he had allegedly violated fundamental law. This line of reasoning also seemed to laymen to give religious sanction to their grievances against unjust taxation and infringements upon civil liberties.

With the exception of occasional hortatory passages, these sermons of the American Revolution tend to be systematic arguments, rather than rousing exhortations. The language is forthright, energetic, unadorned, often disarmingly colloquial. There are few purple passages suitable for quotation or declamation. Beginning with a biblical text, the minister often set forth a series of propositions or topics, linked them to his text, and then developed his sermon from these heads. The arguments are presented with the orderly explicitness of a lawyer's brief. The thought is aligned, the parts laced together, with such transition statements as: "This leads me to show . . .," "But this will appear still more clear if . . .," "From these premises, the following is a natural conclusion," "I proceed therefore to prove. . . . Then, I argue that. . . ." The pervasive forensic tone, created in part by formal devices like these, enhances the clarity of the discourse and makes a strong intellectual appeal.

But there were emotional appeals as well. There could have been no dozing in the pews of the Second Baptist Church of Boston when the Reverend Isaac Skillman delivered his "Oration upon the Beauties of Liberty." In words strikingly reminiscent of Patrick Henry's speech on the Stamp Act resolutions, Skillman inquired: "For violating the people's rights, Charles Stewart, King of England, lost his Head, and if another King, who is more solemnly bound than ever Charles Stewart was, should tread in the same steps, what can he expect?" The king, said Skillman, "can have no more right to America, than what the people have by compact invested him with, which is only a power to protect them, and defend their rights civil and religious: and to sign, seal, and confirm, as their steward, such laws as the people of America shall consent to." "Stand up as one man for your liberty," he urged, "Stand alarm'd, O ye Americans."[12]

A device certain to have had a strong persuasive effect upon audiences familiar with the Bible and responsive to its teachings was the ingenuity manifested by the clergy in selecting texts so astonishingly appropriate that often they seemed to speak directly to current issues and events. The best known sermon of Dr. Jonathan Mayhew of Boston is "The Snare Broken," delivered after the repeal of the Stamp Act on the text, "Our soul is escaped as a bird from the snare of the fowlers; the snare is broken, and we are escaped." After the Boston Massacre, sermons were preached on the text "The voice of thy brother's blood cryeth unto me from the ground." A sermon on the battle of Lexington and Concord by the Reverend William Stearns took for its text "Cursed be he that keepeth back his sword from blood," a biblical reference which was apparently used frequently in sermons to artillery companies. In 1783 Dr. David Tappan, later professor of divinity at Harvard, celebrated the ratification of the peace treaty with a sermon on a text from Psalms, "The Lord hath done great things for us, whereof we are glad."

Testimony as to the effectiveness of the clergy as revolutionary propagandists is to be found in the statements of both friends and foes. Their cooperation was solicited by patriot politicians and their seditious influence denounced by those loyal to Britain. Diaries and letters contain frequent entries commenting on the activities of ministers. Writing to his wife from Philadelphia in July 1775, John Adams inquired concerning his pastor in Braintree: "Does Mr. Wibird preach against oppression and the other cardinal vices of the times? Tell him the clergy here of every denomination, not excepting the Episcopalian, thunder and lighten every Sabbath. They pray for Boston and the Massachusetts. They thank God most explicitly and fervently for our remarkable successes. They pray for the American army." That same month, another representative to the Continental Congress, Silas Deane, told his wife in a letter of hearing "two elegant war sermons."[13]

Others understandably took a different view of this kind of preaching. A letter published in *Rivington's Gazette* excoriates ministers of the gospel "who, instead of preaching to their flocks meekness, sobriety, attention to their different employments, and a steady obedience to the laws of Britain, belch from the pulpit liberty, independence, and a steady perseverance in endeavoring to shake off their allegiance to the mother country. The independent ministers have ever been, since the first settling of this colony, the instigators and abettors of every persecution and conspiracy." The lieutenant governor of Massachusetts, Thomas Hutchinson, wrote to a friend in 1770 of the attempts of the clergy, through their prayers and preaching, to inflame the minds of the people. He tells of the prayer of one minister at an Artillery Election Sermon that the people might have a martial spirit and be instructed in military discipline so as to be able to defend themselves against their oppressors. "Our pulpits," wrote Hutchinson, "are filled with such dark covered expressions and the people are led to think they may as lawfully resist the King's troops as any foreign enemy." Hutchinson may have had reason to resent the clergy. Earlier, at the time of the resistance to the Stamp Act, a mob had looted and destroyed his beautiful home. On the following morning one of the rioters had confessed to having been incited to participation by a sermon he had heard from Dr. Jonathan Mayhew on the previous Sunday. Mayhew, horrified at the charge that his sermon had led to such an act of savagery, wrote Hutchinson, "I had rather lose my right hand, than be an encourager of such outrages as were committed last night."[14]

So prominent in the list of orators of the American Revolution were the names of such clergymen as Jonathan Mayhew, Isaac Skillman, Samuel Stillman, Charles Chauncy, Samuel Cooke, John Cleaveland, and Samuel Cooper that it has been necessary to include pulpit speaking during this period. No depiction of the revolutionary orator as a heroic man of action could possibly omit mention of the patriot clergy. Their status in the community placed them in a commanding position to influence the thoughts and actions of a God-fearing people. Like the secular orators, soldiers of liberty (James Otis called them the "black regiment" and welcomed their assistance), they brought to the battle of ideas the sanctions of religion, enlisting the Lord in the patriot cause. One hundred years after the Declaration of Independence, in a speech pleading for the salvation of Boston's Old South Meeting House, then facing demolition, Wendell Phillips implored: "Let these walls stand, if only to remind us that, in those days, Adams and Otis, advocates of the newest and extremest liberty, found their sturdiest allies in the pulpit; that our Revolution was so much a crusade that the Church led the van."[15]

Most revolutionary orators seem to have cared little about perpetuating their names or reputations in history; their speaking was purposive, utilitarian, directed primarily toward solution of immediate problems or persuasion of an audience rather than personal aggrandizement. Richard Henry Lee left no speech manuscripts. Patrick Henry preserved no letters or speeches; among the few papers left at his death were his will, a copy of his Stamp Act resolutions, and a brief statement describing the occasion of their presentation. James Otis, in the madness of his final years, burned all his papers, including an unpublished treatise on "The Rudiments of Greek Prosody." Samuel Adams, presumably to avoid incrimination of his friends, destroyed bundles of letters.

Opinions of later generations have been molded in large part by writers of the early nineteenth century. Drawing upon the voluminous correspondence of prominent participants, upon diaries, anecdotal material, newspaper accounts, the memories of long-lived eyewitnesses, and sometimes upon their own imaginations, these writers perpetuated, and frequently embellished, legends of glorious oratorical triumphs. Through their efforts a few revolutionary figures have been enshrined in the national Valhalla, while others, possibly as important in their own time, remain neglected and virtually unknown.

Our early national period may be seen in retrospect as a time of searching for a national identity, for establishing symbols of a glorious past to inspire a still more glorious future. The Fourth of July was an appropriate day of national celebration providing opportunities to invoke public recollection of the Declaration of Independence, Bunker Hill, the Liberty Bell, and the Constitution. Prefaces to anthologies and biographies strongly emphasized a patriotic motive. The extent to which the War of 1812 revived old enthusiasms is reflected in Niles's preface to his *Principles and Acts of the Revolution in America*. Niles tells of receiving a letter in 1816 suggesting that he collect and print a volume of revolutionary speeches. In the opinion of the correspondent, "the feelings and sentiments of '76 were never so prevalent as at present. . . . the events of the late war have imparted a glow of national feeling for every thing republican. . . . *What better impression can we make than by rendering the opinions and conduct of our fathers familiar?*" In preparing the volume, Niles solicited the cooperation of those "zealous to catch a spark from the altar of '76, and prepared to enter into the spirit of past times."

An important aspect of the effort to establish a national identity was the creation of national heroes. The story of how Parson Weems laid the foundations for a Washington legend is well known. Somewhat less familiar is the press-agentry of William Wirt in behalf of Patrick Henry.

Wirt was a prominent lawyer and orator who served as counsel for the prosecution in the trial of Aaron Burr and who was appointed attorney general of the United States by President Monroe. Wirt first achieved literary notice with his "Letters of the British Spy," a series of sketches on various topics (the chief of which was eloquence) and portraits of contemporary speakers, which first appeared in 1803 in the *Argus* of Richmond, Virginia, and later went through numerous editions in book form. The remarkable success of this work stimulated his interest in biography. "Do not be astonished," he wrote to his friend Dabney Carr in 1804, "if you see me come out with a very *material* and splendid life of some departed Virginian worthy, — for I meddle no more with the *living*" — a wry reference to the fact that some portraits in *British Spy* had aroused local enmity. "Virginia has lost some great men, whose names ought not to perish. If I were a Plutarch, I would collect their lives for the honor of the State and the advantage of posterity."[16] Wirt's original plan to write the lives of eminent Virginians — Patrick Henry, Edmund Pendleton, Richard Henry Lee, and others — was cut short by the demands of his professional life; the Henry biography was the only one he managed to complete.

The seriousness and dedication with which Wirt approached his task are revealed in his correspondence for the next few years. As early as 1805, immediately after having conceived the project, he wrote to Judge Tucker asking for authentication of an anecdote concerning Henry's alleged fondness for Livy. Since Tucker had frequently heard Henry, and Wirt himself had not, he also asked the judge to sketch as minutely as possible

> a portrait of his person, attitudes, gestures, manners; a description of his voice, its tone, energy, and modulations; his delivery, whether slow, grave and solemn, or rapid, sprightly and animated; his pronunciation, whether studiously plain, homely, and sometimes vulgar, or accurate, courtly and ornate, — with an analysis of his mind, the variety, order, and predominance of its powers; his information as a lawyer, a politician, a scholar; the peculiar character of his eloquence, &c, &c, for I never saw him. These minutiae, which constitute the most interesting part of biography, are not to be learnt from any archives or records, or any other source than the minute and accurate details of a very uncommon observer.[17]

In 1810 Wirt wrote to Thomas Jefferson, asking him "to throw together . . . such incidents touching Mr. Henry as may occur to you." In subsequent correspondence with Jefferson, Wirt enclosed substantial segments of the manuscript, which were returned with revisions, corrections, and expressions of approval. Other letters express a concern for historical accuracy and tell of submitting the manuscript "to several old gentlemen, Mr. Jefferson, Mr. Roane, Mr. Tucker, and two or three others." As the book neared completion Wirt wrote to his friend Francis Gilmer: "The honorable Thomas has given me some flattering encouragement. I can see, however, that he regards my book, rather as panegyric than history," adding poignantly that Jefferson had vetoed most of his favorite passages "as being too poetical for sober narrative."[18]

Repeatedly during the dozen years in which the book was in progress Wirt complained in letters to friends of the difficulties of his task. To Judge Carr he wrote in exasperation, "I can tell you, sir, that it is much the most oppressive literary enterprise that ever I embarked in." And again, a few months later, "As for Patrick — he is the very toughest subject that I ever coped withal." His depression could not have been relieved by a letter from Judge Tucker, with whom he frequently corresponded on the project, declaring that biography in Virginia was a hopeless undertaking — particularly biography of an orator who left no speeches. Listing a number of men once held in high esteem but no longer remembered, Tucker added: "The truth is, that Socrates himself, would pass unnoticed and forgotten in Virginia, if he were not a *public* character, and some of his speeches preserved in a newspaper." It is regrettable, thought the judge, that great men should be forgotten, "But so it is, my friend" — unless they leave their works behind them.[19]

Finding himself without literary remains to work with, Wirt found it necessary to create some. The "Liberty or Death" speech which he reconstructed for his book was to become the most familiar utterance of the revolutionary period and perhaps the best-known piece of secular prose in American English, with the possible exception of Lincoln's Gettysburg Address. That speech did for Patrick Henry what Weems's cherry tree story did for George Washington. Yet it must not be supposed that the speech, like the story, was entirely a figment of the biographer's imagination. Wirt, by his own admission, was not above using "plaster of paris" to cement the gaps in his narrative, but unlike Weems, in this instance he took great pains to render his account as authentic as the materials allowed. In 1887 Moses Coit Tyler, distinguished literary historian of the American Revolution, wrote a biography of Henry for the *American Statesmen* series, which served as a corrective to Wirt's romantic narrative. Although Tyler is highly critical of Wirt, he finds no fault with his treatment of this particular speech. After an examination of the evidence, Tyler concludes that although Wirt does not reveal his source, his account contains the substance of what Henry actually said on this occasion. Three eyewitness reports reinforce parts of the Wirt version: all quote the "Liberty or Death" passage; and one, by St. George Tucker, contains a passage in almost the exact language used by Wirt. It is Tyler's belief that Wirt gathered testimony from all available living witnesses and then from such sentences as these witnesses could recall, and from his own conception of Henry's characteristic method of expression, constructed the speech as we have it today.[20]

The publication of Wirt's *Life of Patrick Henry* in 1817 led to another effort to rescue a revolutionary orator from oblivion. When John Adams read the book he was deeply disturbed by the primacy accorded the Virginia orator over the orators of New England. He wrote a gracious letter to Wirt praising the book, but clearly indicating his concern. Acknowledging the contributions of southern orators, he added: "But, Sir, *Erant heroes ante Agamemnona multi*"; there were heroes before Agamemnon. "I envy none of the well-merited glories of Virginia, or any of her sages or heroes. But, Sir, I am jealous, very jealous, of the honor of Massachusetts."[21] Were he a younger man, said Adams, he would write a biography of James Otis, a man who in the month of February 1761 "electrified the town of Boston, the province of Massachusetts Bay, and the whole continent, more than Patrick Henry ever did in the whole course of his life."

But Adams was an old man, and the task of redressing the balance between Virginia and Massachusetts was undertaken by one of his former law clerks, William Tudor. Of inestimable value to him in this work was a series of long letters from John Adams in 1817 and 1818 in which the old patriot sought to reconstruct from memory and from his notes the dramatic details of pre-Revolutionary events.

Tudor, like Wirt, was forced to work under extreme difficulties; he once compared his search for materials with an attempt to recover parts of a mutilated antique statue — a hand here, a foot there — and he closes his volume with an apology for the imperfect account "derived from the frail recollections of tottering, expiring tradition, the scanty gleanings of forgotten journals, and the formal entries of neglected records."[22] He was obliged to pad out his account with sketches of other revolutionary figures — Samuel Adams, Warren, Hancock, Quincy, Cooper, Mayhew, Chauncy. And like Wirt he collected popular anecdotes and reports of wondrous effects wrought, to create the image of an orator — in Otis's case an orator "bold, argumentative, impetuous and commanding, with an eloquence that made his own excitement irresistibly contagious."

Like Wirt also, Tudor preserved for posterity one classic item in the slender catalog of Revolutionary oratory. This was, of course, Otis's stirring speech against the Writs of Assistance. This speech, which was reportedly more than four hours long, was never committed to writing. The only report was that of John Adams, who, as a young man, attended the court as a member of the bar, and who "took a few minutes in a very careless manner," being as he says in his autobiography, "more attentive to the information and the eloquence of the speaker than to my minutes." These brief notes came into the possession of Judge George Minot, who expanded them into a speech which he inserted in his *History of the Province of Massachusetts Bay* (1803). Years later, in an extensive correspondence with Tudor, Adams commented on the Minot version, offering corrections, calling attention to interpolated passages, and supplying a five-part summary of the argument. He also furnished a much more discursive and substantial account of the event, an account no doubt embellished and augmented by the reflections of fifty-seven years. The original notes, he wrote in one letter, are no better a representation of the speech "than the gleam of a glow-worm to the meridian blaze of the sun."[23] Tudor published the reconstructed speech, together with much of Adams's commentary, in his biography of Otis, whence it has found its way into scores of anthologies and historical sketches.

Two further examples of what historian Daniel Boorstin has referred to as "posthumous ghost-writing" are perhaps worth noting. Charles Botta, Italian author of one of the earliest histories of the American Revolution — a highly successful work which was praised by both Adams and Jefferson — followed the practice of ancient historians of inventing speeches to put in the mouths of his characters.[24] In a special note to the reader, Botta, while insisting that the discourses in his history are for the most part authentic, does admit to making one orator say what has been said by others of the same party, and to adding phrases which seemed to him "to coincide perfectly with the sense of the orator." He mentions specifically two speeches allegedly delivered before Congress in 1776 for and against independence by Richard Henry Lee and John Dickinson. More familiar is the "supposed speech" of John Adams on the Declaration of Independence which Daniel Webster composed and delivered as part of his eulogy on Adams and Jefferson in 1826. The Lee speech is occasionally reprinted as genuine, with no reference to Botta, but the Adams speech on independence is almost always accurately identified as a segment of the Webster oration.

The influence exerted by the works of Wirt and Tudor upon subsequent accounts, the extent to which they created for future generations an image of revolutionary oratory, is readily revealed by an examination of histories and anthologies of literature and oratory published during the next one hundred years. Histories of

American literature usually contained a section on orators of the Revolution, which almost invariably quoted Adams's glowing description of Otis against the Writs of Assistance[25] together with Wirt's dramatic anecdotes of the Virginia orator's personal triumphs — particularly his victory over the Parsons and his "Treason" speech in support of the Stamp Act resolutions. Indeed, one can pick up any one of a score of literary histories of the nineteenth and early twentieth centuries, confidently expecting to find most of the following standard ingredients: 1) a list of revolutionary orators — Otis, Quincy, Lee, Warren, Hancock, John and Samuel Adams — with little or no elaboration; 2) fragments of one or two Boston Massacre orations, "to illustrate the eloquence of the times"; and 3) a biographical sketch of Henry or Otis or both, with numerous quotations from Wirt and Adams (via Tudor).

Indebtedness to the two biographers is especially great among anthologists. As predictable as Edwards's "Sinners in the Hands of an Angry God" for the Colonial period is Henry's "Liberty or Death" for the Revolution. Often included with this staple item is Otis on "Writs of Assistance" or a Boston Massacre oration by Hancock or Warren and quite possibly Washington's "Farewell Address" or Jefferson's First Inaugural. Authors of specialized works on oratory borrow copiously from Wirt. In *Orators and Statesmen,* for example, David Harsha deals with only one orator of the American Revolution, Patrick Henry, though he briefly mentions half a dozen others. Of the twenty-nine pages in Harsha's essay, twenty-five (including the full text of "Liberty or Death") are quoted or paraphrased from Wirt's biography. Magoon's *Orators of the American Revolution* quotes most of Henry's "Liberty or Death" as "a distinguished specimen of his style," with no mention of Wirt's part in its composition. He does acknowledge, however, that the biographical portion of his memoir is "freely copied" from Wirt. Magoon also presents the speech on the Declaration of Independence which Charles Botta has Richard Henry Lee deliver in his *History,* but with no mention of Botta's authorship.

One is struck by the importance of the element of chance in the process of hero-making. What if William Wirt had not completed his *Life* of Henry, with its gem of a speech that has proved so quotable? What if Adams and Tudor had not been stimulated to an elaborate defense of James Otis? In that event would the "forest-born Demosthenes" of Virginia and the Massachusetts "flame of fire" have been acknowledged for over a century as the foremost orators of the Revolution? Or what if Wirt had been able to complete his series of Virginia biographies? What if some New England chronicler with a gift for romantic narrative and striking phrase had chosen to immortalize the Reverend Jacob Duché, or the Reverend Samuel Cooper, or some equally colorful member of the patriot clergy? Would Virginia's Cicero, Richard Henry Lee, today receive equal recognition with her Demosthenes? Would examples of the eloquence of patriot clergymen now be included in the standard anthologies?

Unquestionably chance has played its part; Henry and Otis were extremely fortunate in attracting such able publicists. But the writing of the record has not been entirely a matter of chance. Some men are hero material, likely candidates for glorification. Otis and Henry were such men, as were Richard Henry Lee, Josiah Quincy, and certain patriot preachers. They possessed in abundance qualities highly valued in their time. Others, regardless of the importance of their contributions, do not seem to possess the stuff of which legends are made. John Adams, ablest debater in the Continental Congress, whose powerful pen created political documents still studied with interest and profit, apparently lacked the physical presence, the personal appeal necessary to strike sparks from a popular audience. Oxenbridge Thacher, author of influential pamphlets, James Otis's colleague in the Writs of Assistance case, whom Adams regarded as next in importance to Otis during the 1760s, was said to have turned to the law because his voice was too weak for the pulpit. And Samuel Adams, who perhaps more than any other deserves to be called the father of the American Revolution, though a forthright, logical speaker who always commanded attention, was not regarded by his contemporaries as an "orator" in the same sense as Otis, Henry, Lee, and Quincy were. John, who was transported by the eloquence of Otis, said of Samuel that while on great occasions he made a strong impression on his auditors, "his ordinary speeches in town meetings, in the House of Representatives, and in Congress exhibited nothing extraordinary."[26] It was the possession of something extraordinary — the flashing eye, the thrilling voice, the compelling phrase, the ability to rouse an audience to excitement — that was requisite for preeminence in the "great orator" tradition.

John Adams once distinguished between the American Revolution and the American war. The Revolution, he said, was completed before the war began. If, as he claimed, the "radical change in the principles, opinions, sentiments, and affections of the people, was the real American Revolution,"[27] then the orators and pamphleteers who effected this change were the true revolutionaries — soldiers of freedom, heralds of a new era.

Popular admiration for orators may be seen in the fact that oratory was one of the chief avenues to success. A particularly successful speech often marked a man for future leadership in public office. After his speech in the Parsons' Cause, Patrick Henry's legal practice increased sharply, and within two years he was an elected member of the Virginia House of Burgesses. There he immediately seized leadership and drew national attention with another oratorical triumph, his speech on the Stamp Act resolutions. He took with him to the First Continental Congress a reputation for eloquence and soon managed to impress that august body (all of whom, according to Adams, were orators) not only with his speaking skill but with his general competence and good sense as well. James Otis, too, achieved almost instantaneous popularity and influence as a result of a single speech. Three months after his attack on Writs of Assistance he was elected to the Massachusetts legislature by an almost unanimous vote and was soon chosen Speaker.

Persuasive evidence exists of widespread susceptibility to spoken eloquence. Town meetings, special days of prayer, fasting, and thanksgiving, ceremonial occasions like those commemorating the Boston Massacre and the Declaration of Independence provided frequent opportunities for public address; and if we may trust eyewitness reports, packed houses and enthusiastic audiences were the rule. Newspapers, diaries, and letters contain detailed descriptions of orators' virtuosity, emphasizing manner of delivery, voice, and effect on listeners. Even the prayers of clergymen on secular occasions were analyzed and praised for their eloquence. Of the prayer with which the Reverend Jacob Duché opened the Congress in 1774, Silas Deane wrote that it was worth riding one hundred miles to hear. According to Deane's report, Duché "prayed without book about ten minutes so pertinently, with such fervency, purity and sublimity of style and sentiment, and with such an apparent sensibility of the scenes and business before us, that even Quakers shed tears." Afterward, we are told, a select committee returned him the unanimous thanks of the Congress.[28]

No greater tribute to living orators was possible than to compare them favorably with the orators of antiquity. Representative of such comparisons, of which numerous examples are to be found, are these stanzas in praise of the Continental Congress:

> *Now meet the Fathers of the western clime;*
> *Nor names more noble graced the rolls of fame,*
> *When Spartan firmness braved the wrecks of time,*
> *Or Latian virtue fann'd th' heroic flame.*
>
> *Not deeper thought th' immortal sage inspired,*
> *On Solon's lips when Grecian senates hung;*
> *Nor manlier eloquence the bosom fired,*
> *When genius thunder'd from th' Athenian tongue.*[29]

Among the host of revolutionary orators, celebrated, revered, heeded in their own time, a few became legends before their deaths. It was said of Otis (whom his countrymen liked to compare with Chatham) that so great was his reputation and so magnetic his personal power that his mere appearance at a public meeting would elicit shouts and clapping. And in Virginia, the highest encomium was to say of a speaker, "He is almost equal to Patrick, when he plead[ed] against the Parsons." The legends of Otis and Henry were perpetuated and elaborated by imaginative publicists. But others, less fortunate in their ability to attract articulate disciples or less endowed with qualities which facilitated their translation into "great orators," seem forever doomed (unless destined to achieve heroic stature for other talents, as did Jefferson, Washington, and Franklin) to be remembered only as items in a list of participants — "others who spoke," but alas, not to us.

❧2❧
THE GOLDEN AGE
Oratory as Artistic Expression

The highest bribes of society are at the feet of the
successful orator. . . . All other fame must hush before his. He is the true potentate.
RALPH WALDO EMERSON

The auditor loves to yield himself up to the fascination of a rich, mellow voice, a commanding attitude,
and a brilliant physiognomy. . . . He blends all his
emotions with the speaker, and is subdued or inspired
under his power. He soon becomes stripped of all
defence, and willingly exposed to every blow, so that
the greatest effects are produced by the slightest
words adroitly directed and skillfully expressed.
E. L. MAGOON

We look back today upon the first half of the nineteenth century,
particularly the period between 1820 and 1850, as the Golden Age
of American Oratory. Great Britain's golden age of parliamentary
oratory during the reign of George III — the age of Pitt, Fox,
Sheridan, and Burke — had its American counterpart during the
years when Webster, Clay, Calhoun, and a group of only slightly
less distinguished statesmen and orators participated in a series of
historic "great debates" in the Congress of the United States. But
American eloquence was not confined to the halls of Congress; this
period was characterized by excellence in all forms of public address. The ancient Greeks, with whom early Americans liked to
compare themselves, distinguished three divisions of oratory: deliberative oratory, addressed to parliamentary bodies or public
meetings of various kinds, was directed toward the acceptance or
rejection of future policy; judicial or forensic oratory, consisting of
arguments before judges or juries, dealt primarily with questions of
past fact; epideictic oratory, the oratory of display, had as its province panegyric and inventive — the praise or censure of persons
or things.

The oratory of the Revolution was, with the possible exception of Boston Massacre and Independence Day addresses, primarily deliberative in nature. Speaking in Congress, in town meetings — even sometimes in the courtroom and from the pulpit — was aimed at public persuasion, designed to change opinions or to impel to action. This was true also of the magnificent debates that accompanied the making and ratification of the Constitution of the United States in the late 1780s. Public business of momentous importance was being transacted, and the main emphasis was upon the job at hand. It is true that however much the legends of Henry and Otis may have been the creations of later glorifiers, there were those among their contemporaries who delighted to discuss the dramatic details of their personal triumphs. Even so, it was the effect that ultimately mattered. The Parsons were defeated; the Stamp Act resolutions were adopted; men were aroused to take arms against Writs of Assistance.

But it is one of the outstanding characteristics of the period we are about to discuss that public speaking came to be regarded not only as an instrument of persuasion but also as a medium of artistic expression, not only as a useful art but as a fine art as well. This is not to say that all or even most speeches attained artistic excellence; they most assuredly did not. But there is ample evidence to show that oratory, even when directed at the most practical ends, was regarded by both speaker and audience as an art form, to be cultivated and admired for its own sake. It was accepted as axiomatic that great speeches were part of our national literature, perhaps the most important part. The *North American Review,* foremost literary journal of the day, reviewed dozens of collections of speeches and commented regularly upon current Phi Beta Kappa orations, commemorative addresses, and debates in Congress. Newspaper accounts of speeches analyzed details of style and delivery as well as (sometimes to the exclusion of) subject matter. Essayists and biographers, in depicting spoken eloquence of public men, found analogies in the other arts. Edward Parker, for example, found it an interesting coincidence that American orators typified the same "schools" of manner as were exhibited on the English stage. Henry Clay, he thought, had "much of Garrick's style of effect; Everett follows Kemble; and Choate is of the passionate order of Edmund Kean." Moving from platform manner to a discussion of style, Parker is reminded of painters: Edward

Everett is "the Raphael of word-painters, as Choate and Webster have their somewhat appropriate parallels in Titian and Michael Angelo." Rufus Choate, like Titian, paints with profusion of rich colorings and strong sensuous fancy. Daniel Webster's massive beauty of composition suggests Michelangelo (both architect and painter) planning the dome of Saint Peter and painting "The Last Judgment" on the walls of the Sistine Chapel. Everett's work, on the other hand, is suffused with delicate charms. "His description of Florence Nightingale, in a recent speech, called up an image as warm and sweet as Raphael's own Madonna."[1] Farfetched as such excursions may seem today, they are fairly typical of the rhapsodies inspired by contemplation of oratorical artistry prior to the Civil War.

It is virtually impossible for us today completely to appreciate the importance attributed to public speaking in early nineteenth-century America. Speeches were for many years after the founding of the Republic the chief source of political information, general education, inspiration, and entertainment. As newspapers became more numerous and more available, the influence of the speaker was extended rather than diminished. Columns were devoted to letters, travelers' reports, and articles evaluating the eloquence of one legislator or another, likening it to a mountain torrent, impetuous and foaming, or to a pellucid streamlet meandering through a peaceful valley; remarking upon his allusions and metaphors, his unbroken chain of reasoning, or the organlike quality of his voice. Full texts of important speeches were printed, and extra copies were run off and distributed in pamphlet form, often becoming influential campaign documents. The orator's influence was enlarged, and further practice encouraged, by makers of textbooks. Purple passages, often highly emotional perorations, were reprinted in "readers" and "speakers" to be analyzed, memorized, and declaimed.

The announcement that a celebrated orator was to appear in congressional debate was sufficient to fill the galleries to overflowing. When the star left Washington for trips into the country he was met everywhere by crowds at mass meetings, barbecues, and dinners with rounds of toasts. As the century entered its third decade the lecture platform offered an increasingly attractive rostrum to speakers from all walks of life — statesmen, ministers, lawyers, reformers, professors. The town lyceums of New England in the 1820s and 1830s and the national lecture movement which grew out of the lyceum provided opportunities to confront audiences hungry for instruction and inspiration. Forensic oratory was popular too, as it had been in the days of Patrick Henry. In rural areas, where lawyers and judge rode circuit, court day at the county seat was an event of sufficient importance to bring in an audience from the surrounding countryside. In the cities, and before the Supreme Court of the United States, titans like Rufus Choate, William Pinckney, and Daniel Webster participated in criminal cases and precedent-setting trials on great constitutional questions. Orators of the bar were idolized, eulogized, and compared with one another; for thousands the courtroom was a theater where splendid drama was enacted, the eloquence of the speakers often receiving as much attention as the facts of the case. "Who can wonder at the attractiveness of Parliament, or of Congress, or the bar, for our ambitious young men," Emerson exclaimed in one of his lectures on eloquence, "when the highest bribes of society are at the feet of the successful orator? He has his audience at his devotion. All other fames must hush before his. He is the true potentate."[2]

Speakers responded to this national adulation by devoting immense effort to a cultivation of their art. Rufus Choate formed the early practice of reading aloud from English writers "to give elevation, energy, sonorousness, and refinement to my vocabulary." His ceremonial addresses he wrote out in full and memorized. His eulogy of Webster, a document of sixty-six pages which took three hours to deliver, he worked on for nearly a year during such time as he could spare from his law practice. Charles Sumner, after graduation from college, studied six morning hours on law and devoted his afternoons and evenings to literature, laying in stores of quotations and allusions which were later poured out in such addresses as his Fourth of July oration of 1845, "The True Grandeur of Nations," an erudite but intemperate and interminable denunciation of war which began his oratorical career. Edward Everett, who took pride in his careful preparation, once declined an invitation to speak in Faneuil Hall because the committee gave him only two weeks to prepare — and this after a lifetime of experience, at a time during which he held no office and was free to devote full time to the task. Later, in 1863, the ceremony dedicating a cemetery at Gettysburg (at which the president of the United States also made a few remarks) had to be postponed a month to give Everett time to prepare the principal address. Henry Clay, who was no scholar, began early in life the daily practice of reading and speaking from some historical or scientific book — in the forest, in a cornfield or barn.

This catalog could be extended indefinitely. The assiduous preparation, both general and specific, required to deliver verbatim from memory a two- or three-hour address, as Everett, Sumner, Choate, Phillips, Curtis, and others frequently did, or to speak fluently and cogently for three or four hours at a time from a few pages of notes, as did Webster and Clay on the floor of the Senate, is a feat almost inconceivable in our day. Amazing also is the endurance of the nineteenth-century audiences; a good speaker could apparently depend upon an attentive audience for as long as he cared to address it. And the rewards of eloquence were enormous. Many a contemporary of Henry Clay might with truth have echoed his assertion that "it is to this practice of the art of all arts that I am indebted for the primary and leading impulses that stimulated my progress and have shaped and moulded my entire destiny."[3]

The nature of the oratory of this exuberant period in our national history, as well as the responses it evoked, can best be delineated by considering separately the principal forms or genres, most of which are embraced by the classical headings of epideictic and deliberative. Consideration of judicial oratory, the third category recognized by the Greek rhetoricians is omitted here and in subsequent chapters not because it was unimportant but because the oratory of the courtroom is a specialized study, deserving of separate treatment by technical experts, and because many of the men who distinguished themselves at the bar also displayed their talents in the Congress and on ceremonial occasions. A fourth category, unknown to the ancient Greeks, the oratory of the Christian Church, will receive only passing mention in these pages because of the unique nature of its subject matter and form. It should be noted, however, that during the "golden age" under discussion, forensic and pulpit oratory were regarded as significant forms of artistic expression, and that they, like other forms of public address, were dissected, analyzed, and exclaimed upon in print and by word of mouth by enthusiastic connoisseurs.

CEREMONIAL ADDRESSES

On the last day of July 1826, the president of the United States, John Quincy Adams, gathered his family around him and read aloud a Fourth of July oration delivered a few weeks earlier by Edward Everett at Cambridge, Massachusetts. That evening, noting in his diary that the speech, like all Everett's writings, was "full of thought, of argument, and of eloquence, intermixed with a little humorous levity, and a few paradoxical fancies," the president added: "There is at this time in this Commonwealth a practical school of popular oratory, of which I believe myself to be the principal founder by my own orations and lectures, and which, with the blessing of Him who reigns, will redound to the honor and advantage of this nation and to the benefit of mankind."[4]

Adams's claim that he was the founder of a school of popular oratory was not so immodest as it might seem. While a member of the United States Senate he had served as Boyleston Professor of Rhetoric and Oratory at Harvard, and Edward Everett was only one of many who had come under his influence there. By his precept and practice Adams had helped to revive and extend public interest in the orators and rhetoricians of Greece and Rome. To him, as to the ancients, oratory was an important art form, with its own principles of composition and delivery, and worthy of the most painstaking cultivation. The Adams "school," if school it was, was based on the classical model, with its emphasis upon the canons of invention, style, arrangement, and delivery, and careful craftsmanship applied to exordium, exposition, proof, and peroration.

The address delivered by Everett in 1826 was only one of many celebrating the fiftieth anniversary of national independence and probably differed from scores of others principally in its superior display of learning and its general elevation of tone. After reference to local scenes of the Revolution (at one point he called attention to the very seat General Washington had occupied in the Cambridge church) and tributes to Lee, Quincy, Henry, Otis, Warren, Adams, and Jefferson, the speaker proclaimed the arrival of an age of commemoration. The body of the address is a contrast between arbitrary, tyrannous governments, maintained by force, prior to the Revolution, and American constitutional government founded on equality and consent of the governed. Americans, he asserted, have erected as a model for all nations an example of successful popular government. We have demonstrated to the world that man is by nature "neither a savage, a hermit, nor a slave, but a member of a well-ordered family, a good neighbor, a free citizen, a well-informed, good man, acting with others like him."[5]

It will be remembered that in 1783, the city of Boston, which had previously commemorated the Boston Massacre with an annual oration, officially decreed that it should henceforth be replaced by a celebration of Independence Day, including "a Publick Oration. . . . in which the Orator shall consider the feelings, manners and principles which led to this great National Event as well as the important and happy effects whether general or domestick which already have and will forever continue to flow from the Auspicious Epoch."[6] In the years that followed, the annual Fourth of July oration became established in all parts of the country. As John Adams observed, many a successful public career was launched by a particularly noteworthy address on this occasion. But the sheer quantity of such oratory, plus the demand that each speaker, regardless of his talent, be "eloquent," resulted after a time in establishing the connotations of vainglorious boasting, spurious erudition, and ludicrous rhetorical display which now attach to Independence Day speeches.

By 1826 the Fourth of July oration was only one of a wide variety of occasional or ceremonial addresses which were immensely popular with American audiences for at least half a century. Most important of these was the commemorative address, which took as a starting point an anniversary, a historical character or event, and then frequently ranged far afield. The aim of such addresses was to inspire veneration for American heroes and institutions, to celebrate American values and virtues, to justify and idealize the nation's past, and to herald a glorious national future. Edward Everett, in introducing a second edition of his occasional addresses, called attention to a number of factors propitious to the generation of this type of oratory: the rapid growth of the nation since the Declaration of Independence, the continuing popular interest in our heroic age, and a series of events which cried aloud for commemorative utterance — the death of Washington in 1799, the second centennial of the landing of the Pilgrims in 1820, the visit of Lafayette in 1824, the commencement of the Bunker Hill Monument in 1825 and its completion in 1843, the dramatic coincidence of the death of both Adams and Jefferson on July 4, 1826.

Nowhere has the impulse motivating the commemorative address and the explanation for its enthusiastic popular acceptance been better expressed than in Daniel Webster's oration on "The Character of Washington":

> All experience evinces that human sentiments are strongly influenced by associations. The recurrence of anniversaries, or of longer periods of time, naturally freshens the recollection, and deepens the impression, of events with which they are historically connected. Renowned places, also, have a power to awaken feeling, which all acknowledge. No American can pass by the fields of Bunker Hill, Monmouth, and Camden, as if they were ordinary spots on the earth's surface. . . . But neither of these sources of emotion equals the power with which great moral examples affect the mind. When sublime virtues cease to be abstractions, when they become embodied in human character, and exemplified in human conduct, we should be false to our own nature, if we did not indulge in the spontaneous effusions of our gratitude and our admiration. A true lover of the virtue of patriotism delights to contemplate its purest models. . . . The ingenuous youth of America will hold up to themselves the bright model of Washington's example, and study to be what they behold.[7]

Another variety of demonstrative or epideictic oratory, similar to but distinct from the commemorative, might be termed the "literary address." Some, such as the Phi Beta Kappa oration, the commencement address, or the ceremonial address to literary, historical, and other professional societies, prepared as they were for select academic audiences, tended to be indistinguishable from the essay. Addresses like Wendell Phillips's "The Lost Arts," repeated year after year from the lecture platform, performed much the same function of celebrating national ideals and institutions as did the speeches commemorative of historic persons and events. Of course the public lecture, which remained an American institution for decades after the Civil War, was by no means restricted to literary subjects, but sought to satisfy a growing hunger for education and inspiration by dealing with a varied catalog of subjects from phrenology to foreign travel.

Edward T. Channing, whose influence as Boylston Professor of Rhetoric and Oratory was considerably greater than that of John Quincy Adams and who has been credited with molding the tastes and practices of speakers and writers more than any single educator of his time, observed in one of his Harvard lectures, "We may conceive of a state of society so refined, and perhaps I may add, so luxurious, as to call forth and establish a class of what may be called literary orators, as distinct and acknowledged as that of authors, whose vocation it will be to investigate literary, moral and scientific subjects, or the elegant arts, and make them familiar and agreeable to multitudes in public discourses."[8] A number of nineteenth-century Americans, some of them students of Channing, filled this bill to perfection. With some, such as Ralph Waldo Emerson, Wendell Phillips, George William Curtis, and Edward Everett, this kind of public speaking was almost a vocation; with others, such as Daniel Webster, Charles Sumner, Rufus Choate, and other lawyers and statesmen, it was an avocation which contributed immeasurably to their public reputations.

Quite obviously, the classical division of epideictic oratory, supplemented by an accumulation of subsequent manifestations, had developed into a remarkably heterogeneous category. A classification embracing Lincoln's Gettysburg Address — and Everett's too — Emerson's "American Scholar," Webster's "The Character of Washington," George Bancroft's "Office of the People in Art, Government, and Religion," a Fourth of July oration, and an after-dinner speech is scarcely susceptible of precise description or definition. It generally designates oratory whose basic appeal is to the imagination and the emotions, whose primary function is not argumentation or determination of public policy on specific issues, but to "show forth," to elaborate upon general themes, to illustrate or vivify propositions already accepted by a majority of the audience. During the period under discussion its most significant contribution was to create for the new nation a sense of community by showing the way to future accomplishment through idealization of an heroic past.

No man did more by his oratory to create a spirit of nationalism during the thirty years preceding the Civil War than Daniel Webster of Massachusetts. Alone among the statesmen of his day, Webster achieved preeminence in all three classical divisions of oratory. His fame in senatorial debate and at the bar in such highly publicized cases as the Dartmouth College case or the White murder trial has tended to obscure the fact that he delivered a half-dozen of the finest commemorative addresses ever heard in this country. For examples of American occasional oratory at its best, from an era when it was honored more than at any time before or since, one can do no better than to study Webster's Plymouth Oration, his two Bunker Hill addresses, and his eulogy of Adams and Jefferson. All marked occasions of great national significance; all were hailed as masterpieces by thousands who heard them and hundreds of thousands who read them. It was "The First Settlement of New England," delivered at Plymouth in 1820 in commemoration of the bicentennial of the landing of the Pilgrims, that moved George Ticknor to exclaim: "I was never so excited by public speaking before in my life. Three or four times I thought my temples would burst with the gush of blood. . . . When I came out I was almost afraid to come near to him. It seemed to me as if he was like the mount that might not be touched, and that burned with fire. I was beside myself, and am so still."[9] It should be observed that Ticknor, professor of French and Spanish literature at Harvard, was a man of wide learning and sober critical judgment, not given to indiscriminate bursts of enthusiasm. Another comment on this speech came from John Adams, then in his eighty-sixth year, who pronounced it "the effort of a great mind, richly stored with every species of information." "Mr Burke," wrote Adams in a congratulatory letter to Webster, "is no longer entitled to the praise — the most consummate orator of modern times."

The first Bunker Hill oration, delivered in 1825 at the laying of the cornerstone of the monument, climaxed an all-day celebration which drew thousands into Boston from neighboring towns. Beginning at ten o'clock in the morning, a procession made up of military and fraternal organizations in full regalia, invited guests, and two hundred veterans of the Revolution, forty of whom had fought at Bunker Hill, moved out from the State House. According to one report the procession was of such length that the front nearly reached Charlestown Bridge before the rear had left Boston Common. After General Lafayette had presided over the laying of the cornerstone, Webster addressed an audience described by historian Richard Frothingham as "as great a multitude as was ever perhaps assembled within the sound of a human voice." Estimates of crowd size are frequently on the generous side (Frothingham estimated the audience for the second Bunker Hill oration in 1843 at 100,000), but even after allowances are made for loyal exaggeration, one marvels at the feat (not uncommon in that day) of addressing for two or three hours in the open air, without the aid of electronic amplification, an audience that could scarcely be crowded into one of our largest modern football stadiums. It is an indication of the veneration of the speaker, and the significance attached to public address, that audiences, some of whom probably could not have heard much of what was being said, should have stood crowded together hour after hour just to be in the presence of a great orator on a great occasion and to be part of the ceremony.

Webster's eulogy of Adams and Jefferson in 1826 is considered by some to be his greatest occasional address, as the Reply to Hayne a few years later marked the pinnacle of his deliberative efforts. The death of these two great heroes of the Revolution on the same day — and that day the fiftieth anniversary of the Declaration of which one was the author and the other the most effective champion in Congress — had a tremendous effect upon the nation. For weeks it was the principal topic of discussion in the press, the pulpit, and at public meetings. In all parts of the country commemorative rites were formed and eulogies pronounced. John Quincy Adams reports his attendance at six ceremonies in the space of one week. Of all such gatherings none was more prestigious or more memorable than that held on the second of August at Faneuil Hall in Boston, the "Cradle of Liberty," and addressed by Daniel Webster. This speech contained the two passages which, together with the peroration of the Reply to Hayne, became the most frequently reproduced and (in a day when memorization of elegant extracts was part of every child's education) the most widely memorized of all quotations from Webster. These were his definition of eloquence and the "supposed speech" of John Adams on the Declaration of Independence.

These few addresses, together with three or four eulogies of which his "Character of Washington" was the greatest, and his speech at the laying of the cornerstone of an addition to the national Capitol, were Webster's contribution to the demonstrative oratory of our golden age. They were, indisputably, examples of the grand style — orotund, majestic, sometimes (though not often) approaching the pompous and grandiose. As imitated by a host of lesser men, such a style frequently became ridiculous, but Webster had the intellect, the depth of learning, the impressiveness of features, and the regal bearing to carry it off successfully. Some critics of a later day have denigrated Webster's oratory by dismissing it as "flowery." This characterization, suggesting prettiness or gratuitous decoration, is singularly inappropriate. There were flowery speakers in that day — Rufus Choate comes most readily to mind — but Daniel Webster was not one of them. His gift for sustained, stately diction imparted to his speeches a massiveness and dignity, a sense of great power under control, which is the very antithesis of floweriness.

Webster's great gifts enabled him to breathe life into past events of national significance and to draw from them inspiration for future efforts. His ceremonial addresses were associated with the greatest national scenes and symbols: Bunker Hill, Plymouth Rock, the flag, the Capitol, the character of Washington; his most frequently recurring themes were the Constitution and the Union. Edward Parker, a devoted disciple who went to hear him speak on every possible occasion, once even suggested that if another flood should come, destroying everything on this continent save the volumes of Webster's speeches, "the assiduous explorer might from them pick out, and put together, an outline framework of the American Character and the American History. Every page would tell some characteristic or distinctive national trait or fact, like a slab exhumed from Nineveh."[10]

The beau ideal of demonstrative orators, second only to Webster in his day but now almost forgotten, was Edward Everett. Everett began to acquire a reputation for eloquence in his early twenties as pastor of Boston's Brattle Street Church. One of many admiring young men who took notes of impressive passages from his sermons and committed them to memory was Ralph Waldo Emerson, who wrote later, "He who was heard with such throbbing hearts and sparkling eyes in the lighted and crowded churches, did not let go his hearers when the church was dismissed, but the bright image of that eloquent form followed the boy home to his bedchamber."[11] Everett's subsequent career was brilliant by any standards: he studied in Germany and received the first Göttingen Ph.D. given an American; he became professor of Greek and later president of Harvard, governor of Massachusetts, United States minister to Great Britain, United States secretary of state, and member of both the House of Representatives and the Senate of the United States. Nevertheless, he was best known, both at home and abroad, not as a statesman but as a kind of orator-at-large to the American nation. His sensibilities were too delicate for the rough-and-tumble of political disputation. Although he served five terms in the House of Representatives, he was not happy there, and he resigned from the Senate in the second year of his term, never again accepting public office. Everett was probably as close as we have ever come in this country to a professional public orator. His forte was the ceremonial address. While it remained an important national institution, he was its most eminent practitioner; when it languished, his reputation faded with it. No one got around to writing his biography until 1925.

Everett's speeches, the care he lavished upon them, and the popularity they enjoyed, provide the perfect illustration of pre-Civil War attitudes toward public speaking. For Everett oratory was an art, and he was the most conscious of artists. He labored assiduously for his effects; he ransacked literature and history for images and allusions; he let his fancy soar; he polished his sentences until they dazzled. For him, as for the ancient Greeks, an oration deserved the same careful construction as a temple, or a statue, or a drama. When criticized for the meticulousness of his preparation he replied, "Who but a maniac would undertake to address such an audience without?" Unfortunately, his was not always the true art which conceals art; sometimes it vaunted itself and became pretentious or deteriorated into artifice. But in justice it should be said that Everett himself was aware of his weaknesses and did what he could to modify them. In the preface to a second edition of his speeches he admits to wordiness in his earlier productions and tells of having freely "supplied the pruning-knife" to the style in preparing them for publication. Even so, he feels they may still lack the simplicity which he acknowledges as a desirable quality of such writings.

The four published volumes of Everett's *Orations and Speeches on Various Occasions* contain 186 addresses, a total of nearly three thousand pages. All are occasional addresses. The author's expressed desire is to make a contribution to the literature of the country, and in order that the contribution be "inoffensive," he has omitted all political speeches and "anything of a party character." The range of subjects is astonishing. There are major orations on the same themes developed by Daniel Webster — the landing of the Pilgrims, Bunker Hill, Adams and Jefferson, Washington, the Constitution — the kinds of themes that occupied the attention of epic poets in other lands and other times. There are literary orations, such as the Cambridge Phi Beta Kappa oration on "The Circumstances Favorable to the Progress of Literature in America," which launched his career — discourses which, following Edward T. Channing's prescription, investigated literary and moral subjects, or the elegant arts, and made them familiar and agreeable to multitudes. And there are dozens of shorter speeches at flag-raisings, public dinners, agricultural fairs, and exhibitions. Everett was not always grandiloquent; he did not always soar, though the practice of reproducing only his purplest passages may have conveyed that impression. He was capable of vigorous narrative unencumbered by excess verbiage. He could make a graceful little speech opening Brattle House in Cambridge, or a few appropriate remarks in response to a toast, or presenting awards for declamation at the Boston Latin School. His particular talent was his ability to perceive and give felicitous expression to the spirit, the requirements, and the dramatic possibilities of each occasion.

Ten years after John Quincy Adams had praised Everett's Fourth of July oration at Cambridge, Governor and Mrs. Everett visited the Adamses in their home and left a volume of *Orations and Speeches* as a gift. In his diary Adams pronounced them among the best ever delivered in this country and predicted that they would stand the test of time: "Of the thousands and tens of thousands of these orations, which teem in every part of this country, there are, perhaps, not one hundred that will be remembered . . . and of them, at least half have been, or will be, furnished by E. E. He has largely contributed to raise the standard of this class of composition."[12]

Adams's reference to "tens of thousands" of ceremonial orations is worthy of notice. The celebrations at Plymouth and Bunker Hill, in Faneuil Hall and the Capitol at Washington, had their local counterparts throughout the land. Hundreds of less eminent speakers aspired, on the Fourth of July and other national anniversaries, to emulate the triumphs of a Webster or an Everett. As a speaker on the Missouri frontier put it: "We admire eloquence, and we feebly try to imitate it. We know that ours is but a farthing candle in the sun, but we feel there is no harm in trying."[13] These farthing candles were often feeble indeed, but the themes and the spirit were similar. Adams, of course, was right in predicting oblivion for most of these orations, but he was wrong about the immortality of Edward Everett. Everett's orations are not read today, not even his "Character of Washington," which he repeated over one hundred times in all parts of the nation, turning over the proceeds (nearly $90,000) to the Mount Vernon Fund for the purchase of Washington's home as a national monument. Edward Everett, ornament of the ceremonial platform for more than a quarter of a century, is remembered, when he is remembered at all, as the man who made the other speech at Gettysburg.

The indisputable greatness of Lincoln's address at the Gettysburg cemetery — its majestic simplicity, its poetic quality and depth of genuine emotion, and, not without importance, the fact that it can be quoted in full — has caused us to dismiss the main speaker on that occasion as a faceless figure who emitted two hours of "flowery rhetoric" before Lincoln rose to speak. This is understandable, and probably inevitable. Lincoln's speech that day was the finest thing of its kind ever uttered in the English tongue. There can be no comparing Everett's address with it as oratory, as literature, or by any other criterion. But Everett deserves at least the courtesy of a hearing. Few who read the speech, even now, will be inclined to dismiss it as "mere rhetoric," as those who have not read it invariably do. From the stately exordium ("Standing beneath this serene sky, overlooking these broad fields . . . the mighty Alleghenies dimly towering before us, the graves of our brethren beneath our feet. . . .") to the final benediction recalling the words of Pericles, "the whole earth is the sepulchre of illustrious men," and invoking divine blessing on the Union in whose defense the buried soldiers fell, it is by the severest standards of its day a remarkable performance, product of painstaking specific research and broad general culture.

Everett had been the unanimous choice of seventeen state governors as orator for the Gettysburg ceremony, an impressive testimonial to his eminence. His apparently was the name that naturally came to mind in connection with such an occasion. The president of the United States was invited, belatedly, to make "a few appropriate remarks" dedicating the grounds to their sacred use. One of the myths subsequently attaching to Lincoln's speech was that it was universally denounced in the press and elsewhere as a miserable failure. This is as lacking in foundation as the story that he wrote the speech on an envelope en route from Washington. Nevertheless, there can be no question that Everett, not Lincoln, delivered the kind of speech the audience expected to hear, the speech which in their opinion was called for by the occasion. Beginning with a reference to ancient Athenian funeral customs, Everett moved to a consideration of the present occasion through a comparison of the battles of Marathon and Gettysburg. Following a quick review of the origins of the war came a vivid narrative of the three-day battle and events preceding and following it. (In a note to the published version, he lists his sources: eyewitness reports, a memorandum drawn up for him by the adjutant general, General Lee's official report of the campaign, articles in the *Richmond Enquirer,* and an article in *Blackwood's Magazine* by a British colonel.) The speaker then discussed the causes of the war, fixing the responsibility for it firmly on the South. In the final section he sought to demonstrate through a series of historical allusions to England, France, and Germany that hatreds generated by civil wars, though bitter at the time, are transient. These passages, which Everett considered the most important part of his address, sounded a note of conciliation which anticipated by sixteen months Lincoln's "with malice toward none, with charity for all."

It was a long speech, and many of the audience had been standing for hours before he began. It was not the kind of speech that might be expected to hold a mid-twentieth-century audience spellbound, nor would today's listeners be apt to venerate an Edward Everett, with his studied gestures, his cultivated voice, his patrician air, and his overornate sentences, as he had been venerated a century earlier. But if, as Webster asserted, eloquence lies in the man, the subject, and the occasion (including the audience), it was on November 19, 1863, an eloquent speech. And if Everett does not conform perfectly to the modern model of a hero, if we find him somewhat overfastidious or aristocratic or aloof for our robust tastes, we cannot withhold our admiration for that generous letter he wrote Abraham Lincoln after both men had spoken at Gettysburg: "I should be glad if I could flatter myself that I came as near the central idea of the occasion in two hours as you did in two minutes." Those are perceptive, magnanimous words. Their perfection is matched in Lincoln's reply: "In our respective parts yesterday you could not have been excused to make a short address, nor I a long one."

It seems in retrospect as if that November day at Gettysburg may have marked the end of an era in American ceremonial oratory. Not that such oratory ceased, or even diminished in quantity; the Fourth of July oration, the eulogy, the commencement address, and other varieties of the occasional speech continued after the Civil War and into the next century. But the great commemorative addresses like those given at Faneuil Hall and Bunker Hill and Gettysburg were never again to assume their former national importance. Those and hundreds like them had been acts of public affirmation, occasions when thousands could stand together while an orator gave artistic expression to their thoughts; celebrating the nation's past, honoring its heroes, apotheosizing its ideals. After the Civil War, public attention turned to more practical affairs.

It has sometimes been claimed that Lincoln at Gettysburg established a new style of public speaking in America, that henceforth the national taste moved in the direction of brevity and simplicity. This was not the case; there was to be verbose, heavily ornamental oratory for many years after Gettysburg, much of it infinitely more offensive than anything Everett, Sumner, or Choate ever achieved, because it was unsupported by their learning and artistry. A similar claim was made for Wendell Phillips, that the effectiveness of his "animated conversation" rendered the grand style obsolete. This too was untrue; during much of his long speaking career Phillips's colloquial style was notable because it was so different from that of his fellow orators. But it is certainly true that later generations of Americans have preferred the style of Lincoln and Phillips to that of Everett and Sumner, and it may be significant that twentieth-century textbooks on public speaking have consistently held up as a model for modern platform speakers the example of Wendell Phillips — pure colloquy, a gentleman conversing.

DELIBERATIVE SPEAKING:
THE ORATORY OF CONGRESS

In his Bunker Hill oration of 1825 Daniel Webster observed that great questions of politics and government had for a half-century occupied the thoughts of men in America. Politics, he said, is "the master topic of the age." For more than another quarter-century politics and government continued to be the master topic. The first half of the nineteenth-century was a time of making and revising state constitutions, of differing interpretations of the federal Constitution, and of extension of the franchise to many who had not participated in the democratic process. The basic cleavage between the agrarian economy of the South and the emerging industrialism of the North exacerbated frequent conflicts over the tariff, the settlement of public lands to the west, and the institution of slavery. The necessity of dealing with issues of such vital importance to the nation gave rise to a series of "great debates" in the Congress of the United States.

The debate on the admission of Missouri in 1820 marked the first serious clash between North and South on the slavery question. The battle of the sections continued for three decades in debates on the tariffs of 1828 and 1832, the debate on Foote's resolution, immortalized by the classic exchange between Daniel Webster and Robert Hayne, the clash between Calhoun and Webster on the basic nature of the Constitution during the nullification crisis of 1833, debates on the Bank of the United States, the Oregon question, the war with Mexico, the annexation of Texas, Clay's compromise measures of 1850, and the intensification of personal hostility and vituperation following passage of the Kansas-Nebraska bill. These debates were reported in detail in newspapers and journals. The most notable orations were reprinted by the thousands, admired and discussed, and "elegant extracts" preserved in readers and speakers for study and declamation. Once a man had gained a reputation as an orator, everyone wanted to see and hear him in action. In this early national era, as Daniel Boorstin has remarked, great orations were regarded as "the levers of American history and the formulae of American purpose." "Oration," says Boorstin, "seemed almost to displace legislation as the main form of political action. The 'great speeches' of that era possessed a popular power, a historic significance, and a symbolic meaning difficult for us to understand."[14]

The foregoing discussion of epideictic oratory has sought to make the point that the ceremonial or occasional address was designed by the speaker and perceived by the audience as a form of artistic expression — that it sought to honor an occasion, celebrate a person or event, embellish a theme. Its purpose was essentially to intensify and give felicitous expression to feelings already held, rather than to advance new arguments, change opinions, or solve problems. American audiences did not need to be convinced that George Washington was a great man, but they enjoyed being told in a variety of ways wherein his greatness lay, and when he was compared favorably with the greatest figures of ancient and modern times they felt a thrill of pride in identifying themselves with their eminent countryman.

Still, the demonstrative address could, and frequently did, perform a specific persuasive function. Edward Everett, in a hundred repetitions of his eulogy of Washington, was seeking to save not only Mount Vernon, but the Federal Union as well. He closed this address (delivered up to the eve of Civil War) by urging his listeners to show respect for the memory of Washington by heeding his pleas for union in the Farewell Address. The breaking up of the Union he denounced as unthinkable. Recalling Jefferson's words to Washington in 1792, "North and South will hang together while they have you to hang to," Everett went on to say that though Washington is gone, his memory remains; "I say, let's hang to his memory." Everett could not even close his informal remarks at the laying of the cornerstone of a lighthouse on Minot's Ledge without putting in a few good words for the Union. He expressed the hope that as the solid foundations of the lighthouse were linked with dovetailed blocks of granite and bars of iron, "so may the sister States of the Union be forever bound together by the stronger ties of common language, kindred blood, and mutual affection." Webster, laying a cornerstone at Bunker Hill, pleaded his favorite cause, the Union: "Let our object be, Our Country, Our Whole Country, and Nothing But Our Country." In "Addition to the Capitol" he challenged Southerners to think nationally instead of sectionally and looked forward confidently to the time when "the ill-omened sounds of fanaticism will be hushed; the ghastly spectres of *Secession* and *Disunion* will disappear."[15]

As there was a persuasive element in occasional addresses which were primarily ceremonial and ritualistic, so was there an artistic impulse behind much congressional oratory, essentially deliberative in nature. Great constitutional questions were being discussed; great principles were at stake. National policies had to be agreed upon, opinions and votes influenced, legislation passed, commitments made. Oratory to serve such ends must of necessity be utilitarian, purposive, practical. Nevertheless, apparent in legislative halls as well as on popular platforms was a striving for artistic effect (sometimes with ludicrous results) on the part of speakers and a tendency on the part of audiences to regard "great speeches" of Congress as magnificent performances.

Prominent among those who brought a conscious artistry to their speeches in Congress was Charles Sumner of Massachusetts. Sumner first received national recognition as an orator in 1845 when he delivered a Fourth of July oration entitled "The True Grandeur of Nations" in Boston's Tremont Temple. Gathering from his prodigious reading all the arguments ever advanced against war, he wove them into an oration following the classical pattern of exordium, narration, partition, proof, refutation, and peroration. Clearly intended for a wider audience (Sumner informed the printer that much had been omitted in delivery because of its length, and he supplied several pages of dense scholarly notes), it seemed deliberately designed to antagonize the immediate audience, many of whom were uniformed members of the military establishment. Nearly every page of the 130-page transcript of this "declaration of war against war" contains at least one allusion to or quotation from ancient or modern literature. The orator quotes in translation thirty-two lines from the Agamemnon of Aeschylus to picture the desolation of war. He recites an extended passage from Scott's "Lay of the Last Minstrel" to point up changes in battle dress since knighthood was in flower. Scattered prodigally throughout the manuscript, supplementing tables of military expenditures and other statistical material, are fragments from Plato, Homer, Shakespeare, Cicero, Coleridge, Carlyle, Longfellow, and others. Most are in English, but there is a six-line quotation in Latin from Juvenal and numerous fragments in Latin and French.

Elected to the United States Senate six years later, Sumner brought to his congressional oratory the same formal preparation and impressive delivery, the same parade of erudition, that had characterized his ceremonial addresses. On August 26, 1852, during a debate on the Fugitive Slave Law, he delivered the first of what was to be a long and distinguished series of speeches on slavery, "Freedom National, Slavery Sectional." It was an elaborate oration, written out and committed to memory, and occupying nearly four hours in delivery. It changed no votes (only three senators joined Sumner in voting for repeal), but it elicited widespread response. Predictably, it was denounced by the friends of slavery and praised by its foes. Admirers noted its lofty tone, its dignified language, and compared it with Burke's speeches on America. Theodore Parker wrote: "You have made a grand speech, — well researched, well arranged, well written, and I doubt not as well delivered. It was worth while to go to Congress and make such a speech. I think you never did anything better as a work of art." From an opponent, Senator John B. Weller of California, came a curious compliment which suggests the nature of the speech: "I did not know that it was possible that I could endure a speech for over three hours upon the subject of the abolition of slavery; but this oration of the senator from Massachusetts today has been so handsomely embellished with poetry, both Latin and English, so full of classical allusions and rhetorical flourishes, as to make it much more palatable than I supposed it could have been made."[16]

Sumner's most celebrated speech on slavery was his "Crime against Kansas," delivered in the Senate May 19-20, 1856. After the Kansas-Nebraska Act established Senator Stephen Douglas's principle of popular or "squatter" sovereignty in the disputed territory, proslavery and antislavery forces scrambled to get there first. Armed men swarmed across the border from Missouri in an attempt to secure Kansas for slavery by force, driving out the settlers and voting in their places. Kansas became an armed camp; passions rose in both North and South; and Senate debate reflected the violence and recrimination in the country at large. Charles Sumner's contribution to the mounting tension was a blistering five-hour attack on the slave power. The Massachusetts senator prepared for his task with characteristic thoroughness. Two days before delivering the speech, he wrote to Theodore Parker, "I shall pronounce the most thorough philippic ever uttered in a legislative body." When he rose to address the Senate, all members were in their seats; galleries, lobbies, halls, and doorways were packed despite the ninety-degree heat. The speech had been written out in full, completely memorized, and set in type awaiting final correction before printing. Like all his major orations, it was formally partitioned. The three principal divisions, explicitly announced, were: 1) the Crime against Kansas, its origin and extent, 2) Apologies for the Crime, and 3) the True Remedy. A few sentences will impart the flavor. Summarizing the first main division, he said: "Thus was the Crime consummated. Slavery stands erect, clanking its chains on the Territory of Kansas, surrounded by a code of death, and trampling upon all cherished liberties. . . . And Sir, all this is done, not merely to introduce a wrong which in itself is a denial of all rights . . . but it is done for the sake of political power, in order to bring two new slaveholding Senators upon this floor, and thus to fortify in the National Government the desperate chances of a waning Oligarchy."[17] Earlier, Sumner had compared Senators Andrew P. Butler of South Carolina and Stephen Douglas of Illinois to Don Quixote and Sancho Panza, sallying forth in the same adventure — in this case, the championship of human wrong. Butler, he said, having read many books on chivalry, fancies himself a knight. The mistress to whom he has made his vows is the harlot slavery, whom he defends extravagantly whenever her character is impeached. "He is the uncompromising, unblushing representative on this floor of a flagrant sectionalism now domineering over the republic."

After speaking for three hours, Sumner closed the first part of the oration with a tribute to Massachusetts ("I am proud to believe that you may as well attempt with puny arm to topple down the earth-rooted, heaven-kissing granite which crowns the historic sod of Bunker Hill, as to change her fixed resolve for freedom

everywhere, and especially now for freedom in Kansas") and resumed the next day, holding an undiminished audience for two
more hours. The impromptu exchange between Sumner and Douglas which followed the peroration was, on both sides, considerably
more intemperate than anything in the speech itself. The violent
sequel to this speech is well known. Two days later, presumably in
the name of chivalry, Congressman Preston Brooks of South
Carolina, a distant relative of Senator Butler, attacked Sumner as
he sat writing at his desk in the Senate chamber. While southern
senators looked on, Brooks beat Sumner senseless with repeated
blows on the head with a heavy gutta-percha cane. Miraculously
escaping with his life, Sumner suffered months of agony, was subjected to the most excruciating treatments, and was unable to return to the Senate for more than three years, during which time he
became a heroic figure among antislavery forces. Brooks was
applauded throughout the South. He received dozens of congratulatory canes: citizens of Charleston subscribed ten cents each
and bought a cane engraved with the words "Hit him again"; University of Virginia students passed a resolution to purchase a splendid cane with a heavy gold head bearing upon it "a device of the
human head badly cracked and broken."[18]

Despite its prodigious length (113 pages in his *Works*), "The
Crime against Kansas" was printed in several newspapers. Pamphlet editions were published in Washington, New York, Boston,
and San Francisco, and an estimated one million copies sold. It was
issued as a campaign document in the national campaign of 1856.
Sumner received scores of letters praising the speech — as many as
fifty a day after the Brooks attack. Longfellow pronounced it "the
greatest voice, on the greatest subject, that has been uttered since
we became a nation." Whittier thought it Sumner's best: "A grand
and terrible philippic, worthy of the great occasion; the severe and
awful truth which the sharp agony of the national crisis demanded.
It is enough for immortality."[19]

Such responses from the senator's abolitionist admirers and
close friends, particularly in light of the vicious assault on his person, were perhaps only to be expected. More remarkable, and
illustrative of my point about prevailing attitudes toward oratory,
was the fact that the critical response to this speech — which infuriated the South, triggered the Brooks attack, and intensified

sectional hostility — concerned rhetorical technique as well as subject matter. The address was examined as an example of oratorical art, compared with ancient and modern classics, and its author welcomed into the distinguished company which included Webster, Otis, Everett, and Burke. "In a speech of five hours in length," proclaimed the *New York Evening Post,* "he has exhibited the most signal combination of oratorical splendors which in the opinion of a veteran Senator has ever been witnessed in that Hall." The speech, in the opinion of this writer, deserved comparison with those of Edmund Burke for its satire, appropriate illustrations, clear statement, and close reasoning. The *Missouri Democrat* ventured the opinion that in oratorical ability Sumner had established himself as a worthy successor to Adams, Webster, and Everett. "In vigor and richness of diction, in felicity and fecundity if illustration, in breadth and completeness of view, he stands unsurpassed." Cassius Marcellus Clay, while critical of the studied arrangement (it "smells too much of the lamp"), nevertheless ranked the speech alongside Webster's "Reply to Hayne." Even his adversaries commented on the orator's artistry — or artifice. "A dish of classics," sneered Senator Douglas, who professed to be shocked by reference to the rape of virgin territory; "classical allusions, each one only distinguished for its lasciviousness and obscenity. . . . unfit for decent young men to read." He accused Sumner of having memorized his speech and "practiced every night before a glass, with a negro boy to hold the candle and watch the gestures."[20]

Charles Sumner's congressional speeches on the slavery question were essentially denunciations of evil and evildoers, expressed in as powerful, memorable language as careful premeditation could devise. While the Senate debated the Lecompton constitution for Kansas during his enforced absence, he wrote to a friend, "I would give one year of my life for one week now in which to expose this enormous villainy."[21] When he returned to the Senate his first desire was to deliver a comprehensive denunciation of slavery unrelated to any specific legislative measure. This he did on June 4, 1860, in a four-hour oration titled "The Barbarism of Slavery," certainly the most complete summary of the history and character of the South's peculiar institution ever presented in the Congress.

But the memorized oration in which Sumner specialized, the set speech laboriously constructed, delivered with at least one eye on the larger audience, revised and corrected for the reading public, was not the only brand of congressional oratory which captured popular attention during the pre-Civil War period. Even more attractive than Sumner's works of literary art were the dramatic productions played out in the Senate — clashes of ideas, conflicts of colorful personalities, more exciting than anything taking place in the theater of the day. It was a time when titans, armed only with their wits and a handful of notes, delivered day-long speeches which were reported in the papers and heatedly discussed all over the land. Legends clustered about many allegedly "great debates," but none elicited more superlatives than that on Foote's resolution during the winter and spring of 1830. A brief depiction of one climactic episode may serve to illustrate the importance attached to these encounters by a fascinated public.

Late in December 1829, Senator Samuel A. Foote of Connecticut introduced a resolution to inquire into the expediency of restricting the sale of public lands to those already on the market. The ensuing debate continued from January through May, ranging far beyond the subject of public lands to conflicting interpretations of the Constitution, the national bank, internal improvements, the tariff, and the intentions of the founding fathers. A score of senators delivered several scores of speeches. But the climax, the only part of the Great Debate which is now remembered, came in late January when Robert Hayne of South Carolina and Daniel Webster of Massachusetts faced each other in an oratorical contest which was to produce what is generally regarded as the greatest deliberative address ever heard in America, Webster's second reply to Hayne.

This meeting of southern and northern champions had all the ingredients of a splendid contest. Both men were known to be excellent speakers; each was supremely confident of his powers and the success of his cause, each was backed by loyal supporters with a vital stake in the outcome. The suggestion of personal combat was enhanced by the imagery of a duel. Hayne, referring to an earlier Webster speech, said that since his opponent had discharged his fire in the presence of the Senate, he hoped he might be afforded an opportunity of returning the shot. Webster, folding his arms across his chest, replied: "Let the discussion proceed; I am ready now to receive the gentleman's fire." On the eve of his second reply, changing the metaphor but preserving the spirit of personal struggle for supremacy, Webster assured Judge Story, "I will grind him as fine as a pinch of snuff."[22] Hayne, bidding for the support of the West, had attacked the high protective tariff policy of the North and introduced Calhoun's doctrine of nullification as a weapon against oppressive acts of the federal government. In a strong speech concluded on January 25 he launched an effective attack on Webster himself and on the section he represented. Such attacks could not be left unanswered without serious damage to the prestige of New England, her representative in the Senate, and the stability of the Federal Union.

The dramatic scene of Webster's reply to Hayne on January 26 and 27 has been immortalized in George Healy's enormous painting which hangs today over the platform of Boston's Faneuil Hall. The event was described by overwhelmed eyewitnesses at the time, and their accounts have been embellished by subsequent writers until it is difficult to distinguish fact from fancy. The account most frequently relied upon is that given by Charles W. March in his *Reminiscences of Congress*. According to March, multitudes flowed into the city for several days in anticipation of a speech from Webster. As early as nine o'clock in the morning of January 26 the audience began arriving at the Capitol, filling the Senate chamber long before noon, when the session was to convene. The halls and stairways were dark with men "who clung to one another, like bees in a swarm." Women in gay bonnets occupied seats given up to them by senators. The House of Representatives was deserted, its members having flocked to the Senate. Dixon Lewis, a congressman from Alabama, finding himself wedged in behind the vice president and unable to change his position, managed to poke a hole with his pocketknife in one of the painted glass windows which flanked the presiding officer's chair so that he might see the speaker. March describes Webster as exhilarated by the greatness of the occasion, comparing him to the war-horse of the Scriptures, who "paweth in the valley, and rejoiceth in his strength . . . who smelleth the battle afar off." From the dignified exordium calling for a reading of the resolution before the Senate to the majestic peroration which was to become part of the American heritage, he held his audience — to use a term then popular for expressing the highest possible tribute — "enchained." When he concluded his moving eulogy to the Bay State, a group of Massachusetts men clustered in the balcony, we are told, "shed tears like girls." No man was ever so abundantly endowed by nature as Daniel Webster to play the part of the Great Orator, and this occasion marked the zenith of his oratorical career. Recorders of the event inevitably commented upon the magic of his delivery — his magnificent voice, his imposing countenance and regal manner. Edward Everett, who had listened to the greatest speakers on both sides of the Atlantic, asserted that in this speech Webster approached what Demosthenes must have been when he delivered the Oration for the Crown. To Charles March the peroration was inspired: "Eye, brow, each feature, every line of the face, seemed touched, as with a celestial fire." The entire speech, he said, "was a complete drama of comic and pathetic scenes; one varied excitement; laughter and tears gaining alternative victory."[23]

I have purposely emphasized the dramatic aspects of the Webster-Hayne debate, depicting it as one of several "battles of the giants" which absorbed and entertained the American public in the decades prior to the Civil War. It must not be inferred, however, that this debate and others like it were mere drama, mere spectacle. We have Everett's word for it that "throughout the country Mr. Webster's speech was regarded, not only as a brilliant and success-ful personal defence and a triumphant vindication of New England, but as a complete overthrow of the dangerous Constitutional heresies which had menaced the stability of the Union."[24] Argu-ments advanced in these debates were appropriated by other speakers in the discussion of specific measures and influenced the thinking of the general public. For years, Everett asserts, Webster's speeches constituted a "public armory" from which weapons of attack and defense were drawn by political supporters throughout the Union. The same might be said of the speeches of orators who took the lead in stating opposing positions.

The Foote resolution never came to a vote, but as the *North American Review* pointed out in an eighty-page article on the debate of 1830, debates in a deliberative body are not always intended to settle particular points or dispatch specific matters of business. Sometimes they serve "to produce general impressions by a free interchange of thought," or as we might say, to crystallize public opinion, in Congress and out. Webster's speech won a victory for nationalism and struck a blow to those whose doctrines endangered the Union. The following winter, at a public dinner held in New York in honor of the speech, Chancellor James Kent, the presiding officer, noted its beneficial results in turning public attention to the necessity for national union. As Socrates was said to have drawn philosophy from the skies and scattered it among the schools, Kent asserted, so Webster has rescued constitutional law from the libraries of lawyers and submitted it to the judgement of the American people.[25]

Lest it be supposed that the Congress of the United States regaled the nation with a continuous parade of epoch-making "great debates," it must be acknowledged that these were climactic events, and that for long periods of time between these moments of high drama the halls of Congress echoed little but pedestrian babble and pretentious nonsense. Ironically, some of the worst congressional oratory resulted from the same impulse, a striving for artistic expression, which produced the best.

One of the most valuable sources of information on congressional speaking is John Quincy Adams's diary. After leaving the White House, Adams served from 1831 until his death in 1848 as a member of the House of Representatives. At night he conscientiously recorded the details of each day's debate, though the task was sometimes almost more than he could bear. "The daily repetition of these long sittings in the House," he wrote in 1840, "not only robs me of nightly repose at home, but produces a nervous agitation and musing, which wastes itself in tumultuary thought." The former professor of rhetoric and oratory, student of the eloquence of Demosthenes, Cicero, and Burke, must have found some of those "long sittings" a painful ordeal. Generous in his praise of what he considered genuine eloquence, he was blunt in condemnation of tedious irrelevancy. The diary makes frequent mention of speeches lasting two, three, and four hours. In a debate on the Treasury Note bill, we are told: "Waddy Thompson made a frothy, trashy, silly speech, and Rhett made part of one, alike senseless, against him." On another occasion, when a Dr. Duncan "resumed his rhapsody, repeating his furious, brainless, and heartless speeches of the last session, for about two hours and a half," Adams "sickened at hearing him" and went into the Supreme Court library to do some research. These, of course, are mere explosions —

expressions of annoyance at tedium and ineptitude — but Adams was often more specific about what he found offensive in the speeches of his colleagues. One can imagine him sputtering to himself as he scratched out this critique of a speech on an appropriation bill by Congressman Charles G. Atherton of New Hampshire:

> He had a speech of shreds and patches — scraps of old newspaper, extracts from my messages, from Jefferson's writings, from English reviews, from Blackwood's Magazine, from anonymous pamphlets and electioneering handbills, with school-boy dissertations about the origin of the two great parties, and the contrast of their principles, the Democrats' and the Federalists' responsibility to the people, the eloquence of Tully in support of the Roman democracy, the age of progress, of improvement, of the rights of man, and the unutterable scorn and indignation of his constituents at my recommendation of a university, of appropriations for internal improvements, for clearing harbors, removing obstructions from rivers, and "lighthouses in the skies." About seven o'clock he suspended his speech.[26]

Next day, Adams notes that "Atherton finished his speech of extracts and paragraphs about the people, democracy, oligarchy, and federalism." Examination of the *Congressional Globe* for April 23, 1840, reveals that Adams exaggerated but little. The speech touches upon all the topics mentioned and occupies twenty columns of exceedingly fine print.

In addition to the characteristic wordiness and irrelevancy of much congressional debate, Adams's diary describes verbal abuse and outright violence among the members. Epithets like "liar," "coward," and "scoundrel" were freely exchanged, and challenges to duels were not uncommon. Altercations in Congress ranged in intensity from the relatively civilized encounter reported by Adams "in which the retort courteous, the quip modest, the counter-check quarrelsome, and the lie with circumstance were bandied between them till four o'clock, when the House adjourned," to a threat by Henry A. Wise of Virginia to murder Adams in his seat.[27]

John Quincy Adams was an austere man, not noted for his willingness to suffer fools gladly; it would be reasonable to attrib-

ute his severe strictures upon congressional oratory to tempera-
ment or to misanthropy brought on by an unhappy term as president. His evaluations, however, are corroborated by a variety of
sources. Early records of the proceedings of Congress, though not
verbatim transcripts, are complete enough to substantiate Adams's
observations. Intemperate and even violent language there certainly
was, especially when the subject of slavery came up, as it frequently
did. The personal abuse of Adams by Wise, or of Clay by Randolph, went considerably beyond anything heard in Congress today. As for physical violence, though the assault on Sumner in the
Senate was undoubtedly the most savage example, there were
other times when mere words were inadequate to express inflamed
emotions. For example, in the midst of his account of a debate in
the House of Representatives on the president's message recom-
mending admission of Kansas under the Lecompton constitution —
a debate marked by a continual snarling of parliamentary proce-
dure, a flurry of motions, including motions to adjourn — the
reporter for the *Congressional Globe* writes: "At this moment a violent personal altercation commenced in the aisle at the right of the
Speaker's chair, between Mr. Keitt and Mr. Grow. In an instant the
House was in the greatest possible confusion. Members in every
part of the Hall rushed over to the scene of conflict, and several
members seemed to participate in it."[28] Partial order was eventually
restored by energetic efforts of the Speaker and the sergeant-at-
arms bearing the mace. Though it was well past midnight, more
motions to adjourn were beaten down, and the House remained in
session until 6:25 A.M. When it reconvened the following Mon-
day, Keitt apologized to the House for the "unpleasant incident" in
which he admitted he was the aggressor. Grow, though insisting he
acted only to protect his life and person, tendered "whatever apology is due."[29]

Adams's complaint about the undue length of congressional
speeches is echoed in a multitude of sources. Verbosity had apparently been a weakness of congressmen almost from the beginning.
In the early decades of the century certain members' inexhaustible
capacity for sustained utterance became legendary. John Calhoun
said of a New York congressman, Barent Gardinier, that he could
hold the floor for days. John Randolph of Roanoke, Virginia, often
held the floor for five or six hours at a time, talking of everything or

nothing. As early as 1816, in a debate on standing rules and orders, a congressman proposed eliminating the use of a call for "the previous question" as a means of stopping debate. Randolph predictably favored this action, branding the previous question a "gag law." Henry Clay, attempting to justify the maneuver, said that it was seldom resorted to, and then only when flagrant abuse of debate made it necessary. Clay reminded the House that "a certain gentleman" (probably Gardinier) had once spoken for twenty-four hours without stopping in order to delay action. This debate on "the previous question" ended with no decision made and no action taken.[30]

In 1828 Congressman William Haile, appalled by the inefficiency of the House in transacting its business, remarked that although the most finished oration of Demosthenes or Cicero could be read in forty minutes, modern orators required two or three days, during which they were talking, for the most part, to empty seats. Haile acknowledged the constitutional right to speak but reminded his colleagues of an equally constitutional right not to listen. In the British Parliament, he said, when a member became tedious, the House put him down by coughing and scraping their feet. Haile then expressed the opinion that this practice might one day be resorted to in the American Congress. "At this point of Mr. Haile's speech," we read, "his remarks became suddenly inaudible to the Reporter, from a general coughing and confusion in the House."[31]

Earlier that same year a voice outside Congress had been heard in the same cause. The *North American Review*, whose admiration for spoken eloquence was manifested from time to time in reviews of published volumes of speeches and reports of a variety of speech events including political debates, complained about the proliferation of congressional speeches and sought to establish the proposition that "speeches in Congress have increased, are increasing, and ought to be diminished."[32] The solution proposed for reducing the volume of talk was to stop publishing speeches in extenso, thus frustrating speakers who sought no effect in the House but merely wished to get their speeches into the newspapers.

In January 1841, at about the same time that Adams was expressing greatest irritation at the discursiveness of his colleagues, the same journal published a forty-page blast at "Congressional

Eloquence."[33] At its head are listed three items, apparently congressional speeches printed in pamphlet form and submitted for review. After admitting that much congressional speaking is good, at its best as good as any in the world, the writer proceeds to lambaste congressional oratory in general for its diffuseness, its interminably pointless storytelling, its gratuitous classical allusions, and its bad temper and bad manners. He quotes page after tedious page from two of the speeches listed, by Wise of Virginia and Duncan of Ohio, concluding "with such wretched babble does the gravity of an American Congress submit to be affronted." From Duncan there is a fatuous eulogy to the log cabin (the Harrison campaign was in progress) — its romance, its construction, the frolics, the songs, etc.; from Wise some incredibly wordy passages of which the following fragment is a fair sample. He has, he says, fought valiantly to save public money and combat a corrupt administration, though not without great opposition:

But the blaze of glorification is espied. Thank God, the day-star dawns from on high. There is now hope of salvation; an hour of retributive justice is coming; Truth, though slow, is coming gradually along with her torches. I have been waiting for her long, but never without hope. I have had to carry my life itself in my hand, the harness of deerskin, and cold steel and iron, has often galled my shoulders, an armed arsenal against the king's forces, — they are dangerous when there are such rich spoils; but I have escaped unscathed, thank God! Though my slanderers, and persecutors, and revilers would have the world believe that my war upon corruption has not been bloodless.[34]

Shortly after the publication of this article the House reacted against excessive loquacity by adopting a rule that no congressman could speak for more than one hour except by unanimous consent. Although there was some subsequent evidence of condensation, long speeches did not cease; members were apparently generous in granting approval for extension of time.

Charges of verbosity, irrelevancy, bad taste, and bad manners thus far cited were directed at the House of Representatives. Though observers agreed that the most egregious offenses took place in the House, we have the testimony of at least one distinguished senator that his colleagues in the upper house were not above criticism. Replying in his Seventh of March speech to Calhoun's charge of violence in the northern press, Daniel Webster admitted that the press was violent everywhere, in the South as well as in the North. This, he thought, was to be expected when the press is free, as it should be. When the press is free there will be foolish and violent paragraphs in the newspapers, as there are foolish and violent speeches in both houses of Congress. "In truth," he went on, "I must say that, in my opinion, the vernacular tongue of the country has become greatly vitiated, depraved, and corrupted by the style of our Congressional debates. And if it were possible for those debates to vitiate the principles of the people as much as they have depraved their tastes, I should cry out, 'God save the Republic!' "[35]

Why, we must ask in the face of such widespread agreement concerning the speaking of Congress, why, at a time when public interest in congressional oratory was intense, when great political questions were discussed with an eloquence seldom equaled since, should the general level of quality have been so low? One explanation has already been suggested, the striving for "eloquence" on the part of men unequipped to achieve it. Americans had taken it into their heads, and had been encouraged in the belief by foreign commentators, that they were a race of orators. Oratory had played an important role in winning independence, in establishing and securing acceptance for the new government. Bold voices in and out of Congress had dealt in epic vein with vast themes — nationalism, expansionism, the rights of man. Sumner, Everett, Choate, Webster, and others had created a taste for a classical style of oratory which, though not always completely appreciated, was considered admirable and appropriate in a modern democracy consciously following an ancient model. In attempting to supply the demand and conform to the ideal, men with neither taste, learning, nor a sense of the appropriate succeeded only in pleasing audiences with similar limitations, while making themselves ridiculous to people of discernment.

Foreign travelers, of whom there were many during these years, in their published commentaries upon American customs and institutions, often included evaluations of our oratory. Francis and Theresa Pulszky, noting the magnitude of the themes dealt with by

Congress in the 1850s and observing that great occasions engendered great men, nevertheless felt it necessary to add: "But the crowd of their numerous imitators, anxious to rival them, sink into the bottomless sea of verbiage and false pathos; unable to grapple with the difficulties, they describe them with exaggerating grandiloquence, and hide with flowers of oratory the shallowness of their ideas."[36]

These observers from abroad made frequent comparisons of British and American legislative speaking, arriving at strikingly similar assessments. In Parliament, they agreed, a speaker came immediately to grips with the subject at hand, dealt with it, and sat down. A premium was placed on clear, logical statement, analysis of the facts of the case, and refutation of the opponent's argument. More to the British taste than adornment were wit, irony, invective. In short, the Member of Parliament was a debater, not an orator. In Congress, on the other hand, each speaker rose to "make a speech." And since a speech must by definition have an exordium and a peroration, as well as a variety of divisions in between, its relevance to the specific measure under discussion sometimes tended to become obscured. The congressman, moreover, realizing that oratory was widely regarded as part of the national literature, was tempted to strive for literary immortality each time he took the floor. Because the "Reply to Hayne" or the "True Grandeur of Nations" had become literature, why should not his speech on the tariff or an appropriation bill achieve similar distinction? This lack of discrimination between themes that would support "eloquence" and themes that rendered it inappropriate drew the attention of Alexander Mackay, a perceptive observer of the American Congress who reported the debates on the Oregon question in 1846 for the *London Chronicle*. "The bill before the House may be for the better regulation of the Post-office," wrote Mackay, "but that does not deter a member speaking upon it from commencing with the discoveries of Columbus, and ending with the political exigencies of his own township." For Mackay appropriateness was a prime criterion. "To get poetical over a bank bill is evidently a mistake; to jumble imagery and statistics together, a want of judgment and a defect in taste."[37]

Besides legislators who aspired to rival the great orators and like them to create orations that would live as literature, there were then, as doubtless there will always be, those who simply loved to talk and who having once gained the floor were reluctant to yield it up. Southerners were alleged to be especially susceptible to this weakness, though there was probably little correlation between garrulity and geography. The anonymous critic of congressional eloquence in the *North American Review* asserted (possibly because a speech of Wise was under scrutiny) that most talkative of all were the Virginians. This proclivity he attributed to the fact that they had nothing to do at home but survey solitary expanses of tobacco and read. The southern congressman, according to this critic, read politics and classical history, talked them over with family and visitors, and arrived in Congress having laid away an inexhaustible store on the Greeks and the Romans, the Goths and the Vandals. "All his remembrance of ancient and modern lore, of classical and feudal story, are subject to be brought out on a question of renewing the upholstery of the Representatives' Chamber, or paying the Sergeant-at-Arms."[38]

Further explanation for the diffuseness and sheer quantity of congressional oratory is to be found in the demands and expectations of the American audience. Representatives of the people were expected to make speeches, and the longer and more frequent the better. When Charles Dickens visited Washington during his American tour of 1842 he attended sessions of both houses of Congress "nearly every day" and was not overcome by admiration of anything he saw or heard. The outstanding characteristic of congressional oratory, he believed, was the constant repetition of the same idea, or shadow of an idea, in different words. The most frequent inquiry heard "out of doors" was not "What did he say?" but "How long did he speak?"[39]

The charge was frequently made that the set speeches in the Congress were directed not to senators or congressmen, but to the people back home. The practice of haranguing one's colleagues with a speech with no relevance to the subject under discussion, and no interest for anyone save a few residents of a local district, was known after about 1820 as "speaking for Bunkum." According to a story which was related with several variations, a member of the House from North Carolina whose home district included the county of Buncombe spoke so often, so long, and so irrelevantly, that he drove his colleagues from the chamber. One day, as members made for the exits, he attempted to set the departing legislators at ease by assuring them that their absence would not upset him, since he was speaking not to the House but to "Bunkum."[40] Though such candor was not typical, there is no question that congressmen were aware of the expectations of their constituents and that whether or not the immediate audience listened, the real audience was ultimately addressed through the newspaper reporters and the post office. Constituents who received through the mails speeches in pamphlet form, replete with local references, could take pleasure in the knowledge that Buncombe was receiving national recognition. They could also bask in the reflected glory of their representative in Washington, confident that through his oratory he was influencing his colleagues and helping conduct the affairs of the nation. Speechmaking was regarded as one of the responsibilities of public office and a requisite for retaining favor; silent representatives could be replaced. Alexander Mackay, observing the impact of such popular attitudes upon congressional oratory, believed that hope for change lay in changed expectations: "When constituencies begin to feel that there are other modes in which their interests may be subserved than by seeking for their representative a mere talking machine, there will be more work and less speaking done in the House, and the style of oratory will improve in proportion. Little else can be expected but rant, where speaking is done to order."[41]

Alexis de Tocqueville, an earlier observer of American institutions, had suggested that excessive speechmaking might be an inevitable evil in a democracy. In aristocratic nations, he explained, members of political assemblies are also members of the aristocracy. The member's position in the country at large is often more important to him than his position in the assembly. Consequently he feels no compulsion to make speeches to enhance his public image. In America, it is often the case that a man "becomes somebody only from his position in the assembly." He needs to establish his importance by expressing his opinions in public. In this he is motivated not only by his own vanity but also by the demand of his constituents that he serve them by airing local grievances and honor them by achieving a reputation for eloquence. The legislator in a democracy knows that he is dependent upon his constituents for continuance in office. In an aristocracy, if rejected he may stand for election in another district, or may simply retire and "enjoy the pleasures of splendid idleness."[42]

But though he perceives much pettiness in American political debates, Tocqueville lauds congressional oratory at its best. "I can conceive nothing more admirable or more powerful," he says, "than a great orator debating great questions of state in a democratic assembly."

STUMP SPEAKING

In the autumn of 1840, noting that his son Charles had just attended a meeting at which George Bancroft had delivered "an electioneering Democratic address," John Quincy Adams wrote in his diary: "This practice of itinerant speech-making has suddenly broken forth in this country to a fearful extent. Electioneering for the Presidency has spread its contagion to the President himself, to his now only competitor, to his immediate predecessor, to at least one of his Cabinet councillors, the Secretary of War, to the ex-candidates Henry Clay and Daniel Webster, and to many of the most distinguished members of both Houses of Congress." A few days later he observed that political leaders "are travelling about the country from State to State, and holding forth, like Methodist preachers, hour after hour, to assembled multitudes under the broad canopy of heaven." Instead of attending to the duties of their offices, he complained, they "rave, recite, and madden round the land."[43]

This itinerant political speechmaking which so dismayed Adams was a relatively new phenomenon in his part of the country. No presidential candidate had previously campaigned in his own behalf, and Adams, as a former president, had steadfastly refrained on grounds of propriety from participating in national campaigns. Stump speaking, the appeal to mass meetings for votes or political support, though considered undignified in New England, had long been familiar on the frontiers of the South and West, its very name betraying its frontier origin. Young Abraham Lincoln heard stump speeches in Indiana in 1826-1827. Davy Crockett, a Jackson man in 1827, was exploited by the Whigs as a campaign speaker in 1834. During the campaigns of 1828 and 1832 the supporters of Andrew Jackson, acknowledging the realities of an expanding suffrage, modified traditional political techniques by taking the campaign to the people.

But it was the presidential campaign of 1840, the year John Quincy Adams saw his colleagues traveling around the land, that will be forever remembered for the unrestrained exuberance of its stump oratory. Whether one regards the "log-cabin campaign" as the "nadir of American political intelligence," or as a gratifying manifestation of democracy in action, it surely surpassed in color, excitement, and popular participation everything that preceded it.

After twelve years of Jacksonianism, the Whigs saw a chance to capitalize upon public dissatisfaction with the financial policies of Jackson and the misery accompanying the panic of 1837 and for the first time to place their candidate in the White House. Passing by Webster and Clay, they nominated the aging General William Henry Harrison to oppose Martin Van Buren, the Democratic incumbent. Harrison, the unsuccessful and completely silent candidate of 1836 ("Let him say not one single word about his principles, or his creed — let him say nothing — promise nothing," Nicholas Biddle had instructed on that occasion), had apparently but one qualification for the presidency: he had won a military victory over the British and the Indians at Tippecanoe a quarter of a century earlier. A figurehead, he became a symbol of the opposition to Jackson and Van Buren. The Whigs drafted no platform or statement of principles; their principal aim was to elect a Whig president. Regarded by many as Federalists and aristocrats, they sought to erase their image as the party of privilege, to turn the prevailing democratic impulse to their own advantage — in short, to present themselves as more democratic than the Democrats.

Fortunately, the opposition unwittingly provided them with a most effective weapon. Shortly after the nomination of General Harrison, the Washington correspondent of a Van Buren paper sneered: "Give him a barrel of hard cider and settle a pension of two thousand dollars a year on him, and he will sit the remainder of his days contented in a log cabin."[44] The Whigs, skillfully turning the slight to political advantage, set about the task of portraying themselves as the party of log cabins and hard cider. Harrison, born a Virginia aristocrat, was transformed into a humble, cider-drinking man of the people. The campaign had, if not an issue, a symbol and a slogan.

The nation embarked on a nine-month holiday. Log cabins appeared everywhere — in public squares, mounted on wagons, dangling from watch chains. Farmers drove teams hitched to wagons thirty miles to attend barbecues, listen to speeches, and cheer parades featuring floats, songs, slogans, banners, cider jugs, and coonskin caps. Tom Corwin of Ohio traveled on a huge log cabin mounted on a wagon that served as a platform from which to speak. Crowds of twenty thousand, thirty thousand, or fifty thousand were not uncommon; audiences were calculated by the acre. Democrats, for once finding themselves outdemogogued, fell back on attacks on Harrison's military record and denunciations of intemperate hard-cider drinking, vulgar songs, and vicious lies. More to the point, they pointed out the hypocrisy of professions of log-cabin democracy by the party of aristocracy and wealth.

The tone of the Whig campaign was set by two remarkable speeches delivered in the House of Representatives. In February, during a debate on an appropriation for the Cumberland Road, Congressman Isaac Crary of Michigan, in one of those gratuitous digressions so common in the House, sought to cast doubt upon the vaunted Indian-fighting exploits of General Harrison and to expose him as a bogus hero. Since the Whig candidate's military record was his principal asset, this challenge could not be allowed to go unanswered. On the following day, Tom Corwin, the Ohio Wagon Boy, a speaker with an established reputation for wit and humor, rose to reply. Though much of Corwin's speech was devoted to a defense of Harrison's record, the part that most delighted partisan auditors was his devastating attack upon Crary. In order to discredit Crary and destroy his credibility as a critic, Corwin satirized the peacetime militia, in which the Michigan legislator served as a general officer. Referring sarcastically to "the glorious history of toils, privations, sacrifices, and bloody scenes, through which we know, from observation, a militia officer in time of peace is sure to pass," he portrayed Crary as a ridiculous figure astride a comical horse at the head of troops armed with umbrellas and ax handles. It is parade day, "that most dangerous and glorious event in the life of a militia general." Suddenly, a crisis occurs; a cloud passes over the sun. Decisiveness is imperative.

> A retreat is ordered, and troops and general, in a twinkling, are found safely bivouacked in a neighboring grocery! But even here the general still has room for the exhibition of heroic deeds. Hot from the field, and chaffed with the untoward events of the day, your general unsheaths his trenchant blade, eighteen inches in length, as you will well remember, and with energy and remorseless fury he slices the watermelons that lie in heaps around him, and shares them with his surviving friends. Other of the sinews of war are not wanting here. Whiskey, that great leveler of modern times, is here also, and the shells of the water-melons are filled to the brim.
> Here, again, is shown how extremes of barbarism and civilization meet. As the Scandinavian heroes of old, after the fatigues of war, drank wine from the skulls of their slaughtered enemies, in Odin's halls, so now our militia general and his forces, from the skulls of melons thus vanquished, in copious draughts of whiskey assuages the heroic fire of their souls after the bloody scenes of a parade day.[45]

Members of the House were convulsed with laughter. The speech was hailed as a masterpiece of eloquence, unexcelled for wit, humor, and sarcasm. Crary, known thereafter as "the water-melon general," was rejected for renomination by his constituents, his political career ruined. Crary's humiliation by the Ohioan was somehow construed as a vindication of Harrison; thousands of copies of Corwin's speech were distributed during the campaign.

In April the House heard another speech, equally preposterous and, as it happened, even more influential in the Whig campaign. Congressman Charles Ogle of Pennsylvania, opposing a $3,665 appropriation for repair of the White House, held the floor for three days with an irrelevant and mendacious harangue later published and widely circulated under the title "The Regal Splendor of the Presidential Palace." In a shameless bid for the approval of victims of a depressed economy, Ogle pictured President Van Buren living in kingly splendor in a palace furnished with statuary, royal Wilton carpets, French comforters and bedsteads, and nine-foot golden-framed mirrors, feasting on French cookery from gold plate and sterling silver service, while working men and women perished for want of bread. The speech was, as the *Washington Globe* described it, "an omnibus of lies," but it served perfectly its purpose as a foil to a party campaigning under a banner of log cabins and hard cider. Soon people were singing:

> *Let Van from his coolers of silver drink wine,*
> *And lounge on his cushioned settee,*
> *Our man on a buckeye bench can recline,*
> *Content with hard cider is he.*[46]

Fueled by the intensely personal diatribes of Corwin and Ogle, the log-cabin campaign warmed up during the summer and fall of 1840. One knowledgeable observer, who thought it "the most memorable that has ever taken place," estimated that more than five thousand speakers were on the stump from day to day, from one end of the country to the other.[47] Tom Corwin claimed to have addressed "at least seven hundred thousand people, men, women and children Dogs negroes & Democrats inclusive." John W. Bear, "the Buckeye Blacksmith," campaigning in his leather apron, made 331 speeches. Adams was right; everybody who was anybody was on the stump that year. Speeches were often a melange of hero-worship, gross appeals to prejudice, ostentatious literary allusions, crude anecdotes, and personal abuse. The *Washington Globe* suggested one way of producing a typical Whig speech: Put in a lottery wheel such words as *bloodhounds, Sub-Treasurers, corruption, abuses, credit system, log cabin, hard cider, Tippecanoe, Thames, battles, Indians, women, scalping knives,* etc. "Give it a turn, and let them fly out of an aperture, and the combination will form a fair specimen of the oratory of the tribe."[48]

Even the godlike Daniel Webster descended to the world of men to deliver some hard-hitting, colloquial stump speeches. At Patchogue, New York, he offered by implication to fight anyone who called him an aristocrat. At Saratoga, admitting regretfully that he himself had not been born in a log cabin, he affirmed his deep feeling for log cabins, since his father had built one with his own hands on the New Hampshire frontier, and his elder brothers and sisters had been born there. When the speaker's platform collapsed, hurling Webster to the ground, he recovered himself and resumed his speech atop a wagon, observing grandly that "the great Whig platform was more solid than the frail structure on which he had been standing." The fact that there was no Whig platform in 1840 did not prevent this statement from being added to the list of oratorical tours de force.

Out in Illinois, one of the most effective stump speakers for the Whig party was young Abe Lincoln, the railsplitter, whose homespun humor and bucolic image fit nicely into the motif of the campaign. One of his speeches, delivered at Springfield in December 1839, was considered good enough to be published as a Whig document. The occasion was a three-day oratorical tournament in which three orators from each party presented their cases. The bulk of Lincoln's speech was prosaic and relatively unembellished, but the peroration shows him caught up in the spirit of the day. Replying to the prediction of a Democratic speaker that Van Buren would win a smashing victory in the election, he said:

> I know that the great volcano at Washington, aroused and directed by the evil spirit that reigns there, is belching forth the lava of political corruption in a current broad and deep, which is sweeping with frightful velocity over the whole length and breadth of the land, bidding fair to leave unscathed no green spot or living thing; while on its bosom are riding, like demons on the waves of hell, the imps of that evil spirit, and fiendishly taunting all those who dare resist its destroying course with the hopelessness of their effort; and, knowing this, I cannot deny that all may be swept away. Broken by it I, too, may be; bow to it I never will.[49]

The oratory of political campaigns, or "stump oratory," as it continued to be called long after there were no more stumps, is ostensibly deliberative in nature. Ideally, it enunciates a political principle or stakes out a position on a current issue; it sets forth the qualifications of a candidate and solicits public support. The campaign speaking of 1840 was a prime example of oratory cut loose from the issues. It was more demonstrative than deliberative. Audiences seeking release from the hardships and frustrations of economic depression and the isolation of frontier existence plunged with abandon into the excitement of a political campaign. Entertainment replaced instruction; personalities counted for more than argument. Conflict there was, but it was the conflict of a sporting event rather than the clash of ideas. Colorful speakers staged oratorical jousts for the delectation of partisan crowds. Flights of fancy were more effective than rational argument for scoring points and winning personal advantage. Crary belittled Harrison; Corwin demolished Crary; Ogle ridiculed Van Buren. Speakers were performers; oratory was drama, diversion, spectacle, the manner of expression more admired than the substance.

It is significant that Tom Corwin, the "King of the Stump," despite substantial political talents, was known then and is remembered today as above all an entertainer, a comedian. His feigned astonishment at the Democratic nomination in 1844 was received with delight: "And *who* have they nominated? James K. Polk of Tennessee. *After that,* who is safe?" His skill in dodging an issue was demonstrated before a Whig mass meeting in Marietta, Ohio, where it was important not to offend the abolitionists, whose strength was substantial. An opponent, seeking to put him on the spot, asked, "Shouldn't niggers be permitted to sit at the table with white folks, on steamboats and at hotels?" Corwin, a man of exceedingly dark complexion, replied jocularly, "Fellow-citizens, I ask you whether it is proper to ask such a question of a gentleman of my color?" Ben Perley Poore, to whom we are indebted for this story, reports, "The crowd cheered and the questioner was silenced."[50]

A carnival atmosphere continued to pervade subsequent political campaigns, though the sustained excitement of the log-cabin campaign was seldom if ever duplicated. As property qualifications for voting were eliminated, both parties found it to their advantage to "go down to the people." In 1844 the Democrats, imitating the successful techniques of their opponents, campaigned with songs and doggerel. The campaign of 1856, with its crowds, parades, songs, and fife and drum corps, reminded some observers of 1840. A John Fremont rally in Indianapolis drew fifty bands and 50,000 people. In Wisconsin, two thousand wagons filled with farmers formed a procession seven miles long. In Illinois, Abraham Lincoln made speeches for Fremont and recited Webster's peroration to the Reply to Hayne. Members of the new Republican party sang:

Arise, arise, ye brave!
And let your war cry be!
Free Speech, Free Press, Free Soil, Free Men
Fre-mont and victory.

But political campaigning during these two prewar decades was not all pageantry and foolishness. Important questions — the Oregon boundary dispute, the war with Mexico, the annexation of Texas, and, most basic of all, the dispute over slavery — were debated on the stump as well as in the Congress. A local campaign in Illinois between two candidates for the United States Senate demonstrated what stump speaking could be when the issues were vital, the audience aroused, and the speakers competent. For three months in 1858 Abraham Lincoln and Stephen Douglas stumped the state, participating in seven formal debates and delivering more than one hundred speeches. This was the first campaign in American history to be reported stenographically; shorthand experts accompanied the speakers and supplied the newspapers with remarkably accurate texts. The issues discussed were national, not local; never before had there been such widespread national interest in a local contest.

Spectacle there was in abundance — bands, banners with mottoes and slogans, the roar of cannon, fireworks, special trains bearing supporters, torchlight processions, cavalcades of buggies and farm wagons. But the debate itself was carried on in deadly earnest. The speakers dealt with relatively few issues — the extension of slavery to the territories, the power of states to deal with Negroes as they saw fit, the morality of the slave system — but they were issues uppermost in minds throughout the nation. The general level of the discussion, the seriousness of the speakers, the thrust and parry of genuine debate, the concern with relevant, substantive matters were all in marked contrast to the trivial personal encounters of 1840. Lincoln's humor, sparingly employed, usually served to drive home a point rather than to avoid taking a position or merely to entertain. When asked why he did not more often turn the laugh on Douglas, he replied that he was too much in earnest, adding that he doubted whether turning the laugh on anybody really won votes. The result of it all was a superb debate which not only played a crucial role in the political careers of the two participants, but helped crystallize public opinion on vital national issues. "It may be safely alleged," wrote the editor of the *Chicago Press and Tribune* in October 1859, "that American politics have never developed so close and heated a campaign as the one now in progress. . . . The eyes of the Union are riveted on the combatants, to the exclusion of all other objects of political interest, for all perceive that the history of the Republic is shaping itself around the Illinois battle field."[51]

It would of course be too much to cite the dramatic contrast between Lincoln's empty, grandiloquent campaign speech of 1839 and the earnest, thoughtful argumentation of his contest with Douglas as evidence of a maturing of American stump oratory. It was more likely simply the maturing of one stump orator, caught up in a cause that moved him deeply. But the Illinois campaign of 1858 revealed the enormous potentialities of an institution indispensable to the Democratic process which, despite frequent abuses and excesses, has had the effect of increasing popular interest and participation in political affairs. From time to time, before and since, Americans have managed, amidst the hurly-burly of campaign high jinks deemed necessary to awaken the populace and "get out the vote," to engage in sensible discussion of issues affecting their welfare.

ORATORY OF THE SOUTH

A separate word should perhaps be added concerning the oratory of the prewar South, not because it was essentially different from the oratory of the North, but because it is so often assumed to have been so. Familiar to all is the sterotype of the Typical Orator of the old South, with his flowing white hair, his alpaca coat and black string tie, his exaggerated gestures and florid rhetoric — striving vainly to conceal the poverty of his thought in the richness of his imagery. Like most stereotypes, this one undoubtedly had some basis in fact, but rhetorical excess was not an exclusively southern chracteristic.

Whether or not there existed any such phenomenon as "the typical southern orator," or oratory which could be recognized as unmistakably "southern," there can be little room for doubt about the extreme susceptibility of southern audiences to spoken eloquence. Few historians of the old South have dissented from the judgment of William G. Brown, "It is doubtful if there ever has been a society in which the orator counted for more than he did in the Cotton Kingdom." [52] Eloquence, says W. J. Cash in *The Mind of the South,* "flourished far beyond even its American average; it early became a passion — and not only a passion but a primary standard of judgement, the *sine qua non* of leadership." Southern audiences delighted in oratorical orgies not only at barbecues and political meetings but also at religious camp meetings and even in the law courts. And in all these speaking situations they manifested a willingness, a desire, to be charmed, hypnotized, overcome by the personal magnetism of the orator and the magical power of the spoken word.

This susceptibility to a certain kind of eloquence has been attributed to a variety of causes. Illiteracy was more prevalent in the South than in other sections. An uneducated audience is presumably more easily impressed by the externals of voice and delivery and by language with more sound than sense. Moreover, a rural, agrarian society, deprived of the social stimulation of city life, facing periods of seasonal unemployment, found in the excitement of a camp meeting, a court trial, or a political speaking tournament a rare antidote to loneliness, boredom, and cultural and emotional sterility. But enthusiasm for oratory was not limited to the uneducated. Sons of the southern aristocracy were sent to Harvard, Yale, or Princeton, or to southern academies and colleges emphasizing Greek and Latin studies — including, of course, rhetoric and oratory. Equally important to the acquisition of knowledge was the ability to express it orally. A southern gentleman was expected to excel in both public speaking and private conversation. In a society that liked to regard itself as a recapitulation of Greek Democracy, wherein a slave class made possible the luxury of a leisure class devoted to statecraft and the arts, an emphasis upon classical languages and literature was especially appropriate. Some southern orators, like the erudite Hugh S. Legaré, who viewed eloquence as "poetry subdued to the business of civic life," were men of broad learning and sound scholarship (Parrington thought Legare one of the most cultivated minds in America), but many paraded a superficial acquaintance with ancient lore and Greek and Latin quotations as a badge of rank or as a means of manipulating the common man, to whom such arcane knowledge was impressive. Henry Adams, in his *Education*, spoke disparagingly of the intellectual training of the Southerners he had known at Harvard in the 1850s. He had found them handsome, genial, possessing a habit of command, but little else. And Ralph Waldo Emerson recalled ruefully in later life that as a Harvard student he had been taken in by musical nonsense. He still remembered one sentence from a young Southerner's oration: "And there was a band of heroes, and round their mountain was a wreath of light, and in their midst, on the mountaintop, stood Liberty feeding her eagle."[53]

But the dominance of orators and oratory in the old South is not wholly to be explained by the ignorance and boredom of many of its people or by the ambition of leaders who fancied themselves modern counterparts of Demosthenes and Cicero to display their cultural superiority. It was preeminently the product of an urge for artistic expression and emotional outlet. It ranged literally from the sublime to the ridiculous — from the poetic flights of which John Randolph at his best was capable, to the most primitive, puerile folk art of a traveling evangelist or a backwoods stump speaker.[54]

A similar urge for expression in the North resulted in remarkable literary development — the Flowering of New England which Van Wyck Brooks has described. But southern culture was not a book culture. There were few public libraries or school systems, few literary journals. A literary career was considered beneath the dignity of gentlemen living in feudal splendor on spacious plantations, pursuing more vigorous and virile occupations. William Gilmore Simms, whom Edgar Allan Poe thought the best writer of fiction in America, was disparaged and rejected by his fellow Charlestonians. Legaré, one of the founders of the *Southern Review,* in his anxiety not to be regarded as "a mere literary man," poured his immense erudition into gorgeous, dazzling oratory. John Randolph of Roanoke, an eccentric but also indisputably an artist, observing the low esteem in which literary men were held in southern society, scrupulously avoided cultivating his gifts. Dissipating his considerable talent in arrogant indolence, he adopted the role of mad genius, belaboring and sometimes enchanting the House with interminable orations, remembered today primarily for their elaborate imagery and colorful epithets.

Politics, not art or literature, was the passion of the prewar

South, and the handmaiden of politics was oratory. It was in the political arena that creative impulses found expression. Politics was, as W. J. Cash has observed, "a theater for the play of the purely personal, the purely romantic, and the purely hedonistic." The metaphor of the theater is strikingly appropriate. Oratory was performance; orators were actors. A man might charm his audience with his voice, his actions, his command of language, or a combination of all three, but charm them he must. Personality, dramatic flair, what today would be called showmanship, were all-important. "The powerful man was above all a person; his power was himself. How such a great man mounted the rostrum, with what demeanor he bore an interruption, by what gesture he silenced a murmur — such things were remembered and talked about when his reasoning was perhaps forgotten."[55]

Such things were indeed remembered. The speeches of many southern orators, matinee idols in their time, have perished with them, but anecdotes of their histrionic and literary artistry remain. William Yancey, like many other southern "fire-eaters," left no volume of published speeches, but tradition has preserved a multitude of tales of his personal triumphs on the stump. Contemporaries said of him that it was worth traveling across the continent to hear him pronounce the word *Alabama*. At Uniontown, Alabama, in 1856, climaxing a three-day political meeting featuring relays of orators, Yancey referred in his peroration to the advance of Napoleon's troops against the Austrians. As he described the advance of the troops, he marched with measured tread toward the edge of the stage. At the end of the platform, facing the audience, he hurled the soldier's command, "Keep time, my men! Keep time!" The audience, so the report goes, sprang to their feet, threw their hats in the air, and cheered. Men mounted the platform to congratulate the orator, who was then presented with a bouquet by the ladies.[56]

There is evidence that even Northerners were unable to resist the power of southern spellbinders. W. H. Sparks relates a story told him by "a venerable judge of New Jersey" concerning Seargent S. Prentiss of Mississippi. Hearing that Prentiss had held a New York audience spellbound for three hours and skeptical about the power of oratory thus to obliterate time, the judge took the first opportunity to hear a speech by the Whig orator. Reaching "the place" (the time, location, or circumstances are not revealed), all seats being taken he was forced to stand, jammed in by the huge crowd. He took out his watch to time the speaker, noted the precise minute, and started to replace it, but something said "arrested his attention and his hands from their work." "There was something, sir, in his eye which startled me, and then the words came bubbling up spontaneously as spring water, so full of power, so intensely brilliant, and his figures so bold, original, and illustrating, and the one following the other in such quick succession; the flights of imagination, so new, so eloquent, and so heart-searching — that I found it impossible to take my eyes from his face, or my ears from drinking in every word." At one time, the venerable judge reports, his feelings were so intense that he thought he would faint. Unconscious of the crowd, of time, of everything but the speaker, the seventy-year-old man felt no fatigue. When the speaker finished, the judge found himself still holding his watch in his hand. He had been standing unmoved in the same position for three hours and fifteen minutes. A minister of the gospel standing nearby exclaimed with trembling lips, "Will you ever doubt again that God inspires man?"[57] Nowhere in the report is there any mention of what Prentiss said on this occasion, or even the subject of his speech.

A similar story of oratorical sorcery comes from Henry M. Dawes, a student of Marietta College in Ohio. Having heard of the amazing powers of Henry A. Wise, then a candidate for governor of Virginia, Dawes journeyed to nearby Parkersburgh to hear for himself. Expecting "a person of commanding stature, upright bearing with flashing eyes and noble forehead," he was disappointed to find a small slovenly dressed man with stooping carriage and shambling gait, his chin unshaven and flecked with tobacco juice. But the young student's attention was soon caught up by "an indescribable something" in the speaker's manner. To illustrate the absorbing influence of Wise's oratory he tells of seeing an old bald-headed Virginian seated directly in front of the speaker who listened so intently that he was oblivious of the fact that Wise was splattering him with tobacco juice for three hours as he spoke. "The old man's head was as the back of a trout." Of the speech Dawes wrote to a local newspaper: "I thought him eloquence incarnated. Never in my life have I listened to such an appeal; it set

the blood dashing through my veins like a mountain torrent. . . .
There is an enchantment about his oratory which it is impossible to
resist."[58]

It may be recalled that the speaker on this occasion was the
same Henry A. Wise who for many years had made life miserable
for John Quincy Adams in the House of Representatives, the same
man whom the *North American Review,* in commenting upon his
printed speeches, had accused of affronting the American Congress
with wretched babble. After the Parkersburgh speech Dawes wrote
that it had not changed his opinion of Wise as "one of the veriest
demagogues that ever crouched at the feet of the sovereign people
and whined for office," a man whom he was not anxious to see
elected governor of Virginia. But this did not prevent his adding, "I
have never yet seen a speaker who could obtain such entire mastery
over an audience and could rule their passions with a sway so
despotic as Henry A. Wise," or from writing to a friend, "I tell
you, Mollie, I would rather be an orator and wield the power that
Wise does when he speaks than have all the gold that slumbers in
the mines of Mexico." In a letter to another friend young Dawes
expressed a sentiment widely shared in the North as well as the
South: "I don't know how it affects you, but there is nothing in this
world that stirs me up so much as an eloquent address, whether it
be from the pulpit or the stump it matters not."[59]

Fond as Southerners were of oratory for its own sake, and
important as it was as an outlet for creative impulses which
elsewhere found expression in literature and the other arts, it must
not be supposed that it served no other purpose. As sectional
rivalry intensified, as the South felt it increasingly necessary to
defend and justify its "peculiar institution" and its distinctive "way
of life," oratory became more and more important as a defensive
weapon against the enemies of slavery and as an instrument for
unifying its adherents. Though there were moderate voices speaking out for conciliation and compromise, the intent of much southern oratory was not persuasion but emotional purgation. It was a
rhetoric of defiance and desperation. Southern fire-eaters, particularly after the mid-fifties, were not seeking to convert the North
any more than the abolitionists hoped to change the minds of
southern planters. Argument gave way to public ritual, self-
deluding incantation in which such words as *honor* and *liberty*

(meaning freedom from interference with or criticism of the southern way of life) figured prominently. Voices became increasingly shrill and strident. Extravagance begat greater extravagance. Such displays of defiance as Judah Benjamin's angry farewell to the United States Senate ("You may carry desolation into our peaceful land, and with torch and fire you may set our cities in flames . . . but you never can subjugate us; you never can convert the free sons of the soil into vassals . . . and you never, never can degrade them to the level of an inferior and servile race. Never! Never!") and Yancey's passionate proclamation at Montgomery that he would gather a few brave spirits around him and find a grave which the world would recognize as a modern Thermopylae, give credence to W. J. Cash's depiction of the South as a temple wherein men partook of "the holy sacrament of Southern loyalty and hate." The "bread and wine" of this sacrament, said Cash, was rhetoric — "a rhetoric that every day became less and less a form of speech strictly and more and more a direct instrument of emotion, like music."[60]

THE FINE ART OF ORATORY

During America's Golden Age, oratory, in addition to being an instrument for conducting public business and a means of public education, was valued as an end in itself, a mode of creative expression. This was true not only of the oratory of the special occasion, where it might have been expected, but of forms traditionally deliberative in nature, the political discourse of the stump and the legislative assembly. This thesis should not be carried too far; speeches during this era could sometimes be "levers of history" as they had been in the Revolutionary period. Webster, Clay, and Calhoun, as well as star performers on the stump like Corwin, Legaré, Prentiss, Yancey, Lincoln, and Douglas, were not authors, entertainers, or actors but public men transacting public business. The "Reply to Hayne" was not composed for copy books or elecutionary exercises; it was a historic refutation of doctrines which threatened the Federal Union. Still, popular tastes and expectations unquestionably exerted a powerful influence upon the practice of speaking. The dictum of William Gladstone concerning the relationship existing between the speaker and his audience is relevant here. "His choice," Gladstone said of the orator, "is to be what his age will have him, what it requires in order to be moved by him."

American audiences of the pre-Civil War period required of an orator in order to be moved by him that he be "eloquent" — that is, that he be able to manipulate words in a manner regarded at the time as artistic — and that he be capable through voice, action, and personal magnetism of exerting a mastery over his listeners. Thus, the fine art of oratory was compounded of two principal elements — one literary, the other histrionic. The ideal orator was a happy combination of poet and actor.

"Our people have been tauntingly asked, 'Where is your national literature?' Aside from our historical works, it is in our political speeches, state papers, and newspapers; here are the characteristic germs of a national literature." This confident assertion of Edward G. Parker was accepted as a truism by nineteenth-century Americans. It seemed to them only natural that oratory, a form of literature native to republics, should have been the literary genre to receive the highest cultivation in this country. "Orations and Addresses," wrote one reviewer, "are as natural a product of our institutions, as pines and hemlocks are of our soil." The prestigious *North American Review* showed no reluctance to acknowledge the speeches of Everett, Webster, Sumner, and even Henry Clay as important contributions to the national literature, though it observed editorially on one occasion that orations, addresses, and eulogies were being received in such numbers as to more than fill the entire journal unless selectivity were exercised. Literary critic Edwin P. Whipple pointed out the incongruity of barring a giant such as Webster from literature simply because he was not considered an "author," while hailing minor scribblers and poetasters as literary figures. "Orations," wrote essayist and critic Henry T. Tuckerman, "constitute our literary staple by the same law that causes letters and comedies to attain such perfection in France, domestic novels in England, and the lyrical drama in Italy. They spring from the wants and developments of our national life."[61]

Men of talent, seeking avenues of expression valued by their society, turned to politics and the spoken word. Webster, whose literary gifts might have made him a historian, chose politics instead, as did Sumner, Legaré, and Randolph. Rufus Choate, after a try at politics, found he preferred the law, but continued to address his countrymen through the spoken rather than the written word. Emerson, known today as a literary man, left the clergy for the lecture platform; the majority of his essays were originally delivered as lectures. Even Walt Whitman considered the possibility of publishing his ideas through lectures.

There is no question that orators prepared with the expectation that their words would be accorded a place in literature. Webster revised his speeches thoroughly before publication; Everett polished his sentences before and after he uttered them. Speeches were sometimes too long for delivery and long passages had to be omitted, passages that were restored in the published version, which might also include abundant scholarly notes. Charles Sumner's last years were devoted to a careful editing of his speeches. "I have," he said, "but one solicitude, — it is to print a revised edition of my speeches before I die. . . . These speeches are my life." Sumner meticulously checked quoted material, verified authorities, added explanatory notes drawn from his journals and correspondence, in the process modifying not only the style but sometimes the substance of the addresses. "He hoped," said Whipple, "that his spoken words would become a part of American literature, as the speeches of Burke were indisputably an essential part of English literature."[62]

The conviction that oratory was, and should be, literature was strengthened by analogies with Greece and Rome and generous borrowings from the oratorical literature of antiquity. Rufus Choate kept before him in his library bronze busts of his two favorite orators, Demosthenes and Cicero, and advised young lawyers to "Soak your mind with Cicero" — advice that he took as well as gave. Judge Story said of Sumner that he felt strongest when he could steady himself against a statement by an ancient author. A reviewer of Everett's orations gave voice to the popular sentiment: "We are living over again the classic times of Athenian and Roman eloquence, on a broader stage, in larger proportions, with elements of excitement, hopes of progress, and principles of duration, which never cheered and strengthened the souls of Demosthenes and Cicero."[63]

Audiences delighted in what they regarded as ingenious literary coups, even when they did not completely understand. Unlettered jurors were flattered (though probably baffled) by Choate's quotations from the classics; listeners marveled at the prodigious length and complexity of his sentences and the multiplicity of his adjectives in proportion to his nouns (someone commented that he "drove a substantive and six"). Anthologists and compilers of school readers gleaned purple passages for preservation and admiration; critics analyzed speeches with the same care that they devoted to other literary forms. Particularly beautiful or appropriate figures of speech, felicitously worded tributes, displays of unusual erudition, adroit verbal sallies were enjoyed and repeated appreciatively. John Randolph's imaginative insults were quoted with relish, a great favorite being his characterization of Henry Clay: "this being, so brilliant yet so corrupt, which, like a rotten mackerel by moonlight, shined and stunk." In his most famous speech, Daniel Webster regaled the Senate with one of those examples of scholarly one-upmanship which sophisticated audiences found so impressive. Recalling Hayne's comparison of the ghost of the "murdered coalition" with the ghost of Banquo in Shakespeare's *Macbeth,* Webster seized upon the casual allusion, held it up to minute scrutiny, quoted germane passages from the play, and with a lawyer's skill turned Hayne's witness against him. And after the Massachusetts orator described the power of Great Britain in his vivid image of a world-circling drum-beat, the passage received such wide currency that a reviewer of his *Works* refused to quote it verbatim "only because it has already been quoted a thousand times."[64]

A great oration, in short, was an aesthetic experience, to be enjoyed like a painting or a novel. The mood of appreciative contemplation appropriate to the enjoyment of certain types of oratory is described by Henry T. Tuckerman in this comment on the orations of Edward Everett: "We listen or read, as we roam beside a noble stream, or through an autumnal wood, sure of a succession of pleasing objects, and an ever beautiful and limitless perspective."[65]

But it was not by literary art alone that the speaker exerted his power. Even more admired was his mastery of the skills of the platform, his ability to look and sound and act like an orator. For every quotable passage there were a dozen anecdotes of platform demeanor: Clay's dramatic use of his handkerchief and snuff box; Choate's manner of rising to a vocal crescendo on an ascending scale of adjectives, almost screaming the final adjective, then uttering the noun in a quiet, intense tone; the melodic beauty of Everett's voice and his remarkable feats of memory. Listeners loved to recall dramatic moments of oratorical performance: how Webster, in speaking of the "fox-like tread" of Martin Van Buren, had held out the palm of his left hand and with the other hand had played his fingers with a soft running motion down his extended arm and across the palm; and how at Bunker Hill he had thrilled the great crowd into "long and loud applause" by turning majestically toward the monument and addressing it as the true "orator of this occasion." How Everett, in describing New England's agriculture, had produced at a climactic moment a golden ear of corn, or after an allusion to the Atlantic cable displayed an actual piece of the cable, or in a moment of carefully planned "sudden inspiration" had seized a small American flag from a floral piece on the table and waved it in patriotic fervor.

An anecdote from the diary of Philip Hone, wealthy New York philanthropist and patron of the arts, contains an unconscious revelation of the zeal manifested by both speaker and listener for artistic performance. Hone, an able speaker himself, tells of witnessing a veritable festival of oratory in the Senate in January 1840. Though many celebrated speakers participated, Hone was particularly impressed by William C. Preston of South Carolina. He describes with unrestrained admiration the speaker's voice, manner, and bearing and likens his flood of eloquence to a mountain cataract — now broad and impetuous, now clear and beautiful, and again deep and solemn. After the speech, Hone relates, Preston came over to him and said triumphantly, "There! I made that speech on purpose for you. I had no idea that you should go home without showing you what I could do."[66]

Quite obviously, the orator gloried in showing what he could do, and the listener derived pleasure from being shown. People went to hear great speakers as they attended a concert or a play, hoping to be thrilled, enchanted, lifted out of themselves. The scholarly Ticknor, his temples throbbing as he listened to Webster's Plymouth Oration, the New Jersey judge standing transported before Prentiss, too engrossed to return his watch to his pocket, the college student bewitched by Henry Wise, feeling the blood dashing through his veins like a mountain torrent — all seem to bear testimony to Magoon's startling assertion that "assembled multitudes love that which dazzles them, which moves, strikes, and enchains them."[67]

Few revelations of the conception of oratory as a grand performance, an exalted spectator sport, are as vivid as Edward Parker's poignant recollections of the days he sat in the Senate gallery watching his heroes in action:

> Webster, Calhoun, Clay, in the American Senate! How grand a vision that was! No spectacle of physical grandeur or splendor, to our eyes, could compare with that scene of surpassing moral interest. We have spent whole hours, when nothing but dry routine business was in progress in the Senate, in gazing upon them there. . . . What a sight it was to see! Those three men in their seats in the Senate! That *was* a Senate. They alone would have made up a Senate fit for the empire of the world; the true Triumvirate of the Republic, — the triumvirate of transcendent talent. . . . When *they* spoke, America listened. . . . To have lived in the same age with these three great beings, and seen and known them face to face . . . exalts our whole ideal of human nature, as well as all our standards of oratoric excellence.[68]

ॐ 3 ॐ
THE BRAZEN AGE
Obfuscation and Diversion

The age of the heroes is over, and the age for their
statues is come. A brazen age, anti-sentimental, suc-
ceeds; an age when sordid, calculating interest rather
than conscious merit dares to run after renown.
EDWARD G. PARKER

The quarter-century following the Civil War was not, it is emi-
nently safe to assert, American oratory's finest hour, nor did the
political orator enjoy anything like the same veneration he had
known since revolutionary times. Politics, Daniel Webster had said
at Bunker Hill in 1825, is "the master topic of the age"; politics (as
Webster had conceived the subject) was most certainly not the
master topic of the postwar decades.

Changing conditions brought new national emphases and
priorities, and with them new heroes. There was a continent to be
developed, unlimited natural resources to be exploited, factories
and railroads to be built, new inventions inviting new applications.
There were individual fortunes to be made, industrial empires to
be created, gigantic business enterprises to be undertaken. The
average American had seen played out before him enough real-life
rags-to-riches stories to encourage the belief that he too might one
day become a Carnegie or a Rockefeller. In such circumstances it
was not strange that the tycoons of business and industry, men who
in Matthew Josephson's words "spoke little and did much," should
be elevated in the public estimation above the "politicos" who
willingly served their purposes — men who "did as little as possible
and spoke all too much."

The national priorities are illustrated in Chauncey Depew's
story of how he came to choose a business career. In 1866 Commodore Vanderbilt offered Depew a job as attorney for the New
York & Harlem Railroad. The young lawyer who after his graduation from Yale had launched upon a promising political career had
at the time of his encounter with Vanderbilt just been nominated

and confirmed as United States minister to Japan at a salary of $7,500 and an "outfit" of $9,000. Vanderbilt's offer was substantially less than the ministerial salary, a fact that Depew respectfully called to his attention. "Railroads are the career for a young man" was the financier's reply; "there is nothing in politics. Don't be a damned fool."[1] Depew was convinced. He took the railroad job, in ten years becoming general counsel and director of the "Vanderbilt System" and ultimately president and chairman of the Board of Directors of the New York Central Railroad.

Rich men, men who could exert great economic power, were becoming the popular heroes of the day. Money was power. Money, it seemed, spoke more persuasively in legislative chambers and city halls than the voices of politicians. The Commodore's admonition made sense to young men of talent and ambition: "There is nothing in politics. Don't be a damned fool." Occasionally a periodical of the time would recall wistfully the earlier days of the republic when men of intelligence, legislative or administrative ability, and skill in oratory were selected for public office — times when ministers, judges, successful lawyers, college presidents or professors, and not "mere men of property," were the great men of the day. During the national centennial celebration of 1876 the *Nation* took note of a number of commencement and Phi Beta Kappa addresses on the subject of educated men in public life and expressed the opinion that the proportion of college graduates filling governmental positions was steadily diminishing. Control of politics, according to this writer, was passing more and more into the hands of "self-made men," "men of little education who through shrewdness and ruthlessness had managed to accumulate fortunes." Where once a seat in the United States Senate or a state legislature had been considered a high honor, when the announced intention to seek public office had been enthusiastically encouraged, now such an announcement on the part of a promising young man was enough to dismay his friends and family. When young Theodore Roosevelt decided to run for the state legislature in 1881, his horrified friends told him that this was no field for a gentleman, but more appropriate for saloon keepers, horse-car conductors, and other "low" types.[2]

In the postwar industrial society, with its emphasis upon material wealth and economic development and its admiration for the practical man of business affairs, the role of the public orator, his importance in the republic, the nature and quality of his utterance were all to change remarkably. Quite understandably, congressional debate was altered by the diminished stature of the public official and the changed nature of subjects under discussion. But it was not only political oratory that changed. The new business orientation of society had an impact on other forms of speaking as well. An examination of the principal genres reveals the close relationship between the oratory of an industrial age and changing societal institutions, emphases, and expectations.

"Everyone, of course, knows what the 'great speech' of the average Congressman has become. It is usually a diffuse written essay, full of quotations, often far-fetched and sometimes absurd, which he expects few people to listen to, and only lets off that he may get it printed."[3] So it seemed to E. L. Godkin, influential editor of the *Nation* and unrelenting critic of the excesses of the Gilded Age. For many years Godkin and his colleagues on the *Nation* carried on a running commentary on political orators and oratory which is probably unmatched in American journalism either before or since. Godkin's criticism of public speaking was but one aspect of his criticism of American institutions. A firm believer in the democratic principle that public office is a public trust, an effective crusader against the evils of the spoils system, he brought to his comment on the speaking of public men the same demands for honesty and civic responsibility, the same hatred of ostentation and bad taste that characterized all his social criticism. Again and again the idea is reiterated that the speaking of congressmen has little relation to, or effect upon, the transaction of public business. Again and again the "bastard eloquence" of politicians is ridiculed for its bogus erudition and tiresome volubility.

There is, the *Nation* reported in 1866, "all over the country a growing impression that Congressional debates are farces intended to amuse or befog the country people," exerting no influence on legislation and staged only to demonstrate party loyalty.

> The discussions in the House are, in fact, much like the duels one sees on the stage, in which there is a prodigious clicking of foils and a good deal of wriggling of the body, leading

children and servant girls to fear that when one of the combatants flops on his back, and tosses his manly legs in the air, it is all over with him. But the regular attendants and the intelligent public generally knew well that it is all gammon, and that the whole thing was settled at the rehearsal, and that the dead Smith will that night eat a heartier supper than ever in consequence of the thrusts of the foeman's steel.

Real parliamentary fighting — controversies that influence votes, outlines of policy, arguments pro and con — has, in the opinion of this writer, apparently become a thing of the past.

As for the speeches given on these occasions — they were not speeches at all, but ponderous essays.

Suffice it to say that every subject, from the opening of a sewer to the stopping of a salary, is treated with as much solemnity and grandiloquence as if the orator considered it just the theme for an epic poem, and was driven to discussing it in prose simply through want of time. Sometimes, too, when the display promises to be more than usually bombastic, and Xenophon, Cyrus the Great, Cato the Censor, Sesotris and Nebuchadnezzar are likely to play a more than usually prominent part in the discourse, the services of one of the New York daily papers are enlisted, and he telegraphs in his "special dispatches" what the French call an "appreciation" of it. He describes it as "Mr. Smith's great effort in the House today" — a "magnificient burst of eloquence."[4]

The *Nation*'s charges of verbosity, irrelevance, and rhetorical display were echoed by a host of writers and speakers. In a discourse on Edward Everett in 1865, Frederick H. Hedge named as the prevailing vice of American oratory "extravagance, exaggerated statement, hyperbolic imagery, overdone sentiment, counterfeit enthusiasm, superfluous verbiage, riotous invective, and all that straining after coarse effect commonly known as 'sensation.'" The following year James Russell Lowell wrote in the *North American Review* of the dangers of popular oratory: "Even a speaker in Congress addresses his real hearers through the post-office and the reporters. The merits of the question at issue concern him less than what *he* shall say about it so as not to ruin his own chance of re-election." A. R. Spofford, sharing with the Columbia Historical Society his recollection of the deliberations of twenty-three congresses, noted the compulsion of congressmen to deliver an oration. "They quite forget that grandiloquence is not eloquence, and so indulge in a reckless expenditure of physical exertion and of the English language."[5] James Bryce, distinguished British commentator on American institutions, devoted a chapter of his *American Commonwealth* to an evaluation of our oratory. While finding much to praise, he observed its commonest defect to be "a turgid and inflated style." Noting that speaking in the Senate maintained a consistently higher level than that of the House, he judged English parliamentary oratory to be more "eloquent" than that of the American Congress.

Many explanations for the decline in congressional oratory have been advanced. Both the Senate and the House moved to larger quarters in the late 1850s, and the new halls, cluttered by scores of desks, lacking the intimacy of the former chambers, were inappropriate for protracted public speaking.[6] The tremendous increase in the number of bills to be considered annually precluded long debates; as more and more congressional business came to be transacted in committees, the scene of decisive debate was transferred from the floor of Congress to the committee room. Moreover, differences once aired in public debate were now reconciled in party caucuses where party position was solidified and recalcitrant members brought into line.

Added to such organizational and procedural factors was the fact that the best men were apt to choose business, rather than politics, as a career. Henry Adams's melancholy assessment that "one might search the whole list of Congress, judiciary, and executive during the twenty-five years 1870-1895, and find little but damaged reputation," was only slightly exaggerated. If the debates were different from those of an earlier day, so too were the topics being debated. Many of the great questions that had evoked the eloquent utterances of Daniel Webster and his colleagues had been settled by the Civil War. Such subjects as the protective tariff, railroads, revision of the currency or the Civil Service would seem to offer limited possibilities for inspired or inspiring public address.

This is not to say that there were no vital issues. With increased industrialization and urbanization came a multitude of social and economic problems: increasing centralization of wealth and power, depletion of natural resources through reckless exploitation, large-scale unemployment, urban crowding, poverty, crime, the spoils system in politics, the difficulty of preserving political democracy in the face of growing economic plutocracy. But political speechmaking both in and out of Congress more often than not was designed to obscure rather than clarify such issues. The principal preoccupation of the nation was the accumulation of wealth; the contribution of the politician was to maintain a favorable climate for undisturbed moneymaking, not to engage in the agitation of unpleasant social issues. The efforts of those who, like Carl Schurz and George W. Curtis, sought purification of a corrupt political system were an irritation to be countered with ridicule. Party discipline was rigorous; the rank and file of politicians were rendered virtually unpersuadable by allegiance to party and to the economic interests to which they owed their political lives.

Such conditions were scarcely propitious for meaningful parliamentary debate. Small wonder that writers for the *Nation* saw little relation between speechmaking and legislation and compared congressional debating to mock duels on the stage. Small wonder that intelligent observers came to regard the speeches of politicans as window dressing to conceal machinations taking place in back rooms. The senator or congressman who found it impossible to resist the urge to compose an occasional oration discovered a convenient ally in the device of "extension of remarks" — the printing in the *Record* of speeches not actually delivered. By this means he could display his rhetorical virtuosity, real or imagined, parade his command of elaborate metaphor and classical allusion, have the creation printed and mailed at public expense, and thus address his constituency through the post office, while continuing to vote as directed.

Under the circumstances, it is not surprising that we have little to show for twenty-five years of post-Civil War congressional oratory. After the debates on reconstruction there was little worth preserving until near the close of the century. Indeed, if we may trust the judgment of those conservators of rhetorical excellence who compile the anthologies of public speeches, the most memorable congressional utterances of the period were Lamar's eulogy of Sumner and Blaine's eulogy of Garfield — both, it will be noted, demonstrative rather than deliberative in nature.

After the death of Senator Charles Sumner in March 1874, both houses of Congress suspended business for the customary delivery of memorial addresses. Among numerous tributes offered on that occasion, the speech delivered in the House of Representatives on April 27 by Lucius Quintus Cincinnatus Lamar of Mississippi stands preeminent. It was a dramatic situation. Sumner had been an abolitionist, an uncompromising, often arrogant, enemy of the South; Lamar was known as a southern "fire-eater," a secessionist Democrat. What would the Southerner say, what could he say, on such an occasion? Instead of making a perfunctory statement, acceding to the formal demands of the situation and going only so far as courtesy and decorum required, Lamar used the occasion for a stirring plea for restoration of sectional harmony. After speaking briefly of the Massachusetts senator's intellect, his scholarship, broad learning, and eloquence, Lamar went on to emphasize his "high moral qualities" — his love of freedom, his unswerving devotion to duty, his unrelenting warfare against what he considered to be evil. The peroration was an earnest attempt to blend eulogy with an appeal for reconciliation between North and South, two estranged sections of a common country: "Shall we not, over the honored remains of this great champion of human liberty, this feeling sympathizer with human sorrow, this earnest pleader for the exercise of human tenderness and charity, lay aside the 'concealments which serve only to perpetuate misunderstandings and distrust, and frankly confess that on both sides we most earnestly desire to be one; one not merely in community of language and literature and traditions and country, but more, and better than that, one also in feeling and in heart?" The effect on the House was electric. Visitors in the galleries joined the members in applause. Some wept openly; James Blaine in the Speaker's chair reportedly turned aside to conceal his tears. The speech, as predicted at that moment by Lyman Tremaine of New York, rang through the country. It was printed in newspapers across the land. Editorial comment proclaimed the end of the war, a packing away of the bloody shirt, and a new spirit of brotherhood and unity.

But deep hatreds are not so easily dispelled, and miracles are seldom wrought by a single speech. Lamar's eulogy of Sumner, admirable as it was, did not put an end to the waving of the bloody shirt. The tears of James Blaine dried quickly, and soon he was excoriating Jefferson Davis on the floor of the House and stirring up old sectional animosities in a presidential campaign. Still the celebrated eulogy was not without importance. It evoked for a brief moment a spirit of understanding between hostile factions, and it established on the national scene a new symbol of pacification. Lucius Lamar went on to become a United States senator, secretary of the interior, and associate justice of the United States Supreme Court, and until his death in 1893 his was a voice of moderation and reconciliation. There is still power to move in the concluding words of his tribute to Sumner: "Would that the spirit of the illustrious dead whom we lament today could speak from the grave to both parties to this deplorable discord in tones which should reach each and every heart throughout this broad territory: 'My countrymen! *know* one another, and you will *love* one another.'"

A similar opportunity for the oratory of tribute came after the assassination of President Garfield. On February 27, 1882, the new president and his cabinet, the Supreme Court justices, members of the House and Senate, and the diplomatic corps assembled in the chamber of the House of Representatives to listen to a eulogy by the slain president's friend, James G. Blaine of Maine. Blaine's address, prepared with meticulous attention to detail (it is said to have undergone eleven revisions) was proclaimed a classic of American eloquence. It had, at least, the merit of simplicity. Read today, it seems (except for the peroration) a prosaic recitation of Garfield's ancestry, education, military and political career, administrative abilities, and traits of character — a rather pedestrian effort to cast in heroic mold the life of an undistinguished politician. The elevated peroration doubtless satisfied the expectations of the audience, but the assertion of the senator's most competent biographer that "there is no finer passage in the literature of eulogy than the prose poem with which Blaine closed his oration" is certainly an overgenerous appraisal.

Such ceremonial addresses are dramatic interludes, moments when the regular business of Congress is interrupted. What of the regular business of Congress? One searches the record in vain for parliamentary debates comparable to those of the prewar decades.

Where Webster, Clay, and Calhoun had employed their great talents in the discussion of the issues of human freedom or slavery, disposition of the public lands to the West, interpretations of the federal Constitution and the nature of the government founded upon it, now was heard the acrimonious bicker of the "Stalwart" defenders of Grantism and their "Half-Breed" adversaries. It is indicative of the level of political discussion that the conflict that most aroused public enthusiasm was the purely personal battle for supremacy between James Blaine and Roscoe Conkling.

James G. Blaine was by common consent the master politician of his age. Warm, amiable, persuasive, irresistibly charming, he was one of the most popular public figures of his generation. Member of Congress for nearly twenty years, Speaker of the House, senator, secretary of state under Garfield and Harrison, his name was prominently mentioned at five national conventions as his party's nominee for the presidency. When in 1884 he secured the nomination his defeat came about as the result of a number of unfortunate events not entirely within his control. Never able completely to escape the taint of charges that he had used the influence of his office as Speaker for personal financial gain, he died without having attained the highest office.

Roscoe Conkling, powerful boss of the New York political machine, was essentially a parochial figure who nevertheless had his moments of prominence on the national stage during long terms of office in both the House and the Senate. A proud, arrogant, distant man and something of a dandy in dress and manners, Conkling was for years the dominant leader of the pro-Grant Stalwarts. From the time in 1866 when Blaine in a speech before the House of Representatives referred derisively to Conkling's "majestic, super-eminent, overpowering, turkey-gobbler strut," to long after Conkling's contemptuous refusal to campaign for Blaine in 1884 because "I don't engage in criminal practice," the two men hated each other. Yet the continuing Blaine-Conkling controversy which divided the loyalty of Republicans throughout the nation was little more than a fight for political advantage. No important issue divided the two men. Each believed unquestioningly in high tariffs, "sound money," and the spoils system; each opposed civil service reform and reconciliation with the South.

Both Blaine and Conkling were men of great political gifts.

Each was regarded as an outstanding orator, capable of compelling the allegiance of large audiences through public speech — the one by his charm, the other through force of personal presence and a wit that could wound. Men loved Blaine and feared Conkling; both appeals attracted a following. Yet despite long careers in the highest councils of the nation neither is remembered today, either as orator or statesman, because neither is identified with any significant legislation or with any great cause or principle. They compelled public attention for a time because they were capable, articulate foemen engaged in dramatic personal encounter. But they demonstrated as have other spellbinders before and since that great themes as well as technical skill are requisite to true and abiding eloquence.

Political speaking outside Congress was, if anything, less illustrious than that within, displaying the same empty rhetorical flourish, the same lack of relevance to vital issues. James Bryce, who pronounced congressional oratory inferior to that of Parliament, felt that Americans excelled in stump speaking. This may be regarded as a somewhat dubious compliment, however, since Bryce defined this type of oratory as "speaking which rouses an audience but ought not to be reported." Stimulation, not conviction or education, Bryce observed, was the aim of the stump speaker. He praises American speakers for their extemporaneous skill, animation and grace in delivery, quickness in catching the temper of a particular audience and adapting to it, but finds deficiencies in their invention (the power of finding good ideas and constructing effective arguments) and style (skill and taste in the choice of appropriate words). He attributes these deficiencies to a deterioration in public taste since the days following the Revolution "when it was formed and controlled by a small number of educated men" and to a desire on the part of speakers not to appear wiser or more refined than the multitude. In England, speakers (who generally belong to the cultivated classes) obey their own tastes, rather than those of their audiences; trained in Parliament, they carry their formal parliamentary style with them into public meetings. In America, where stump oratory is as old as congressional oratory, the fashion is set not by the cultivated few but by the uneducated many. "The taste of the average man," according to Bryce, "was not raised by the cultivated few to their own standard, but tended to lower the practice, and to some extent even the taste, of the cultivated few."[7]

This is a perceptive analysis, but we must look further for an explanation of the debasement of public address. The sorry state of American political oratory was directly traceable to the sorry state of postwar American politics. Both major parties were dedicated to the task of facilitating the expansion of business and industry. Both parties were opposed to reforms that might reduce the power of the spoilsmen; it mattered only whose spoilsmen were to be in control. No major difference of principle divided the leadership of the two parties. Together they opposed reduction of the tariff, expansion of the currency, reform of the Civil Service system. In the open alliance between business and government, business corruption begot political corruption. In the blunt words of historians Samuel E. Morison and Henry Steele Commager, "Business ran politics, and politics was a branch of business." A small band of independent Republicans, among them some of the best minds in the party, strove valiantly to keep alive the hope of reform, but were repeatedly brushed aside as dilettantes and nuisances. When in 1884 they bolted the party in an attempt to stem the tide of corruption and restore a measure of dignity to public affairs, they were ridiculed as "Mugwumps" and effectively disowned by both parties.

There can be little doubt that the oratory of obfuscation heard at political conventions and on the hustings was a deliberate attempt to maintain the status quo by diverting public attention from the real issues through appeals to personal and sectional hatreds. For the Republicans, who managed in a series of close elections to keep control of the governmental machinery through most of this period, the most serviceable diversionary tactic was a waving of the bloody shirt. Since the strength of the Democratic party lay primarily in the Solid South, war emotions were kept hot by exhortations to "vote as you shot." Union generals were inflated to heroic proportions (until near the end of the century every Republican candidate for the presidency except Blaine was a war veteran); political meetings featured barbecues, parades, and Civil War songs: "Marching through Georgia," "Battle Hymn of the Republic," "Rally round the Flag, Boys." "Every man that endeavored to tear the old flag from the heavens that it enriches was a Democrat," cried Robert Ingersoll in the fever of a political campaign. "Every man that tried to destroy this nation was a Democrat. . . . The man that assassinated Abraham Lincoln was a Democrat. . . . Soldiers, every scar you have on your heroic bodies was given you by a Democrat." In the campaign of 1880, Senator Conkling gave a less emotional, but equally clear expression of the singleness of the Republican appeal. Called upon to support Garfield, who desperately needed his help, Conkling gave a three-hour speech at the New York Academy of Music on "The Issues of the Campaign."[8] "The general issue confronting us," said the senator (the singular noun is significant), "is in itself and in its bearings sectional." "It is not a question of candidates," he declared (refraining throughout from mentioning the candidate by name), it is a question of which of the two parties it is "safer and wiser to trust." The bulk of the address is devoted to picturing the horrors of turning the country over to the party controlled by "men of the South who were against the Union and the Constitution."

An event that occurred at the Republican national convention in 1876 is indicative of the distance oratory could stray from reality and still be acceptable. The occasion was the nomination of James Blaine for the presidency by Colonel Robert G. Ingersoll, a man greatly renowned for his oratory whom Henry Ward Beecher pronounced "the most brilliant speaker of the English tongue of all men on this globe." Nominating speeches are not traditionally marked by restraint or strict adherence to factual accuracy, but the discrepancy between the man as known and as presented to this audience was unusually striking. The times demanded a candidate, said Ingersoll, with a "political reputation spotless as a star." The people called for the man "who has torn from the throat of treason the tongue of slander, the man who has snatched the mask of Democracy from the hideous face of the rebellion." Then, in the passage that fastened upon the Maine senator an appellation which clings to this day, the orator declaimed: "Like an armed warrior, like a plumed knight, James G. Blaine marched down the halls of the American Congress and thrust his shining lance full and fair against the brazen forehead of every traitor to his country and every maligner of his fair reputation." Blaine did not secure the nomination, and the taint of corruption from a series of suspicious personal financial transactions clung to him to the end of his life.

But Ingersoll's speech nearly stampeded the convention; it was hailed at once as a "classic" and as such was declaimed by a generation of schoolboys. The fact that a national audience saw nothing incongruous in this idealization of a flawed politician says something about its values, as well as its apparent lack of a sense of humor.

What had brought about the decline of serious instructive political oratory? What had happened since the days when the public had awaited the pronouncements of public men before forming their judgments upon the issues under discussion? E. L. Godkin thought he knew the answer. At first he was inclined to attribute it to "the absence of really exciting questions in the political arena." But he later placed the blame upon the growth of party machines dominated by powerful political "bosses."[9] As politicians' responsibility to the boss increased, their responsibility to the public diminished. Since the machine controlled entrance to and continuation in public life, the machine and not the public had to be pleased. It was Godkin's fervent conviction that "there is nothing in a democracy so important as persuasion." The chief inducement to public speaking is the desire to persuade, to affect opinion. When the machine and not the public is in control of political careers, it becomes more important to please the boss by votes than the people by speeches. The machine does not prosper through public instruction; it discourages instruction, preferring diversion and deceit.

Looking back on the seventies and eighties, William Allen White pronounced it "an era of gorgeous spoilation, a time when bombast concealed larceny." It was, he said, "a day when waving the bloody shirt passed for argument, when the bronze button of the G.A.R. was unquestioned in the North as a badge of courage, merit, and distinction; when patriotism was often marked by a swagger, and when it was always popular to 'twist the lion's tail,' meaning thereby to insult Great Britain; when the cynicism of the day declared that 'a public office is a private snap.' "[10]

Fortunately, there is more to the story than this bleak depiction of the plight of political oratory. The most notable speaking of the period took place outside the political arena. The most celebrated speakers — Henry Ward Beecher, Wendell Phillips, George W. Crutis, John B. Gough, Henry Grady, Robert Ingersoll, Ralph

Waldo Emerson, Susan B. Anthony, Anna Dickinson, T. Dewitt Talmage, Phillips Brooks (the list is a long one) — were not politicians; they spoke from the lecture platform, not in the halls of Congress or on the hustings.

For nearly a century the public lecture in its various manifestations remained a continuous source of education, inspiration, and entertainment. The beginnings of the lecture movement may be traced to the organization of the first local lyceum by Josiah Holbrook in Millbury, Massachusetts, in 1826. Originally conceived as a kind of mutual education or cultural improvement society, the lyceum featured informal discussions and occasional lectures delivered without fee by local citizens or visitors from neighboring towns. The idea caught on, and soon there were scores of town lyceums through Massachusetts; within five years lyceums were to be found in nearly every state in the Union. By the 1840s these informal discussion groups had been transformed into lecture audiences. To the platform came many of the educators, statesmen, scientists, and literary men of the day — Emerson, Thoreau, Lowell, Holmes, Webster, Parker, Agassiz, Greeley, Mann, and Holbrook himself. In the fifties and sixties, the lyceum (for the term was still commonly used) became a forum for the discussion of public problems. Lectures on literary and scientific subjects were replaced by speeches advocating temperance, woman suffrage, and the abolition of slavery. For a decade preceding the Civil War the reformers practically took over the lecture platform. After the war there were unmistakable evidences of the decay of the lyceum, and some who had participated in the prewar days of glory sadly predicted its demise. But in 1868 James Clark Redpath organized the Boston Lyceum Bureau, introduced lecture brokerage methods, and set in motion machinery that was to make the lecture system a really "big business." Under Redpath's successor, Major James Pond, entrepreneur extraordinary, the lecture business was to reach its highest point (quantitatively, if not qualitatively) during the last quarter of the century.

In the 1870s the lecture system received unexpected impetus from an apparently unlikely source. In 1874 Lewis Miller, a manufacturer of farm implements, and John H. Vincent, later a bishop in the Methodist Church, established a summer institute for Sunday school teachers on the shores of Lake Chautauqua in New

York. Chautauqua soon became a national institution: branches were founded throughout the nation; the curriculum was expanded to include all manner of secular subjects; lecturers were recruited from all areas of American culture. As time went on it became increasingly difficult to distinguish between lyceum and Chautauqua lecturers, for they were often the same people. Chautauqua became "the summer manifestation of the Lyceum"; as one Chautauqua lecturer put it, "In winter, we played the lyceums." Initially conceived as an instrument for moral uplift, Chautauqua moved steadily in the direction of mere entertainment. With the advent of the tent Chautauqua (an altogether different phenomenon from the institute founded by Miller and Vincent) lecturers found themselves competing with Swedish bell ringers, Scottish bagpipers, magicians, jugglers, and trained dog acts. Chautauqua, like the lyceum, ultimately succumbed to commercialism, becoming in its latter days little more than third-rate vaudeville.

There is no doubt that the commercialization of the lecture system affected the quality of platform speaking.[11] As the lecturer became a professional (or perhaps more accurately, a businessman), attention had to be paid to the salability of the "product." The lecturer who depended upon fees for a living had to be concerned with what the public would buy. And, as later generations would discover in their experience with radio and television, a readier market seems to exist for entertainment and diversion than for education and enlightenment. Still, it is a mistake to be persuaded by contemptuous references to the "Chautauqua lecture" to dismiss all late nineteenth-century lecturing as unworthy of serious attention. Generalizations concerning lectures and lecturers are inevitably inaccurate, for the variety was almost limitless. As J. G. Holland explained, "The word 'lecture' covers generally and generically all the orations, declamations, dissertations, exhortations, recitations, humorous extravaganzas, narratives of travel, harangues, sermons, semi-sermons, demi-semi-sermons, and lectures proper, which can be crowded into what is called a 'course,' but which might be more properly called a bundle."[12] The so-called inspirational lecture, a staple item of the platform, ranged from the spoken essays of Ralph Waldo Emerson or the sermons of Phillips Brooks and Henry Ward Beecher to the vacuous moralizings of undistinguished clergymen — effusions like "Helping God Paint the Clouds," or "Luck and Pluck," which Glenn Frank described as the "always - room - at - the - top - mother - home - and - heaven - never - say - die sort of lectures." Humorous lectures, which, then as now, could be excruciatingly bad, were often remarkably good. Mark Twain, Josh Billings, Artemus Ward, and Petroleum V. Nasby (whose newspaper columns President Lincoln had admired and occasionally read to his cabinet) managed frequently to convert the humorous lecture into an effective vehicle for social satire.

Though it was probably true that entertainment ultimately triumphed over education, there was no lack of excellent informative lectures — what Holland probably meant by the category "lectures proper." Thomas Huxley's lucid expositions of Darwin's theories evoked defenses of religion against the claims of science as well as attempts to reconcile the conflict. There were lectures by such visiting men of letters as Charles Dickens and Matthew Arnold, and lectures on travel, history, biography, geology, and astronomy. Difficult to classify were discourses such as Wendell Phillips's "The Lost Arts" and "Toussaint L'Ouverture." Combinations of the essay, the lecture, and the oration, they were sometimes referred to as "literary addresses." Other examples of the genre were Ingersoll's "Shakespeare" and Curtis's "Sir Philip Sidney." Each of these was repeated many times, season after season. "The Lost Arts," first given on the lyceum platform in 1838, was repeated over two thousand times over a period of forty-five years.

Nor must it be forgotten that, as had been the case before the war, the lecture platform became a branch of the stump. The lecture hall offered a free forum for the discussion of issues deliberately avoided by party politicians and offered speakers without party affiliations a chance to be heard. Wendell Phillips, who had earlier used the lecture as a formidable antislavery weapon, now took to the platform in behalf of "Temperance," "Woman," "The Irish Question," and "Agitation." George William Curtis proclaimed the necessity for civil service reform; Frances Willard advanced the cause of temperance; Susan B. Anthony, Dr. Anna Howard Shaw, Anna E. Dickinson, Lucy Stone, and their associates waged the battle for women's rights. Booker T. Washington delivered hundreds of lectures in his crusade to provide vocational training for uneducated blacks and to reduce racial tensions in the

South. John B. Gough, whose histrionic abilities enabled him to combine entertainment with reform, made his denunciations of the evils of drink so irresistible that he remained year after year one of the top box-office attractions. Major Pond, who as much as any man was in a position to know, named Gough as one of three "Kings of the Platform," the others being Wendell Phillips and Henry Ward Beecher. Robert Ingersoll, whose unorthodox religious views barred him from election to public office and whom the large bureaus were reluctant to book, carried on his own campaign of reform, seeking to purge organized religion of cant and superstition in a series of lectures whose sparkling prose style and moments of genuine emotional power more than atoned for the fatuity of his bloody-shirt diatribes in political campaigns.

Audiences were impelled by a variety of motives to pay money to hear men and women make speeches. After the horrors of the Civil War there was a need for release, a wish to be diverted and amused. A nation in transition from a rural to an industrialized, urban society felt a craving for "culture" and for increased knowledge. Attendance at a lecture meant an opportunity for sociability, of which there were all too few. And not to be discounted was the element of curiosity — the desire to see the stars (many of whom had come to the platform as a result of notoriety in other fields) in person — to sit in the presence of the great man, to hear his voice, to see him perform.

Whether for these or other reasons, the American public gave amazing support to the lecture system. In its heyday, an estimated forty million people attended Chautauqua in a single season. John B. Gough was said to have delivered over nine thousand addresses before nine million people in his forty-year speaking career. Favorite lectures such as Phillips's "The Lost Arts" and Ralph Parlette's "University of Hard Knocks" were demanded again and again, season after season; it has been claimed that Russell Conwell's "Acres of Diamonds" was repeated six thousand times. Whatever one's judgment concerning the intrinsic merit of these lectures (and, like examples of most literary and rhetorical genres, they ranged from the excellent to the execrable), they satisfied the public appetite and met the public need. A study of representative lectures is a useful index to what millions of Americans living at that time found amusing, uplifting, and instructive. No form of public utterance which was so influential for so long can be dismissed as unimportant.

The oratory of the special occasion continued undiminished during the postwar decades. Speechmaking played an important role in the celebration of numerous anniversaries and in marking such public events as unveiling statues, dedicating monuments, opening expositions, or laying cornerstones. Bryce noted that the oration of the occasion was much more fully developed in America than in European countries and attributed our characteristic inflation of style partly to the fact that speakers commemorating special events felt it necessary to talk their "very tallest." The tallest talkers were probably the Fourth of July orators, whose rhetorical excesses had become a favorite target of satirists. Still, the Fourth continued to be the greatest of all American patriotic holidays, year after year attracting enthusiastic crowds and eliciting frequent comment in contemporary journals. Surprisingly, much of the comment on the oratory of this occasion is written in a spirit of tolerance and understanding toward those whose exuberance on their country's birthday leads them to rodomontade. There are the inevitable cautions not to lose sight of the original significance of the day in the noise and confusion that accompany its celebration; there are exhortations to higher aims and nobler dedication for the future. But the writers seem, for the most part, to be more grieved than outraged as they seek to point out the difference between chauvinism and genuine patriotism. George William Curtis, who from the "Editor's Easy Chair" in *Harper's* issued periodic reminiscences and reflections on Phi Beta Kappa orations, commencement addresses, and lectures, seldom let a Fourth of July go by without some observations upon the speaking of that occasion. Godkin's *Nation,* which in 1872 had pronounced the Fourth of July oration "synonymous with blatant nonsense or platitudes in thought, tawdry rhetoric in diction, and crude, egotistical chauvinism in spirit," published in mellow, good-natured report of the centennial celebration in 1876. The reporter does not begrudge the celebrants their indulgence in panegyric. When a man gives a birthday party, he admits, the guests are supposed to dwell on his good qualities and not drink to the times when he has made a fool of himself. Still, self-reproach and repentance may not be postponed indefinitely. It is well to remember, he counsels, that without constant improvement in government, social legislation, education, and justice, all oratory in praise of the past is hollow.[13]

The centennial celebration of the Declaration of Independence, on July 4, 1876, called by one writer "probably the proudest day in the history of Demonstrative oratory," was only one of a series of centennials, which included those commemorating Lexington and Concord and Bunker Hill in 1875, and the surrender of Cornwallis at Yorktown in 1881, in which both Northerners and Southerners participated in a spirit of unity and reconciliation. Indeed, it seems in retrospect as if much of the occasional oratory of the time constituted an antidote to the bellicose speeches of Congress and the stump. Whereas the politician running for office or seeking party ascendancy usually considered it necessary and profitable to accentuate sectional differences and keep open the wounds of war, the holiday speaker often sought to strengthen common bonds and heal old wounds. A new holiday had its beginnings on May 30, 1865, in Charleston, South Carolina, when James Redpath led a group of black children in strewing flowers on the graves of Union soldiers. The event attracted attention in the North, where it was sponsored by the Grand Army of the Republic; during the seventies state after state declared Memorial Day a legal holiday. In time joint services were held honoring veterans of both Confederate and Union armies, in which audiences demonstrated their longing for an end to sectional hatred and strife by warmly applauding tributes paid by orators to the dead of both North and South. A later example of the conciliatory nature of occasional oratory was Booker T. Washington's celebrated Atlanta Exposition Address in 1895, not in this case a plea for the reconciliation of the sections but for an accommodation between blacks and whites in the South.

Though there was little to compare in grandeur or national significance with the eulogies attending the death of Adams and Jefferson or the commemorative rites at Bunker Hill or Gettysburg, the postwar period was not without its opportunities for epideictic oratory. One of these was the unveiling of the Bartholdi Statue of Liberty in New York Harbor in October 1886. The speaker on this occasion was Chauncey M. Depew, president of the New York Central & Hudson River Railroad. Since taking the advice of Commodore Vanderbilt in 1866 to choose business instead of politics, Depew had prospered mightily.[14] He had also acquired a national reputation as a public speaker. Like Edward Everett thirty years earlier, he had become something of an orator-at-large to the nation. In the next few years he was to deliver the principal oration at the centennial of the inauguration of George Washington, the laying of the cornerstone of the Grant Mausoleum, and the dedicatory ceremonies on October 12, 1892, of the Chicago World's Fair. His choice for such assignments must have seemed as inevitable as that of Everett at Gettysburg.

Depew's Statue of Liberty speech was an adequate response to a situation that called for somebody to say something: to dignify the occasion, if possible with winged words. The speaker dealt with predictable themes — the spirit of liberty, the friendship between France and the United States, the statue as symbol. Fully half the address was devoted to a narrative detailing Lafayette's contributions to the American Revolution and his subsequent activities in France. There is an occasional felicitous touch ("When Franklin drew the lightning from the clouds he little dreamed that in the evolution of science his discovery would illuminate the Torch of Liberty for France and America") and some striving for "eloquence" ("As the centuries roll by, and in the fullness of the time the rays of Liberty's torch are the beacon lights of the world, the central niches in the earth's Pantheon of Freedom will be filled by the figures of Washington and Lafayette"). After enumerating the assets of this blessed land — the abolition of privilege, the equality of all men before the law, freedom of speech, the right to rise, and equal opportunity for honor and fortune — Depew predicted with characteristic optimism, "The problems of labor and capital, of social regeneration and moral growth, of property and poverty, will work themselves out under the benign influences of enlightened law-making and law-abiding liberty, without the aid of kings and armies or of anarchists and bombs."[15]

The similarity of the roles of orators Everett and Depew invites a comparison of the speaking of the two men. Since each apparently served admirably the needs of his time, such a comparison may suggest changed requirements for oratorical success. Everett was a man of dignity, refinement, and taste; a scholar of sufficient distinction to serve as professor and president of the nation's most prestigious college. Though elected or appointed to a series of high public offices — governor, secretary of state, foreign minister, congressman, and senator — he was not the kind of man people referred to as a "politician." Handsome, intelligent, imperious, dramatic, he was the very archetype of the Grand Orator. For him oratory was an art, and very nearly a profession. He showed respect for audiences by devoting months of preparation to a single speech; his ceremonial addresses were crafted, rehearsed, and delivered with meticulous attention to detail. Through them he sought to adorn and immortalize great American ideals, symbols, and events; to illuminate the future by glorification of the past. A reviewer of his published *Addresses* in 1850 summarized the themes of the orator: "The importance of knowledge, the necessity of popular education, the value of public improvements, and of inventions in the arts, the practical applications of science, the obligations of charity, the duties of an enlarged love of country, and more than all, and above all, the indispensable necessity of enlightened Christian faith; — in short, all the vital themes connected with the peculiarities of American existence."[16] Everett was a master of demonstrative oratory at a time when such oratory was universally admired. To some he was vastly more than this. The *North American Review* observed that at his death "He was by common admission our foremost civilian, our most accomplished man."

Chauncey Mitchell Depew embodied and gave public expression to the dominant values and aspirations of a budding industrial nation. Corporation lawyer and business executive, "A busy man of affairs" as he characterized himself, friend of tycoon and politician, intimate of presidents, his outstanding characteristics were geniality, affability, optimism, and good humor. A man of business, he was not a "typical" businessman. Articulate, polished by a Yale education, broadened by travel, possessing the glamour of one who knew personally the great of many nations, able to quote apposite passages from history and literature, he impressed the merchants, bankers, and mass audiences to whom he spoke. The recurrent themes of his addresses on ceremonial occasions, at the banquet table, and on the stump (he campaigned for every Republican presidential candidate from Fremont to Coolidge) were these: the opulence and power of the United States, the superiority of good old American know-how, the glory of the Republican party, the unlimited development of commerce and industry, the beneficience of the railroads — bringers of the comforts of civilization, the worth of the individual, the hallowed traditions of liberty and equality, harmony between capital and labor. Concentrating always on the smiling aspects of American life, he celebrated "the marvellous development and progress of this republic." At a dinner given in his honor on Washington's birthday in 1896, Depew was introduced as one of two typical Americans. "We commemorate today the Father of our Country," said the president of the Lotos Club, "by paying our tribute of affection to Chauncey M. Depew. And there is much propriety in linking together these two names, for as one represents the highest type of character at the birth of our country, the other represents its oldest development near the opening of the twentieth century."

Noted as he was as an opener of expositions and dedicator of monuments, it was as an after-dinner speaker that Depew became preeminent, and as such he deserves to be remembered. His output was prodigious; he is survived by fifteen volumes of speeches, mostly of the after-dinner variety. Near the end of his life he estimated that he had attended eight thousand public dinners, at most of which he spoke. This is roughly equivalent to twenty-two years of uninterrupted public dining, seven evenings a week, but the estimate may not be exaggerated since he lived to the age of ninety-four and seemed to grow more voluble the longer he lived. Much in demand, he was asked back repeatedly to the same table. He addressed banquets of Republican clubs, ethnic groups, bankers, war veterans, chambers of commerce, alumni associations, and appreared frequently at dinners given by the Lotos Club, the Union League Club, the Gridiron Club of Washington, and the New England Society of New York. The Montauk Club of Brooklyn gave birthday dinners in his honor (at which he always delivered the major address) every year for more than thirty years. In 1925 he told an interviewer he belonged to twenty-eight clubs, "all of whom want to celebrate my birthday."

Speechmaking was for Depew a hobby, a form of recreation. He related with obvious satisfaction how unlike others who played cards, kept late hours, drank too much, and died young, he went home from the office, worked for an hour or so on his speech of the evening, attended the banquet, and was home in bed by eleven o'clock. By way of preparation, he first read one of Macaulay's essays

— any one; "it rehabilitates me and clothes my soul in a more intellectual and critical garb." He then walked around his library table thinking about the subject of the evening; "Everything I have ever read or heard about that subject comes back to me." His preparation for ceremonial occasions was presumably more extensive, though perfunctory when compared with that of Everett or Sumner. He admits that he had only a few days to prepare the oration dedicating the Statue of Liberty. George William Curtis, whose scholarship and culture were infinitely broader and deeper than Depew's, though he lacked the latter's appeal for the business community, was first asked to deliver the oration on that occasion. Curtis, a superb occasional speaker, declined because there was only one month for preparation. He required three months for a major address: one month for research and preparing a first draft; one month to put it aside and let his mind work on it; and one month for leisurely revision. In his account of the incident in his memoirs, Depew betrays manifest pride in his own ability as a quick study; if he had followed Curtis's example, he says, his many volumes of speeches would never have seen the light of day.[17]

Chauncey Depew was a glad-hander, a jollifier — an expert in "public relations." His affability and wit, together with his enormous capacity for making friends and creating goodwill, made him an effective apologist for the business community. It was often said that he never made an enemy, but he was not without his critics in the press, who portrayed him as either a superficial lightweight or a mouthpiece for unscrupulous business interests. Years before Depew had donated to Peekskill, New York, a statue of himself and delivered the dedicatory oration at its unveiling, the acidulous Ambrose Bierce had written this "ante-mortem epitaph":

> Stranger, uncover; here you have in view
> The monument of Chauncey M. Depew.
> Eater and orator, the whole world round
> For feats of tongue and tooth alike renowned.
> Pauper in thought but prodigal in speech,
> Nothing he knew excepting how to teach.
> But in default of something to impart
> He multiplied his words with all his heart.

David Graham Phillips, in one of his muckraking articles on "The Treason of the Senate," charged that Depew, through his lobbying with state legislatures and his aid to Vanderbilt in swindling the public, had cost the people of New York State "a thousand million dollars." Yet as Phillips himself ruefully acknowledged, Depew remained throughout his long speaking career immensely popular with the public. Criticism of his personal wealth and the power and corruption of the railroads he represented was adroitly turned aside with the pleasant jest. Audiences were continually reassured concerning the rosy future of the nation, the well-being of the farmer, the "almost brotherly" cooperation with which capital and labor shared in the fruits of industry. His memoirs recount stories in which men with every reason to dislike him have succumbed to his charm and acclaimed him a "good fellow" or a "peach." He tells, for example, of speaking at a Christmas dinner given by the *New York World* for one hundred men picked from a breadline. Afterward, one of the guests, who identified himself as an anarchist, came forward and according to Depew spoke as follows: "You do more than any one else in the whole country to create good feeling and dispel unrest, and you have done a lot of it tonight. I made up my mind to kill you right here, but you are such an infernal good fellow that I have not the heart to do it, so here's my hand."[18] One is entitled to some skepticism regarding the mellow reminiscences of an octogenarian, but this story and others like it reveal unmistakably that Chauncey Depew considered it his mission "to create good feeling and dispel unrest." He performed this mission in thousands of banquet rooms by satisfying a voracious public appetite for entertainment, diversion, and assurance that everything would inevitably turn out all right in this best of all possible worlds. By means of his charming, witty, anecdotal, postprandial discourses he helped create an atmosphere in which unpleasant problems of an industrial age could, for the moment at least, be dissolved in cigar smoke and a warm surge of good fellowship.

It is significant that Chauncey Depew, regarded by many as the foremost ceremonial speaker of his time, chose to specialize in the light-touch after-dinner speech. His instinct for self-advancement, his feeling for what would "sell," led him to discern, and to devote his considerable talents to augmenting, the immense popularity of this genre.

The rise of the after-dinner speech to preeminence among all other forms of occasional speaking was one of the most striking developments of the postwar decades. One writer, deploring the decline of serious oratory, noted a tendency "to substitute the dining-table for the rostrum." After-dinner speaking, he said, is presently "the style of oratory most cultivated among us." "Nothing today gives a man more of a certain kind of fame and popularity than excellence in it. Indeed, we may say that through no channel can a man acquire so much influence with so little expenditure of labor or money. Our young men are today really more anxious to acquire it than any other style of oratory. There is far more demand for it than for any other. A man's chance of being called on to speak at a dinner are twenty times greater than his chances of being called on to speak on any other occasion."[19] Most after-dinner speaking, delivered to well-fed listeners often pleasantly narcotized by cigars and brandy, was designed neither to instruct nor to provoke thought but to amuse. Almost any subject would do, so long as it was treated with a felicitous fluency. James Russell Lowell once described this type of speech as containing a platitude, a quotation, and an anecdote. Some, indeed, were little more than strings of anecdotes. The humor, often topical in nature and appropriately linked to audience and occasion, was frequently so volatile as to have lost much of its point even before being printed in next day's newspaper.

But not all after-dinner speaking was of this nature; some of the best speeches of the day were delivered in banquet halls. It is useful to preserve a distinction made at the time between speeches following Lowell's recipe and speeches of genuine substance. One commentator described the difference between "after-dinner oratory" and "after-dinner speaking" as that between a good play and a bad burlesque. James Bryce too was careful to distinguish between light after-dinner speeches and what he called "epideictic speeches at public dinners." These latter were delivered at banquets in honor of national heroes or foreign guests, alumni or commencement dinners, annual dinners of literary and historical societies, chambers of commerce or organizations such as the famed New England Society. These addresses, delivered by such men of intellect and culture as Wendell Phillips, George W. Curtis, Oliver Wendell Holmes, Jr., Thomas Wentworth Higginson, Brander Matthews, and Woodrow Wilson, were often quite similar to those delivered by these same men and others from the lecture platform, before such academic societies as Phi Beta Kappa or on ceremonial occasions. The fact that speeches were presented after dinner did not necessarily render them frivolous or unworthy.

Sometimes the speaker would deal directly or obliquely with matters of serious social or political concern. In the midst of the Hayes-Tilden controversy, while the election was still being bitterly contested, George W. Curtis spoke at a dinner of the New England Society of New York on "The Puritan Principle: Liberty under Law." Before three hundred influential business and professional men, a group sharply divided in opinion as to whether Hayes or Tilden had actually been elected, Curtis went beyond postprandial pleasantries to meet the "terrible subject" head-on. His friend Edward Everett Hale later credited him with convincing these leaders of public opinion that a court of arbitration must be appointed to settle the controversy. "At a great moment in our history," Hale asserted, "George William Curtis spoke the word which was most needed to save the nation from a terrible calamity."[20]

The most celebrated after-dinner oration of the 1880s was Henry Grady's "The New South," also delivered at an annual dinner of the New England Society of New York. In this urbane and witty address to some of the most influential members of the eastern business community, the newspaper editor from Atlanta, Georgia, made an eloquent plea for conciliation between the two sections and sought to give assurance that the new South was a fertile field for the investment of northern capital. It was exactly the right speech at the right time, and it stirred the imagination of the entire country, making the young Grady a celebrity overnight. Predictably, it was pronounced a "classic" and was added to the collections of models for declamation. Francis P. Gaines, a student of southern oratory, reports that by the end of the century "The New South" had replaced Patrick Henry's "Liberty or Death" as the favorite declamation of southern schoolboys. As a member of the audience and sometimes as a judge, he says, "I am convinced that I have heard this oration one hundred times, maybe one thousand times."[21]

The many changes in postwar America resulted in a modification of attitudes toward oratory, changes in the nature and quality of oratory itself, and a changing perception of the role of the orator in society. No longer a national hero as in generations past, the political orator was with considerable justification regarded as a lackey to the new heroes of industry and finance. Congressional "debate," too often intended to obfuscate rather than illuminate, was ridiculed by thoughtful observers as a device to cloak undercover activities of spoilsmen. Campaign oratory, traditionally short on substance and long on exuberance, continued the tradition of pageantry but took on dimensions of ugliness in its deliberate perpetuation of Civil War hatred to divert attention from genuine issues. With the commercialization of the public lecture came a deterioration in quality as entertainment shouldered instruction from the platform. Chautauqua, born of a genuine impulse for intellectual and moral uplift, was gradually being transformed into a traveling circus. And demonstrative speaking, the oratory of the special occasion — which had once attracted the talents of the nation's greatest men — became debased and neglected, while the trivial banter of the dinner table was elevated to a position of eminence among the various types of occasional speaking.

Still, despite these disheartening central tendencies, the oratory of this brazen age was not completely without redeeming aspects. By no means all the oratory of this period was devoted to obfuscation and diversion. Independents in politics, unwilling to yield to party discipline, continued to expose the evils of the system and speak out bravely for reform. Bloody-shirt oratory of the political campaign was countered, as has been illustrated in the references to Lamar, Grady, and Washington, by occasional oratory which appealed to the finer impulses and sought to soften hatred with conciliation. The lecture platform remained as in prewar days the freest forum for the discussion of vexing social questions as well as a medium for public enlightenment. Even the oratory of the dinner table, despite its frequent triviality, was not without beneficent influence and moments of genuine excellence.

ॐ 4 ॐ
THE SPEAK-OUT AGE
America Finds Her Voice Again

"The era of frankness and publicity has come, and
come to stay . . . the 'speak-out' age has arrived."
R. N. MATSON

When Edward Parker asserted that "the age of heroes is over," he
added "the age for their statues is come." Despite a low regard for
contemporary speakers during the postwar decades, the "orator"
remained a revered ideal.[1] In his book *The Golden Age of American
Oratory,* Parker sought to erect enduring statues to nine orators of
the Congress, bar, and platform. Looking back wistfully to the days
when giants strode the halls of Congress and strains of eloquence
filled the air, he contrasted the heroes of that golden age with the
"pygmies of the present day who . . . aspire to the purple of their
honors." Another attempt to keep alive a "great orator" tradition
was made by William Mathews, author of a rhapsodic tribute to
Oratory and Orators. Mathews apparently ransacked the popular
magazines, biographies, the works of Parker, Magoon, Edward
Channing, and others for anecdotes relating dramatic oratorical
triumphs. A series of chapters on the influence of the orator, qualifications necessary to oratorical success, the nature of eloquence,
and the like is followed by eulogistic sketches of celebrated English, Irish, and American speakers. An idealized picture emerges
of the orator as a godlike creature, endowed with magical gifts
which enable him to rule the minds and passions of lesser mortals.

But it is noteworthy that the orator thus idealized is a dead
orator. Appraisals of living orators were, more often than not, satirical in tone. Ammunition for subsequent attacks on speakers and
speechmaking was provided by Thomas Carlyle in a strident,
hyperbolic essay on the "Stump-Orator."[2] In a harangue of more
than forty pages, the Scotsman derogated "the faculty of eloquent
speech" and called for an economy of words. Deploring the emphasis on speech in the schools and in public life, he affirmed that
speaking is by no means the highest human faculty and is no test of
general excellence and ability. Most of the principal arguments and

assumptions present in attacks upon the orator to the present day are to be found in Carlyle's essay, originally published in 1850: 1) Silence is preferable to speech. "The Age that admires talk so much can have little discernment for inarticulate work, or for anything that is deep and genuine." 2) Skill in speaking is a sign of intellectual shallowness; one talks because he is incapable of thinking. 3) Talkers are seldom doers; one talks as a substitute for action. Professing to believe that to utter an idea is to impoverish oneself, Carlyle propounds a bizarre law of the conservation of ideas: "The idea you have once spoken . . . is no longer yours; it is gone from you, so much life and virtue is gone." Better that one keep silent, allowing his ideas to activate him to do good things.

> Probably there is not in Nature a more distracted phantasm than your commonplace eloquent speaker, as he is found on platforms, in parliaments, on Kentucky stumps, at tavern-dinners, in windy, empty, insincere times like ours. The "excellent Stump-Orator," as our admiring Yankee friends define him . . . is not an artist I can much admire, as matters go! . . .
>
> Be not a Public Orator, thou brave young British man, thou that are now growing to be something: not a Stump-Orator, if thou canst help it. Appeal not to the vulgar, with its long ears and its seats in the Cabinet; not by spoken words to the vulgar; *hate* the profane vulgar, and bid it begone. . . . Love silence rather than speech in these tragic days, when, for very speaking, the voice of man has fallen inarticulate to man; and hearts, in this loud babbling, sit dark and dumb toward one another.[3]

Endorsements and elaborations of these themes soon appeared in this country, some obviously inspired by Carlyle's excoriation of the orator. Disparagers of eloquence expatiated with relish upon the theme that "full men are seldom fluent" and exalted the virtues of silence. Especially censorious were the literary men. Nathaniel Hawthorne deplored the practice of selecting orators for leadership in government. "The very fact . . . that they are men of words makes it improbable that they are likewise men of deeds. And it is only tradition and old custom, founded on an obsolete state of things, that assigns any value to parliamentary oratory. . . . The speeches have no effect till they are converted into newspaper paragraphs; and they had better be composed as such, in the first place, and oratory reserved for churches, courts of law, and public dinner tables." Samuel Gardner echoed Carlyle's denunciation of the talking power as a low faculty, seldom conspicuous among men of high intellect: "It requires only a tongue, which most people have, to be able to talk in private or in public either, — and he who can do one tolerably, can do the other also, — but to be silent shows brains, a higher organ than the tongue." The American people, Gardner suggested, fearing too much legislation, send orators to Congress knowing that they will dissipate their energies in talking and will not harm the Republic by acting.[4]

The anonymous author of "A Plea for Freedom from Speech and Figures of Speech-Makers"[5] complains of two epidemics, eloquence and statuary, which threaten to render the country unfit for human habitation except for the deaf and the blind. Boston, he thinks, is especially unfortunate, having more statues and more speakers than any other city on the continent. He mentions a book that he has seen called *The Hundred Boston Orators.* This, he believes, is ample justification for renaming her the *tire,* rather than the *hub,* of creation, and he shudders to think of all those orators commemorated in statuary. Every time we manage to get one orator safely underground, this writer laments, there are ten to pronounce eulogies, and twenty more to repeat the ceremony later around the inevitable statue. But, he admits, "I am falling into the very vice I condemn, — like Carlyle, who has talked a quarter of a century in praise of holding your tongue."

While such sentiments as these were finding expression in the *Nation* and the *Atlantic Monthly,* the humorists were busy satirizing the orator on the platform and in the columns of daily newspapers. Behind such pseudonyms as Artemus Ward, Bill Nye, Petroleum V. Nasby, and Orpheus C. Kerr, men of considerable talent ridiculed the themes and the styles of contemporary oratory. Particularly vulnerable were the Fourth of July oration, the set speech in Congress, and the emotional, rabble-rousing effusions of the stump speaker. One of Bill Nye's contributions to this satirical literature was the announcement of his invention of "a patent oratorical steam organette for railway stumping." This ingenious aid to political campaigning was a small organ operated by steam to be mounted on the rear platform of a railroad car, out of sight under an American flag. A speech prepared on punched paper is inserted into the machine, and the speaker simply stands behind it "with his hand socked into the breast of his frock coat nearly up to the elbow, and while his bosom swells with pardonable pride the engineer turns on the steam." These prepunched speeches insure the orator against inappropriate local references, such as praising a soap works in a rival town. George Ade supplemented this image of the political speaker as a pompous ass with his fable of "a Bluff whose Long Suit was Glittering Generalities. He hated to Work and it hurt his Eyes to read Law, but on a Clear Day he could be heard a Mile, so he became a Statesman." He was invited to speak at picnics because his voice "beat out the Merry-Go-Round." "The Habit of Dignity enveloped him. Upon his Brow Deliberation sat." "He loved to talk about the Flag." When on the brink of exposure by an investigating committee for indiscretions involving corporations, "he put on a fresh White Tie and made a Speech about our Heroic Dead on a Hundred Battlefields," and people found it impossible to believe that such a patriot could be a crook.[6] Martin Dooley was impressed by the lyrical beauty of speeches he had heard. He claimed to have listened to speeches that were subsequently set to music and played by a silver cornet band, and he told of walking home humming to himself snatches of a speech on the tariff. Of Albert Beveridge's Senate speech on the Philippines he said, "Twas a speech ye cud waltz to." After hearing William Jennings Bryan's Cross of Gold speech he went over to Hogan's house and picked out the tune with one finger on the piano; "it was that musical."

A favorite device for pointing up the most egregious excesses of platform speaking was the parodied oration. These imagined addresses displayed for the entertainment of readers and lecture audiences the characteristics which had become all too familiar in more serious efforts at oratory — exaggeration and verbosity, patriotic bombast, gratuitous quotations and allusions, inappropriate imagery, lofty apostrophes, and the tendency to preface the discussion of almost any subject, however trivial, with an interminable excursion into the remote past. Orpheus C. Kerr emphasized this final characteristic in his synopsis of a speech accompanying the presentation of a sword to the colonel of the Mackerel Brigade:

He spoke of the wonderful manner in which the world was called out of chaos at the creation, and spoke feelingly of the Garden of Eden, and the fall of our first parents; he then went on to review the many changes the earth had experienced since it was first created; and described the method of the ancients to cook bread before stoves were invented; he then spoke of the glories of Greece and Rome, giving a full history of them from the beginning to the present time; he then went on to describe the origin of the Republican and Democratic parties, reading both platforms, and giving his ideas of Jackson's policy; he then gave an account of the war of the Roses in England, and the cholera in Persia, attributing the latter to a sudden change in the atmosphere; he then went on to speak of the difficulties encountered by Columbus in discovering this country, and gave a history of his subsequent career and death in Europe; he then read an abstract from Washington's Farewell Address; in conclusion, he said that the ladies of Washington had empowered him to present this here sword to that ere gallant colonel, in the presence of these here brave defenders of their country.[7]

Kerr reports that at the conclusion of the speech the regiment was near starvation and the colonel so weak from lack of sleep that he had to be carried to his tent.

Several of this group of humorists demonstrated their mastery of the devastating parody, notably Artemus Ward on Webster's Glorious Union theme and Nye and Nasby on the Fourth of July oration, but none was more skillful than Finley Peter Dunne, the creator of Mr. Dooley. One example must suffice to illustrate his castigation of the orator as a purveyor of senseless sound. Dooley's friend Carney wanted a bridge built across a creek. On the way to the banquet he offered Dooley a persuasive argument in favor of the project. Consequently Dooley expected his friend to make a speech along these lines: "We need a new bridge; the old one is a disgrace; if we don't get one we'll defeat the politicans responsible." Instead, he made an oration.

"Gintlemen: We ar-re th' most gloryous people that iver infested th' noblest counthry that th' sun iver shone upon," he says. "We meet here tonight," he says, "undher that starry imblim that flaps above freemen's homes in ivry little hamlet fr'm where rolls the Oregon in majestic volume to th' sun-kist wathers iv th' Passyfic to where th' Pimsicoddy shimmers adown the pineculed hills iv Maine," he says. "Th' hand iv time," he says, "marches with stately steps acrost th' face iv histhry, an' as I listen to its hoofbeats I hear a still, small voice that seems to say that Athens, Greece, Rawhn, an' Egypt an' iver on an' upward, an' as long as th' stars in their courses creep through eternity."[8]

The orator was only one of many tempting targets for these nineteenth-century satirists who were ever alert to manifestations of the pretentious and the phony wherever found. Their aim was so accurate, their victims so vulnerable, and their access to the public eye and ear so extensive, that they were able, while masquerading as mere entertainers, to serve as effective social critics and to exert a considerable influence upon public attitudes and tastes. It is unlikely that members of the American electorate, long familiar with certain rhetorical devices of public men, could fail to recognize them in the parodies of the humorists or could ever again be quite so susceptible to the more obvious attempts at "eloquence" after seeing them subjected to such merciless exposure, One testimonial to the effectiveness of the parodist may be found in the subsequent lament of an editor of a collection of orations that one by one orators had abandoned "the old traditions" because of "the sneer of the inconoclast."

Nostalgia for the oratorical giants of an earlier day and derision of the pygmies of a brazen age stimulated speculation concerning the likelihood of a permanent decline in oratory. Early in the new century Edward Everett Hale could write, "It is one of the conventions of the age to say that parliamentary oratory is a lost art." And Champ Clark, the Democratic leader of the House of Representatives, recalling Wendell Phillip's celebrated lecture, ventured the opinion that if Phillips were to return to earth he would doubtless list among "The Lost Arts" the one "of which he was a master and upon which his reputation rests — the art of oratory."[9]

Actually, of course, such proclamations (and responsive denials) of the decline of oratory had been heard since ancient times. Dionysius of Halicarnassus spoke in the first century B.C. of the decline and revival of oratory. British writers, both before and after the golden age of Pitt and Fox, had lamented the death of eloquence. In the United States, Edward T. Channing observed in his inaugural address as Boylston Professor of Rhetoric and Oratory at Harvard that "oratory, now, is said to be almost a lost art. We hear constantly that it has fallen from its old supremacy." This was in 1819, in the childhood of the new republic, when Lincoln, Phillips, and Sumner were schoolboys, and before Webster, Clay, and Calhoun had reached their prime. During the decades prior to the Civil War, connoisseurs of oratory debated in print the relative merits of ancient and modern eloquence in one of many attempts to share the ethos of the republics of antiquity. One reviewer of a collection of speeches wrote: "We are living over again the classic times of Athenian and Roman eloquence, on a broader stage, in larger proportions, with elements of excitement, hopes of progress, and principles of duration, which never cheered and strengthened the souls of Demosthenes and Cicero." While a few answered in the affirmative the persistent question "Is Ancient Eloquence Superior to Modern?" the consensus seemed to be that although modern eloquence was different, it was not necessarily inferior. In a lecture on "The Orator and His Times," Edward T. Channing disparaged the worship of Greek orators, suggesting that their style "might now be despised, even if it could be perfectly acquired." "I think it unquestionable," said Channing, "that the oratory of modern free countries is, in character, as precisely formed by and suited to our state of society, as that of the ancients was accommodated to theirs; and that it would be scarcely less ridiculous to lament over the decline of their oratory amongst us, than it would be to lament over the decline of good government, morals, and philosophy since the days of the triumvirate."[10]

After the Civil War, less interest was manifested in the question of whether Cicero and Demosthenes were superior to Webster and Clay than in whether there was anyone in postwar America to compare with Webster and Clay. Disgusted with the quality of speaking in Congress, in the courts, and on the public platform, writers proclaimed an oratorical decline. In 1872 the *North American Review* announced the decisive victory of the press over the orator. The speaker, it argued, realizing that much wider audience can be reached through the press, no longer relies upon histrionics to affect an immediate body of listeners. Admitting that as "a useful incidental appliance" it must continue to be cultivated "more or less assiduously," the writer asserted that "by comparison with the days when oratorical eminence was among the supreme ambitions of statesmen, it must be admitted that oratory is, not certainly a lost art, but a declining one, and that the orator has abdicated his power in favor[11] of the journalist." Shortly after the appearance of this article, the *North American Review,* formerly a prolific source of commentary on speakers and speaking, abruptly ceased publication of such comment for the remainder of the century.

But elsewhere the discussion became more intense. When in 1879 William Mathews, motivated by a desire "to aid in awakening a fresh interest in oratory in this country," published his *Oratory and Orators,* he titled his second chapter "Is Oratory a Lost Art?" In the 1890s a number of articles with such titles as "The Passing of the Art of Oratory," "The Neglected Art of Oratory," and "Has Oratory Declined?" appeared in the popular journals. Numerous reasons for the alleged decline were suggested: rigid party control and the committee system in Congress, the lack of competent men in politics, decreased susceptibility of audiences to emotional appeals, the nature of subjects discussed, and, as asserted earlier by the *North American Review,* the growing influence of the press. Some, convinced that oratory was as important as ever, cited the phenomenal success of Grady's "New South" and Bryan's "Cross of Gold," but they were answered by others who recalled that Bryan had been charged with being a "mere orator," a charge that had proved a handicap in his bid for the presidency. Animated as the debate became, the lack of agreement as to terminology rendered it in a large measure meaningless. To some disputants the term *oratory* designated artistic speaking cultivated for its own sake — highly emotional, richly imaginative, abounding in figurative language and classical allusion, delivered verbatim from memory, or ignited by the inspiration of the moment. To others, oratory meant all effective persuasive speaking. Such antagonists might conceivably give different answers to the question "Has oratory declined?" while being in essential agreement as to the facts of the situation.

Perhaps the most striking aspect of this controversy which had its beginnings in antiquity and continues to the present day is the fact that these statements almost invariably conclude by sounding the same note. Regardless of his individual conception of the nature of "oratory," or of the extent of its "decline," each commentator feels it necessary to assure us that when the time comes, when the crisis arrives, when the nation is in danger, when great subjects need ventilation, the orator will appear. It requires only the occasion or the issue to call him forth. So compelling was this theme that it moved classical scholar and encyclopedist Harry Thurston Peck to conclude an article on political oratory in his literary journal *The Bookman* in this most unscholarly fashion: "As it has always been true in the past, so will it always, we believe, be true throughout the future, that when great bodies of men are stirred by intense emotion and when the wind of passion is blowing over human hearts, then will the fire once more descend and touch the lips of some born orator, who will as heretofore smite down all opposition, take reason and imagination captive, and impose his single will on all who hear him, by the indescribable magic of the spoken word."[12] When the time comes, when the need arises, it was confidently predicted, orators will arise to meet the need.

The time came near the turn of the century. America's infatuation with the titans of trade diminished, and new heroes took their places as a growing interest in the discussion of pressing public questions became apparent. In a New Year's editorial in January 1904 reviewing the events of the year just past, *Collier's* observed: "The centre of attention has to some degree shifted from commerce to politics, and the protagonist is now rather President Roosevelt than J. P. Morgan." With amazing suddenness the politician rose in public interest and estimation, while the prestige of the businessman declined. In the first decade of the century the number of business biographies in the popular magazines dropped markedly, while biographical articles devoted to political leaders, notably the dynamic Progressive speakers, more than doubled.[13] Orators of the Progressive era, together with the muckrakers, their colleagues in the press, were seen as heroic advocates before the court of public opinion — exposing the venality of bosses and industrialists, appealing to the public sense of justice and mercy, engaging in the always exciting battle between the good guys and the bad guys.

No longer was it considered madness for men of good character and good family to choose politics as a career. In his *Twenty Years of the Republic* Harry T. Peck recalled that from 1890 to 1905 it became more and more usual for young men of cultivation and intelligence to enter public life. And James Bryce, who had devoted a chapter of his *American Commonwealth* to the question of why the best men do not go into politics, noted that a tendency, observable since the Civil War, of the ablest men to turn to business instead of public service, had apparently been arrested. "There is more speaking and writing and thinking . . . upon the principles of government than at any previous epoch. Good citizens are beginning to put their hands to the machinery of government." In a revised edition Bryce added this footnote: "This seems to be even more true in 1914 than it was when first written in 1894."[14]

Godkin, who had earlier reported in the *Nation* a revival of British parliamentary oratory, thought he saw evidence in 1902 of a similar revival in this country. The increased amount of space in the press devoted to Washington dispatches he interpreted as evidence of an unusual public interest in the proceedings of Congress. The reason, he was convinced, was that Congress had been debating for a change. Votes, he observed, have actually been changed by give-and-take argument. Discussion preceding voting has affected the outcome. He hopes the leaders of Congress will take heed of this new interest evoked by genuine debate: "In a word, let them make Congressional debate what debate ought to be everywhere — a means of bringing out the better reason and the wiser policy — and we shall hear much less of the decadence of Congress, or the growing indifference of the people to what goes on in the Capitol at Washington."[15]

It is difficult in analyzing this oratorical renaissance to distinguish clearly between cause and effect. Did an aroused public interest in political issues encourage capable speakers to enter the arena, or did the emergence of articulate spokesmen stimulate public interest? Both influences were probably at work. But that there was a revival of interest in instructive and persuasive public speaking during the years immediately preceding and following the beginning of the twentieth century, there can be no doubt. Nor is there much question that two remarkable but dissimilar men, William Jennings Bryan and Theodore Roosevelt, helped provide the impetus.

The story of Bryan's dramatic triumph at the Democratic National Convention in Chicago in July 1896 has been told again and again; it needs no repetition here. But it must be recalled that the events of that day reminded millions of Americans of the potential power of the voice of a single human being raised in behalf of an idea whose time had come. It has been said with much truth that the "Cross of Gold" speech presented no new facts; that many of its memorable passages, including the famous peroration, had been used by the speaker on other occasions; that the speech probably convinced no one not already converted to the cause of free silver. But in that speech Bryan demonstrated his genius for articulating what was in the minds of his listeners, for saying far more effectively than they would have found possible precisely what they wanted to hear. He dramatized what was a potentially dull subject, monetary policy, heightening the elements of conflict — the West versus the East, the farmer versus the combinations of economic power. In cadences reminiscent of Patrick Henry's "Call to Arms" in 1775, he hurled his defiance at the forces of organized wealth: "We have petitioned, and our petitions have been scorned; we have entreated, and our entreaties have been disregarded; we have begged, and they have mocked when our calamity came. We beg no longer; we entreat no more. We defy them!" At those words, recalls Henry T. Peck, "the great hall seemed to rock and sway with the fierce energy of the shout that ascended from twenty thousand throats."[16] Throughout the latter part of the address, applause punctuated every sentence (Bryan later described the audience as a trained choir, responding in unison to every point). When the speaker finished, the scene, according to Peck, was "indescribable." "Twenty thousand men and women went mad with an irresistible enthusiasm."

But Bryan was no one-speech man; his influence did not fade after the enthusiasm generated by this oratorical tour de force had cooled down. He campaigned for the presidency as no man had ever campaigned before, traveling 18,000 miles to deliver 600 speeches to an estimated five million people. He was called a demagogue and worse by men who far outdid him in demagoguery. Actually, his gentlemanly conduct throughout the campaign, his sweetness of spirit, his courtly generosity to his opponent, his patience, moderation, and good humor were in dramatic contrast to the furious hatred displayed by those who opposed him on the platform and off.

Bryan lost the election, and two more elections after that. He was ridiculed and reviled by his opponents as virulently as any public figure before or since. He was, they said, like the Platte River, six miles wide at the mouth, and only six inches deep. But his achievement in seizing the leadership of a national protest movement in one irresistible speech elicited the admiration even of many who had little sympathy with his cause. "It was," wrote William Allen White, certainly no Bryan partisan, "the first time in my life and in the life of a generation in which any man large enough to lead a national party had boldly and unashamedly made his cause that of the poor and the oppressed." And Bryan's evangelical fervor, his power as a political preacher, enabled him to lead for a time what Richard Hofstadter has called "a Great Awakening which swept away much of the cynicism and apathy that had been characteristic of American politics for thirty years."[17]

Even more influential, because he spoke from a loftier pulpit, the office of the president of the United States, was another political preacher, Theodore Roosevelt. The connoisseurs of oratory, those who yearned for the likes of Everett, Choate, and Webster and whose spirits were quickened by the magnificent voice, the flawless articulation, and the majestic bearing of William Jennings Bryan, would not have considered Roosevelt "eloquent," nor even, perhaps, have admitted him to the ranks or the "orators." His high-pitched voice and prominent white teeth, his eccentric gesticulation, his juvenile ebullience, all invited caricature. But he was a tremendously effective stump speaker, and he always brought out the crowds. Some, it is true, came primarily to hear, and to see, Roosevelt; there is no denying that many were more interested in his colorful personality than in the subject matter of his speeches. There was a zest, a flair, to everything the man did and said; he quite literally commanded attention.

In 1910, former President Roosevelt while on a European tour delivered the Romanes Lecture at Oxford. Later, in a discussion of the lecture with a distinguished American scientist, the archbishop of York gave this evaluation: "In the way of grading which we have at Oxford, we agreed to mark the lecture 'Beta Minus,' but the lecturer 'Alpha Plus.' While we felt that the lecture was not a very great contribution to science, we were sure that the lecturer was a very great man."[18] It is likely that a wider application of the archbishop's evaluation can be made. By no means all the thousands of political addresses which were so ardently applauded constituted a very great contribution to the science of government or the solution of complex economic problems, nor did they always exemplify the best in rhetorical artistry, but those who listened were usually persuaded of the greatness of the speaker.

That Roosevelt, the most prominent political figure on the national stage during the Progressive Era, exerted leadership in ways other than by making public speeches goes without saying. But certainly his enormous hold on the public must be explained in part by his speaking. He dramatized himself and his policies and prepared the way for political action through vivid pronouncements from the public platform which spoke directly and forcefully to those middle-class elements in American society whose support he sought. So firm was his hold on the public imagination, so devoted his followers, that even the histrionics of the Milwaukee speech in October 1912, delivered immediately after he had been shot by a fanatic, were not perceived as being absurd. The bullet still in his chest, he refused to be taken to a hospital: "I will make this speech or die. I have a message to deliver and will deliver it as long as there is life in my body." The audience, it is reported, was sick with horror and overcome with genuine concern.

In his speaking, as in everything else he did, Roosevelt was indefatigable. As president, he was constantly on the stump, the lecture platform, Chautauqua — seizing whatever opportunity offered itself to deliver his homilies and exhortations, carrying his fight against the railroads, the trusts, and all manifestations of special privilege. Like Bryan, whom he maliciously attacked as a dangerous radical, but many of whose policies he later appropriated, he brought to the discussion of public questions a moral fervor and an exciting personality. In addition, he brought to programs of reform a respectability they had not previously possessed. The protests reiterated during the eighties and nineties by the ragtag Populist orators somehow sounded different from the mouth of a Harvard-educated patrician, unassociated with the outcasts and the dispossessed.

As it turned out, the young man whose family and friends had warned him against entering the political arena because it was frequented by low types became an important influence in raising the level of politics. As a public official he made it a point to seek out good men and appoint them to office. His own participation in national politics led other men of education, principle, and talent to follow his example. And for a time at least, able men engaged in the kind of public discussion which had long been missing from the American political scene. After the 1904 election campaign, a campaign in which President Roosevelt himself had been the principal issue, a writer in the *New England Magazine* heralded the arrival of a new area of "frank, open-hearted expression of opinion."[19] Recalling past decades of secrecy in the conduct of public affairs, times when bosses dominated politics, when puppet candidates sought to commit themselves as little as possible, and when speeches were made up of meaningless platitudes, he hails a new spirit of candor and openness. It began, he thinks, in 1896, when one party declared unequivocally for free silver, the other for the gold standard, and William Jennings Bryan deserves most of the credit. Then came Roosevelt, who like Bryan said what he thought but won. Roosevelt put his views on record in a series of books, articles, and speeches; he issued an unevasive letter of acceptance; and he received a record-breaking public endorsement. What, asks this writer, does all this mean? "It means that the new method of campaigning has been fixed beyond the possibility of recall; that the era of frankness and publicity has come, and come to stay; that the 'speak-out' age has arrived, and that Theodore Roosevelt was its chief founder."

Actually, signs of this renaissance and a concomitant interest in public discussion were evident much earlier — even before Bryan's oratorical triumph at Chicago in 1896. Early stirrings can be seen in the campaign of 1884, when a group of liberal Republicans, many of whom had for years waged an impotent battle for reform, bolted their party to support Grover Cleveland, the Democratic candidate. This campaign, it is true, deteriorated into an exchange of almost unprecedented personal abuse. But the sense of moral outrage that spurred the Mugwump defection to Cleveland and forced men of the caliber of Carl Schurz, Henry Ward Beecher, George W. Curtis, E. L. Godkin, Charles F. Adams, as well as President Charles W. Eliot of Harvard and numerous members of his faculty into open opposition to Republican candidate James G. Blaine, symbol of the spoils system, gave promise of more significant public discussion and an end to acquiescence in things-as-they-are. This campaign also marked the end of the Republicans' most serviceable "issue," the bloody shirt, as an effective means of beclouding more pressing issues; Blaine's attempts to revive memories of the Civil War and the specter of a South again dominant in national affairs proved disappointing.

The corruption of the campaign of 1888 has been thoroughly chronicled by historians; Arthur M. Schlesinger has called it the most venal political campaign in American history. In it the crass, open purchasing of individual votes for cash reached its most outrageous limits; before the next national election the adoption of the secret ballot system had made direct bribery considerably more difficult. But another aspect of this campaign is more relevant to the present discussion.

In December of 1887, just prior to the opening of the campaign, President Cleveland devoted his annual message to Congress exclusively to a plea for revision of the tariff. This courageous speech, published in full in the newspapers and widely read and discussed, clearly drew a line (hitherto deliberately blurred) between the two major parties and provided an issue for the presidential campaign. Democrats somewhat reluctantly united behind the president, while Republicans closed ranks in support of the principle of protection. The national debate which followed impelled the *Nation* to rejoice in "The Educational Value of the Present Campaign."[20] For many years, says this writer, "there has been little that was educational in politics." But now, thanks to the courage of the president, voters are provided with an important subject and the necessity for clear, reasonable arguments in opposition and support. Admitting to a preference for the Democratic position, the writer affirms that it is preferable to appeal to the intelligence of the country through reasoned argument and lose, than to win by avoiding such an appeal. Cleveland did lose, though he polled over 100,000 more popular votes than Harrison. But he and his supporters looked on it as a campaign of education, which, while temporarily lost, would triumph in the end.

The campaign of 1888 also added a new word to the American political lexicon. Employed originally as a term of jocular self-depreciation, it became useful before the end of the century as an opprobrious epithet. Shortly after the election, on November 14, 1888, two hundred Republican campaign orators attended a Spellbinders' Dinner at Delmonico's in New York. The dinner was the inspiration of Colonel Cassius M. Goodloe of Kentucky, head of the Speakers' Bureau of the National Republican Committee, who had coined the term *spellbinders,* applying it to the orators who throughout the campaign would invade his office, seize him by the lapels, and report "Last night I addressed two thousand voters for 2½ hours on the tariff. Not a man left the hall til I finished. I held them spell-bound."[21]

The dinner, "a spell-binding affair," was reported in detail the following day by both the *Times* and the *Tribune.* The hall was adorned with flags and portraits of Harrison and Levi P. Morton. Frequent reference was made to "the glorious victory at the polls." Songs were sung, among them one made famous in the campaign, "Goodbye, Old Grover, Goodbye." Even the fact that the banquet was a total abstinence affair did not prove an insuperable obstacle to merriment, though it did seem to the *Times* reporter that "the hauteur of the waiters as they poured out the crystal ice water into the cut-glass goblets had a depressing effect upon the guests." After the coffee and cigars had been served, letters and telegrams from those who could not attend were read: Benjamin Harrison sent cordial regrets, as did Ingersoll, Morton, and Mrs. J. Ellen Foster, who pointed out sadly that no woman's voice would be heard at the victory celebration but hastened to add her assurance of continued support from organizations of Republican women. Then came the inevitable speeches — though not so many as there might have been, for Chauncey Depew revealed in his opening remarks that 111 of those present had requested a chance to speak. Colonel Elliott Shepard praised Depew as "our American Cicero" and extolled the power of the press: "you spell-binders who talk as tonight to an audience of two hundred, or as did our Cicero at Binghamton, to an audience covering a ten-acre lot, find yourselves in the morning addressing millions, covering pretty much the whole country."

The main speaker was Depew himself, whose "witty speech" the *New York Tribune* printed in full. The speech contained the usual felicitous references to the occasion, the pleasant anecdotes, the warm appreciation of Republican policies, which audiences had come to expect from this virtuoso of after-dinner speakers. Noting the changes which had occurred in speaking styles, he observed that speeches which had once aroused the enthusiasm of multitudes could no longer be given to American audiences. He had heard them all — Lincoln, Douglas, Corwin, Seward, Sumner, Phillips — and the only one who would be acceptable to "the highly cultivated and thoroughly informed audiences" of 1888 was Wendell Phillips, still without equal or superior. Depew's description of the requisites of the stump orator is revealing: "the power of so stating what he believes that his hearers of the same party, from passive members become active enthusiasts, the tact to so impress and yet not offend the doubtful that they are thenceforth converts to his faith, and the talent to both irritate and dishearten the enemy." Revealing also is the acknowledgment of the vocation and the motivations of his fellow spellbinders:

> Now the campaign speaker retires from the canvass into his business and disappears from the public eye. But there is something of the dramatic spirit aroused in him. He loves the platform, the cheering audiences, the wild acclaim; and it is difficult for him, if he has been a long time out, to settle back again into the trend and current of life. *It is the peculiarity of this canvass that the professional speaker had little part in it, but that the great business community furnished the orators.* From every profession and vocation men volunteered who felt that their highest duty to their country, and their best service to their business was to instruct their fellow-citizens in those principles to which they had pinned their faith.[22]

No clearer indication is needed that the spellbinders, many of them, were Republican businessmen with a stake in the maintenance of a high protective tariff. They were defending their selfish interests. Nevertheless, like the followers of Cleveland, they were convinced that they were engaging in an educational campaign. They were citizens of this republic, personally participating in a political campaign, mounting platforms for the purpose of instructing their fellow citizens "in those principles to which they had pinned their faith" — just as others were to do in subsequent campaigns.

If, as Depew had said, in 1888 "the great business community" furnished the orators, it was the stricken farm communities of the West that supplied another host of them in state and local campaigns of the eighties and nineties. Scores of men and women who had never made a public speech before rose in town halls, schoolhouses, and in open air meetings throughout Kansas, Nebraska, and the Dakotas, in Minnesota, Iowa, and Illinois to preach with a religious fervor the gospel of Populism. The great climax came in the campaign of 1896 when Bryan led the combined Democratic and Populist parties against the superior forces of wealth and power represented by William McKinley and directed by Mark Hanna. Flaunting the tradition that the candidate must not actively seek the office, Bryan sought it zealously, campaigning in twenty-seven states and making twenty-seven speeches on the final day. The Republicans were able to martial hundreds of speakers and almost the complete power of the press against him; Bryan himself, it was said, waged his battle virtually alone. But in a speech at Ottumwa, Iowa, near the end of the campaign, he acknowledged the unselfish devotion to his cause demonstrated by nameless, inexperienced speakers: "If they had taken from us every man who had made a public speech before, we would have had sufficient of public speaking from these new men who have demonstrated that eloquence is the speech of one who knows what he is talking about and believes what he says."

Though the defeat of Bryan in 1896 marked the effective end of the Populist party, the spirit of reform which the populists had engendered did not die. The sense of frustration and moral outrage expressed by farmers and laborers during the eighties and nineties spread to the middle class during the Progressive Era of the early twentieth century as orators of the stature of Robert LaFollette, Theodore Roosevelt, Woodrow Wilson, Jonathan Dolliver, and Albert Beveridge carried on the battle against many of the same enemies. Issues long festering — conservation, workmen's compensation, women's rights, methods of curbing the malefactors of great wealth, political measures such as the direct primary, initiative, referendum, and recall for restoring democratic control — were brought by able spokesmen to the platform and into print. The supreme issue, said Robert LaFollette, was "the encroachment of the powerful few upon the rights of the many," and during the turbulent period which reached its apex in the campaign of 1912 both the few and the many spoke out vigorously by tongue and pen.

By the turn of the century *spellbinder* had become a generic term for all stump speakers, used without apology by the speakers themselves. Articles by and about spellbinders in the popular journals reported revolutionary changes in political campaigning.[23] Formal speeches in the large cities were supplemented by hundreds of shorter speeches from rear platforms of special railroad cars. From such a peripatetic rostrum a speaker could address a score of audiences in a day. Depew was said to have made over a hundred speeches in forty-three counties in a single week; Roosevelt as vice-presidential candidate made 673 speeches to an estimated three million listeners. Speakers' bureaus were established at strategic points; "campaign textbooks" were prepared containing materials for spellbinders. Managers supplied with huge maps of the nation moved speakers around like train dispatchers. There were speakers for every audience and occasion — black speakers, speakers able to address ethnic groups in their own tongues, even, it was reported in 1904, a deaf and mute orator who delivered speeches in sign language.

Not only were speeches shorter, they were more colloquial. There was more give and take between speaker and audience; dialogue encroached upon monologue; hecklers challenged the pompous declaration and the vacuous abstraction, placing more demands upon speakers to keep at least one foot on the ground. In his recollections of the 1896 campaign Bryan notes that his remarks were often "enlivened by witty remarks" from the audience. Sometimes these interruptions were merely embarrassing; sometimes they provided an opportunity to score an additional point. Many speakers, of course, persisted in the devices traditionally associated with campaigning — the string of funny stories, the appeals *ad hominem* and *ad populum,* the patriotic flights. But there is reason to believe that audiences were becoming less susceptible to such stratagems. As Senator Jonathan Dolliver remarked: "Fourth of July stuff went to pieces under fire of questions from the audience." William D. Foulke quotes a local authority on spellbinding who gave him this prescription for the art: "Fill yourself with your subject, knock out the bung, and let nature caper." Even such a flippant recipe as this, Foulke adds, acknowledges the necessity for being informed. No one, he was convinced, is of much use in a political campaign who has not studied the issues.

Speakers began to discover that audiences were sometimes as smart and as knowledgeable as they were, and that an audience was usually worthy of the best a speaker could deliver. "No one," wrote a veteran Republican campaigner, "could take an active part upon the stump in such a campaign as that of 1892 and not come out of it with an increased respect for the good faith and excellent sense of the multitudes who attend our public meetings." Such testimonials to the intelligence of audiences are numerous, as are comments upon the improved qualtiy of political speaking. James Bryce, while observing that American stump speakers had traditionally aimed at stimulation, rather than instruction or conviction, was moved in later editions of his *American Commonwealth* to make this qualification: "In the campaign of 1896, however, the currency question was argued before the electors with a force and point which were both stimulative and instructive: and the habit of appealing to the intelligence as well as the feelings or prejudices of the voters has since been maintained.[24]

Commenting on the campaign of 1900, another writer reinforces these observations regarding audiences and speakers. Never since pre-Civil War days, he thinks, has political speaking attracted such widespread interest and such vast audiences. "Far from the voice having lost its power as an instrument of instruction, one may well question if a new career for the orator has not just begun."[25]

This rebirth of interest in public speaking manifested in the reappearance of first-class men on the political platform and increased public interest and involvement in the serious discussion of vital issues was also strikingly revealed in journalism and book publishing. More articles concerning orators and oratory appeared in the popular journals from 1896 to 1900 than had been published during the two decades from 1870 to 1890. Readers at the turn of the century were introduced to "The Ten Best Speeches Ever Made," "Great Speeches by Eminent Men," and "Happy Hits in Oratory." In 1901 *Scribner's* presented two articles by Senator George F. Hoar of Massachusetts: "Oratory" and "Some Famous Orators I Have Heard." The *Nation* carried a series on British and American orators, including James Bryce's tribute to the eloquence of Gladstone; T. P. O'Connor, a Member of Parliament, contributed six articles to *Harper's Weekly* on "Orators Who Have Influenced Me"; in the *Bookman,* Harry T. Peck offered "Some Notes on Political Oratory."

Indicative of public interest in speaking techniques is the appearance of a little book by Brander Matthews, professor of dramatic literature at Columbia University, entitled *Notes on Speech-Making,* a composite of two articles previously published in *Cosmopolitan* and *Century.* This was followed by T. W. Higginson's *Hints on Writing and Speaking,* a book containing two articles which had appeared in *Atlantic* and *Harper's.* James Bryce, during his residency in the United States as British ambassador, gave a lecture at the State University of Iowa entitled "Some Hints on Public Speaking," which was published in his *University and Historical Addresses.* Suggesting that his audience may soon join, or may already have joined, the "Great army of orators," Bryce states, "It is natural that you should desire to have a few hints given you on the subject."

The year 1896 saw the publications of two histories of oratory, the first, and for another thirty years the only, such works in America. Noting indications of revived interest in oratory and failing to find its development over a period of twenty-four centuries traced in a single work, Lorenzo Sears of Brown University set about to remedy the situation. Shortly thereafter, Henry Hardwicke, a member of the New York bar and the New York Historical Society, brought out a book with a similar purpose and motivation.[26] Both volumes sought to record the history of oratory and orators from the age of Pericles to the end of the nineteenth century; both authors hoped to inspire their contemporaries and encourage further study of eloquence. As Sears put it, "The necessity remains of gathering up the lessons left by masters of the art in the past, that, profiting by their successes and their failures, the men of the present and the future may know how they can best instruct, convince, and persuade."

Even more surprising than the appearance of two such works in a single year was the publication of a phenomenal number of anthologies of speeches a few years later at the turn of the century. The enthusiasm manifested at this time for enshrining oratory in handsome, multivolume sets exceeded anything seen before or since. More than a score of these collections appeared, many featuring on their title pages impressive editorial boards drawn from the political and intellectual elite of the time. Representative works were *The World's Best Orations* (10 vols.) edited by David Brewer of the United States Supreme Court, William Jennings Bryan's *The World's Famous Orations* (10 vols.), and Chauncey Depew's fifteen-volume *Library of Oratory.* Julian Hawthorne contributed volumes of American and British orations to the *World's Great Classics* series. T.B. Reed, Speaker of the United States House of Representatives, was editor-in-chief of *Modern Eloquence,* published as a ten-volume set in 1900 and soon expanded to fifteen volumes. The most ambitious (though by no means the most distinguished) undertaking was the twenty-five volume *Masterpieces of Eloquence,* prepared by a board of editors including Mayo W. Hazeltine, Henry Cabot Lodge, Albert Beveridge, and Archbishop John Ireland, which ran to something over 11,000 pages. The anthologists were, for the most part, professional educators, historians, literary men, and statesmen. Brewer's "Advisory Council" included four college presidents, six professors, two deans, and a Member of Parliament. The advisory council for Guy Carleton Lee's ten-volume anthology of *The World's Orators* consisted of twenty-two college and university presidents; his associate editors were professors of Latin, Greek, history, rhetoric, and literature.

In introductions and in critical essays distributed throughout their works the editors revealed a variety of motivations for undertaking these impressive collections of oratory. The patriotic impulse is clearly in evidence; there is a strong desire to show the link between oratory and freedom, to acknowledge the debt owed to eloquence by democratic institutions. "Evermore," says Lorenzo Sears in an essay in *Modern Eloquence,* "eloquence and liberty are seen hand in hand — Hellenistic resistance to Asiatic despotism; Roman warfare against imperialism . . . the protests of the Reformation, and in France against courtly corruption and oppression; in England against tampering with British freedom; in America for equal rights and for general liberty under the laws to all inhabitants of the land." These examples of eloquence are provided in the confidence that they will serve as models for future orators, be used as pieces for declamation in the schools, and impart inspiration and zeal for liberty to future generations.

Even stronger, perhaps, is the literary impulse. Oratory is the literature of Democracy; it must be honored and preserved. Every effort must be made to insure that oratory not be allowed to fall among the lost arts. The reader is continually reminded that only masterpieces in the literature of platform oratory have been chosen. According to one preface, "the single test has been, is it oratory? the single question, is there eloquence?" This precious quality, "eloquence," though seldom defined is apparently immediately recognizable when encountered. It may be strong and beautiful, like Webster's; or elegant and graceful, like John Randolph's; or natural and energetic, like Clay's. Unmistakably, eloquence is to these anthologists a literary quality, a matter of style. One selection committee in quest of genuine eloquence claims to have included only "those addresses which are characterized by attractiveness of style, clearness and force of thought, and appropriateness of illustration." It is noteworthy that *Modern Eloquence,* edited by that most practical of politicans, "Czar" Reed of the House of Representatives, has a strong literary emphasis. The editors, we are told in the introduction, have excluded all parliamentary speeches and "all other speeches delivered in the heat of debate." Only speeches regarded as "oratorical literature" have been selected.

However, when three years after its initial publication five volumes of political oratory were added to *Modern Eloquence,* the emphasis and bases of selection were radically different. Professing little interest in literary excellence, the author of the introduction presents these political speeches as illuminators of history, casting light on subjects of national importance. In fact, he adds, "It would be a broad, but scarcely inaccurate generalization to state that such a collection as 'Political Oratory' contains a history of liberty or political freedom and independence." Other anthologies of the time also emphasized the role of orations in influencing or illuminating history rather than exhibiting them as models of stylistic excellence.

The essays by eminent statesmen and scholars which studded the more pretentious anthologies offered historical sketches of oratorical periods and genres and celebrated the power of eloquence. T. B. Reed's *Modern Eloquence* featured fourteen of these "introductory essays and special articles." Reed himself discussed "Oratory Past and Present." Lorenzo Sears, in an abridgment of his earlier book, attempted an account of twenty-four centuries of oratory in twenty-two pages. Edward Everett Hale wrote of "Lectures and Lecturing," Hamilton Wright Mabie of "The Literary Address," and Jonathan Dolliver of "The Oratory of the Stump." George F. Hoar contributed a reprise of his *Scribner's* article on "Oratory" — this time titled "Eloquence" — and Charles W. Emerson praised "The Power of Oratory."

The essayists took this opportunity to revive the familiar paeans of praise for great orators of the past and to defend the art against its detractors. For detractors there still were; ridicule of political orators had not ceased, and echoes of Carlyle's "Stump Orator" were still heard in the land. The urbane, aristocratic Henry Cabot Lodge, for example, had spoken contemptuously of Bryan's "stump speaking mind." "With him," said Lodge, "words take the place of actions. He thinks that to say something is to do something." Such condemnations, it is true, were often attributable to personal animosity: Lodge is not on record as having accused his friend Theodore Roosevelt, or other Republican campaigners, of possessing the stump-speaking mind. Such charges were also regarded by some as revealing a lurking distrust of democratic processes. Curtis Guild, later an able and respected governor of Massachusetts, once characterized criticism of his fellow spellbinders as coming from "that class whose vociferous censure of all men in political life is only less marked than their own abstention from the simplest political duties of the American citizen." But it was Senator Jonathan Dolliver in his essay on the oratory of the stump who articulated the most forceful response. Of Carlyle's "fierce satire" printed fifty years earlier he said, "It is easy to see that this clumsy criticism is only a part of his general complaint against the progress of society — the voice of the old regime recording its malediction against the new era." Satire of stump speaking, "bred in high intellectual atmospheres," was to Dolliver criticism of Democracy itself. It is aimed, he said, "at our form of government; at the management of their own affairs by the people themselves; at parliaments and all manner of representative assemblies; at that tremendous revolution which is gradually preparing the whole world for the new order of things; at 'the count of heads' as much as at 'the clack of tongues.'" The conclusion of Dolliver's impassioned defense epitomized the spirit of the anthologists, and very possibly the prevailing attitude of the Progressive Era toward the political speaker:

> The candidate standing before the people seeking a commission to act in their behalf is not a figure to be despised. He stands for our form of government at the very sources of authority by which the nation itself acts. Wherever speech is free, liberty is safe. The democracy of England and America is no fierce mob, bewildered by the babble of tongues or the scribble of pens. It is an eager citizenship, anxious for the national welfare, having within it a tribunal of reason and conscience before which all causes are to be heard, and from which must emanate the final judgments that direct the progress of mankind. While that tribunal stands, the stump orator, whether he be a country lawyer . . . or an ex-President of the United States . . . ought not to be disparaged in any sane estimate of the forces which control the national life.[27]

Less than a decade after its first manifestations, the passion for collecting and publishing models of oratory waned. Never again were professors of literature to show much interest in compiling collections of speeches, though this function was later preempted by members of developing departments of speech. Articles on the glories of eloquence or the exploits of great orators appeared less and less frequently in the popular journals. The outbreak of a world war ended, for a time at least, the period of political, economic, and social reform which Frederick Lewis Allen termed "the revolt of the American conscience" and extinguished the wave of popular enthusiasm for public discussion of domestic problems. In the decade of prosperity following the war the "orator" was to become a "public speaker," and public speaking was to be put to very different uses.

❧5❧
THE TWENTIES
Oratory Becomes Public Speaking

There are few places today where the oratory of
twenty years ago is not a joke.
ALBERT E. WINSHIP (1923)

Were I unable to make an address — remember, I
am just a plain, ordinary speaker, not an orator in any
sense of the word — I would not be worth half the
salary I am receiving today.
FREELAND HALL (1927)

Americans of the 1920s prided themselves in their modernity.
Among numerous outmoded customs repudiated by the new age
was "oratory." One observer, the editor of an educational journal,
contrasting anachronistic "oratory" with modern "public speaking,"
compared the old-fashioned oratorical style of Bourke Cockran
with a cupolated dome on a Cambridge mansion, a silk hat in a
Boston street, or snuff-taking at an afternoon tea.[1] Speakers and
writers went out of their way to proclaim that although oratory had
declined, public speaking, its modern successor, was steadily gaining ground. Senator Albert Beveridge, who at the turn of the century had made the welkin ring with stirring exhortations to march
with the flag and follow the star of empire to the uttermost Heb-
rides, wrote an article for the *Saturday Evening Post* (later published
as a book) calling for brevity, simplicity, sincerity, and naturalness
in speech and expressing the opinion that American audiences
would no longer tolerate a Webster or even an Ingersoll.

Though there was near-unanimity in condemning "oratory," it
was not always easy to determine precisely what was being condemned. The odious term apparently carried connotations of insin-
cerity and pomposity; oratory was "flowery" and highfalutin — the
antithesis of plain, honest talk. "Speech-makers are very different
from orators," it was affirmed," and what the world has lost from
the ranks of one it has gained in the ranks of another." But wherein

the difference between orators and speakers lay was not often explained. Even when a distinction was made, it was not always helpful. Leonard Woolf, for example, is admirably clear: "Oratory is an art, which can exist as an end in itself like a sonnet or a symphony; public speaking is a useful instrument, like a pamphlet or a plough, to serve a practical purpose. The orator's object is simply to speak, to speak winged words; the public speaker's object is not to speak, but to persuade."[2] This is a bit too neat, for persuasion has at least since the time of Aristotle been regarded as the very raison d'etre of the greatest oratory. Still, such a distinction is probably more defensible than that of numerous despisers of eloquence to whom "oratory" is mere bombast and emotional effusion, whereas respectable public speaking is "plain talk" designed to inform and guide.

The new era moved at a different tempo. The automobile brought increased mobility and release from isolation. Competing interests and modes of recreation multiplied. As in the nineteenth century humorists, prestidigitators, and Swiss yodelers had crowded serious lecturers from the lyceum platform and as entertainment had ultimately replaced uplift on the tent Chautauqua circuit, so did radio and the movies provide distractions for a citizenry weary of war, fed up with reform, and longing for normalcy. An erosion, if not a dissolution, of old forms of public discourse followed. Radio discussion programs, featuring the lively exchange of attitudes and views, began to replace sustained discourse in which themes were elaborated and arguments developed. Shortened attention spans and diminished concentration called for shorter speeches, shorter sermons, and shorter magazine articles. The *Reader's Digest,* founded in 1922 by DeWitt Wallace, was phenomenally successful, becoming in time the most popular magazine in America and inspiring a host of imitative digests, abridgments, condensations, and summaries. The same craving for what was short, snappy, and not too intellectually demanding resulted also in a reduction of the length and complexity of public speeches. Clergymen were warned, "You've got to save 'em in a sermon of twenty minutes or you'll never get 'em back to save 'em." Politicians noted that long speeches were no longer welcomed in the Congress. Businessmen were advised to be brief, simple, and above all persistent. Significantly, this latter piece of advice was offered in a cele-brated address by Bruce Barton, an advertising man.[3] The new modes of discourse, regardless of the type of audience addressed, tended to be geared more and more to the hard-sell tactics of the advertiser, the gimmicky persuasive techniques of the salesman.

The influence of business was felt everywhere. The business of the nation, as Calvin Coolidge later proclaimed, was business. To be called "businesslike" was the highest praise, whether one was a clergyman, an educator, or a public administrator. This national preoccupation with business and business methods was to have immense implications for the practice of public speaking. One man-ifestation was the emergence of a new genre, the business speech. Acknowledgment of the importance of this new form appeared in a 1923 revision of the impressive collection of *Modern Eloquence,* first published in 1900.[4] The revised edition included one entire vol-ume of speeches "by business men on business occasions and on business subjects" — the first such collection ever attempted. The preface notes a great change since publication of the first edition, when speeches by businessmen were few, and when meetings of the Board of Trade or Chamber of Commerce were likely to be addressed by visiting clergymen or politicians. However, "the growth of trade and commercial associations and the rapid progress of the art of salesmanship have made speech-making an indispens-able adjunct of commerce and industry and have greatly altered the field of modern eloquence." The volume of business speeches is introduced by an essay on "The Business Man as a Public Speaker," written by the dean of New York University's School of Com-merce, who observes that the businessman is more and more a factor in civic affairs and must be prepared to speak if called upon. Schools, civic organizations, and churches, he says, are looking to the businessman for leadership, and these wider duties make it necessary that he cultivate the arts of public speech.

The proliferation of business speeches by businessmen stimu-lated the publication of several more such collections before the end of the decade.[5] Editors invariably stress the significance of the new speech type and note the importance of speaking skill to indi-vidual businessmen and their contribution to the stature of the business community. The speeches chosen for preservation are for the most part prosaic, anecdotal, informal, self-consciously chatty.

Executives addressing college audiences are generous with advice, as when Charles Schwab of United States Steel speaks at Princeton on "How to Succeed," or Charles Kettering of General Motors returns to his alma mater, Ohio State University, to give a commencement address. Flowers of oratory, the editors are careful to point out, are replaced by straight-from-the-shoulder talk. Lest there be any misunderstanding, the speakers repeatedly announce that they are not "orators"; they do not "make speeches"; they wish simply to say things in a straightforward fashion, to "chat informally." "I have not made a single bit of preparation except the preparation that may come to one on the spur of the moment," said Charles M. Schwab to the Princeton men. He was, he said, "just talking as if you were in my drawing room . . . just as if you were my own sons." Thus did the captain of industry assure his listeners that he was no orator delivering a premeditated speech, but a plain, blunt man speaking the plain, blunt truth.

Not only the manner but also the matter of the business speech was distinctive. Several subcategories of the genre are discernible. There was the promotional speech, the pep talk to employees (brutally parodied in Sinclair Lewis's *Babbitt*) with exhortations to serve, to boost, to sell, to have the right attitude. There was the policy speech, directed primarily to high-level executives, on such subjects as "Good Business Practices." There were speeches designed to establish business as a profession or to endow it with the ethos of religion. A celebrated effort in this direction was Bruce Barton's "Which Knew Not Joseph," delivered to the public relations section of the National Electric Light Association. Barton is perhaps best known as the author of a best-seller of the 1920s, *The Man Nobody Knows,* which portrays Jesus Christ as the forerunner of modern business, the first popularizer of the idea of service.

Most important of all was the Goodwill Speech, delivered to a variety of audiences — luncheon clubs, community organizations, school assemblies, trade associations — and designed to improve public relations, to attract favorable attention to a particular company or industry, or to glorify business in general. The activities of the muckraking journalists and reform orators of the Progressive Era had inflicted grievous wounds in the ego of the business community. The extent of the hurt was revealed by Elihu Root when in 1915 he addressed the Union League Club of Philadelphia.[6] Root called attention to the great change which had come over the nation since the days of McKinley, when businessmen controlled the elections of 1896 and 1900. "The scepter has passed from the business man," Root observed ruefully. "The distinguishing characteristic of recent years has been the conduct of the government of the country by men who have but little concern with the business of the country, by men who distrust the man of business, who suspect the man of business." Root attributed the rejection of the businessman to the age-old hatred of wealth and to a general failure to understand "the processes, the conditions, the requirements and the results of the vast and complicated business by which the wealth of the country is created and maintained." To dispel this ignorance he called for "a campaign of education and instruction for a clearing of the air; so that all over our broad land every American may come to respect every other American in whatever business he may be engaged."

No longer, it appeared, would "the public be damned" response of the nineteenth century suffice. Industrialists were forced to realize that they must be concerned not only with the operation of their businesses but also with what they should say to the public. The flood of self-justificatory goodwill speeches delivered during the early 1920s constituted a significant part of the conservative defense against the reform spirit of Progressivism. An indication of the importance attached to this effort is found in a report that 18,000 goodwill addresses were made in one year by public utilities representatives in a single state. A remarkably candid expression of the motivating spirit of this campaign of public education is found in the remarks of Preston S. Arkwright, president of the Georgia Railway and Power Company at a convention of the American Electric Railway Association in 1922. Talking on "Public Speaking as a Publicity Medium," Arkwright urged his business associates to participate actively in public speaking and not to leave it to politicians and demagogues to lead the people. "You never heard of anybody elected to any political office of any importance for what he did. They're elected for what they say." Since politicians had stirred up the people against the electric railway industry, picturing them as the enemy, Arkwright urged his colleagues also to adopt the effective weapon of the spoken word. He was confident that speeches by businessmen would create sympathetic understanding:

"If we can but lead the people into a correct understanding of the business and an appreciaiton that their prosperity depends on the railway's prosperity, we will have no trouble in getting just consideration from Commissioners, Legislators and Councilmen, and then we won't have any need for courts or injunctions. This is a great deal better than to let public sentiment be crystalized against us by the orators, and at the last moment hiring professional orators to off-set them."[7]

But public speaking was not only a valuable publicity medium for the business community as Arkwright pointed out, it was also a key to personal success. "That efficiency in speaking, public and private, is an aid to success is a point too well accepted to need argument here," wrote the editors of a collection of business speeches. "Students of business, and younger business men, are studying the art of speaking in ever increasing numbers." Hundreds of companies offered public-speaking courses to their employees, often paying half or all of the costs. Clearly, business executives wanted their men trained in public speaking. But not, they were quick to add, in oratory. Conversational delivery, down-to-earth talk, the ability to "sell" one's self and one's ideas, were more to be desired than artistic expression. A survey of eighteen academic schools of business administration in 1924 revealed that twelve offered no instruction in public speaking. The investigator thereupon sent a questionnaire to fifty business executives in New York, Boston, and Philadelphia asking their opinions on whether such instruction should be given, and if so whether specialized and practical or general and cultural. An overwhelming majority of the executives replied that speech training was needed, and that it should be practical. "Business demands results . . . competition demands convincing speaking. Learned speaking is of little value."[8]

Few men did more to promote the cult of personal success through public speaking than Dale Carnegie, who after a series of early failures discovered the key to rapid advancement. The key was the ability to stand on one's feet in public and "say a few words." For this all that was needed was a compelling idea, boundless enthusiasm, and, above all, self-confidence. Carnegie persuaded the New York YMCA to permit him to offer a course for businessmen. Finding existing textbooks too academic and impractical, he wrote his own, *Public Speaking and Influencing Men in*

Business. In the opening chapter he dangled irresistible prizes before potential disciples: "Think of what additional self-confidence and the ability to talk more convincingly in business will mean to you. Think of what it may mean . . . in dollars and cents. Think of what it may mean to you socially; of the friends it will bring, of the increase of your personal influence, of the leadership it will give you. And it will give you leadership more rapidly than almost any other activity you can think of or imagine." The book became the official text of the United YMCA Schools, the American Institute of Banking, and the National Institute of Credit. By the time a new edition was issued in 1936, Carnegie could claim that more than 11,000 businessmen had enrolled in courses personally conducted by the author. Lowell Thomas, in his introduction to the 1936 edition, asserted that more adults were going to Dale Carnegie for training in public speaking than were attending similar courses conducted by both Columbia and New York universities. Thomas attributed his own success to Carnegie's unique system of training, which he described as "a striking combination of Public Speaking, Salesmanship, Human Relationship, Personality Developmen, and Applied Psychology."[9]

The wide appeal of the Carnegie formula was reflected in a number of articles in such popular journals as the *Saturday Evening Post* and the *American Magazine*. One writer revealed the secret of his meteoric rise from mere salesman to sales manager to vice president. He took public speaking in high school and won several competitions. When someone was needed to address a sales convention, he volunteered. So great was his triumph that he became in time the best-known person in his line because he was on the rostrum and not in the crowd. Great are the rewards, he testified, for a person who can get up before a crowd and please it with wit and wisdom. "Oratory," he affirmed, "in its lesser degrees, at least, is indispensable to the person who would accomplish the greatest success, I care not what his work or ambitions." Another business executive, introduced editiorially as a "unique combination of seriousness and humor" who, despite the fact that he has declined hundreds of invitations, "has spoken on some 1500 occasions," discloses his perception of audience expectations. He answers his question "Why am I in such demand?" in this way: "Well, I have a voice that can be heard in any corner of the worst of the halls that are handed out to speakers. I pack all my personality into my voice, so that it will carry the punch. I give people my honest convictions in the plainest language, and, no matter how serious my subject, provide them with a little relaxation in the way of a laugh."[10] According to this veteran of the platform, people are not interested in being shown that the speaker is of superintelligence but whether he is "a regular fellow."

Students of the 1920s have observed that the America of that day was a nation of "joiners." The affluent businessman belonged to a service club, a chamber of commerce, and an industrial organization for business associations; to a country club for recreation; and with his wife to additional church, school, social, and civic organizations. The existence of such a multitude of clubs and societies provided almost unlimited opportunities for speechmaking.

After-dinner speaking flourished and, despite the cavils of detractors, continued to be as popular as it had been in the preceding century. The 1923 edition of *Modern Eloquence* followed the example of the original edition by devoting three volumes to after-dinner speaking, but of the three hundred items presented, more than half (including speeches by four women) were new. Books and articles appeared on after-dinner speeches and how to make them, with admonitions to be brief, to "get on the good side" of the audience, and not to be too serious. Some included treasuries of poems, illustrative anecdotes, quotations, jokes, and inspirational fragments, which the reader was invited to use in his own speeches, with or without acknowledgement. Weekly and monthly journals made their pages available to popular speakers for first-person accounts of postprandial adventures. Typical is an article in the *American Magazine*, "The Confessions of an After-Dinner Speaker," in which "Martin W. Littleton, the distinguished lawyer, who is famous for his eloquence, tells you about toastmasters, witty retorts, long-winded speakers, embarrassing situations, and ways in which audiences show whether they are interested, convinced, hostile, or bored." Almost anyone, it seemed, might expect to be called upon at almost any time to say a few words in public upon almost any subject, and it behooved one to be prepared. Even the military were given instruction in this popular art form. At the United States Naval Academy a professor of English introduced a course which he enthusiastically recommended to other institutions. The mess hall was converted into a banquet hall. After dinner, cigars and cigarettes were passed out and the postprandial ceremony began. A toastmaster introduced each speaker, who delivered a short, carefully prepared speech on one of several subjects suggested earlier by the instructor, for which he was required to submit an outline, with the first and last paragraphs written out in full and preferably committed to memory.[11]

Speaking after lunch during the 1920s became nearly as common as speaking after dinner. Such service clubs as Rotary, Kiwanis, and Lions, founded during the early decades of the century, flourished and drew into their ranks the leading businessmen of every city and small town in America. Dedicated to the ideal of service, their weekly luncheon meetings were conducted in a spirit of hearty friendliness. Here businessmen made contacts, addressed one another by their first names, sang songs, listened to speeches, performed their rituals, and proclaimed the loyalties and values of middle-class America. Speeches delivered under such circumstances served purposes similar to those of ceremonial addresses of the early nineteenth century, in that they were devoted to the affirmation of shared values. But these ceremonies and these speeches apotheosized business values, business goals, and business heroes. It has been suggested that Kiwanis, Rotary, and Lions may have contributed to the decline of Chautauqua by preempting the functions of the mother-home-and-heaven lecturers who specialized in faith, optimism, patriotism, and uplift. Certainly "business" as idealized by service-club orators, came close to being a religion for many. It was not considered incongruous to speak of "the redemptive and regenerative influence of business" or to assert that Kiwanis was doing God's work "by bringing the Golden Rule into the business lives of men." "I like to think," said a speaker to the International Convention of Kiwanis in 1924, "that God looks down with a benign smile every time a Kiwanis club meets."[12]

Meanwhile, the appeal of the serious public lecture grew steadily. Hundreds of colleges and universities, community forums, and public-service agencies like Cooper Union in New York offered an attractive and lucrative circuit for traveling speakers. The *Literary*

Digest, observing that "the great public have regained the lecture habit," predicted a lecture deluge, brought on in part by postwar hero worship and a desire to see celebrities in person.[13] Also contributing to the popularity of the lecture was the desire on the part of the newly rich to acquire "culture" befitting their station. The quicker and more efficient this acquisition, the better, hence the immense vogue during the twenties of such books as *Outline of History, Outline of Science, Story of Mankind, Story of Philosophy,* and similar compendia which encouraged some to expect mastery of a subject through familiarity with a single volume. Culture could be even more quickly and effortlessly acquired through the medium of the public lecture. A century earlier, when Holbrook originated the lyceum, books and magazines were hard to come by, and lectures were the primary source of information. In the 1920s it is not likely that many lectures offered anything that was not readily available in print, but a populace forever in a hurry and regarding efficiency as one of the higher virtues found it easier to listen than to read. Besides, there was in the lecture hall the additional benefit of the living presence of the communicator. The audiences of literary figures like Bertrand Russell, William B. Yeats, John Masefield, and Alfred Noyes included both those who had become disciples through reading their works and those who wished merely to see and hear celebrities "in the flesh."

Managers, paid to know what audiences wanted and to supply it, reported that the greatest demand was for information — for facts about scientific developments, foreign lands, strange customs — discussed by experts. The old "inspirational" lectures, delivered by retired clergymen, judges, educators, and sundry purveyors of spiritual uplift, went out of fashion and were replaced by informative lectures given by men and women who had other means of making a living and who talked about their fields of expertise. A writer in *Scribner's* (obviously a lecturer himself) called attention to "a great national thirst for information" which in his opinion was calling forth lectures of greater substance and quality. "From Bellingham, Washington, to Corpus Christi, Texas, the country burns with a passion for facts. The small-town waitress who wants to hear about Italian Corfu or the Bolsheviki or the Ruhr, is one of many millions who want to hear what is going on in the outside world, beyond the end of Main Street."[14]

One distinguished educator envisioned for the lecturer a loftier destiny than that of a mere conveyor of interesting facts about travel, science, and the arts. Glenn Frank, editor of *Century* magazine and later president of the University of Wisconsin, dreamed of a revivification of a revered American institution, the public forum. Writing in the *Century* in the summer of 1919, Frank recalled that Woodrow Wilson, during the 1912 campaign, had stressed the need for the restoration of a "parliament of the people," a meeting for free discussion and debate; between as well as during political campaigns.[15] Noting that Americans had become a press-reading and lecture-hearing people, allowing their genius for debate to atrophy, Frank urged the creation of an agora or forum. Admitting the impossibility of restoring the New England town meeting, which had served the needs of simpler times, he maintained that genuine public debate — the "common counsel" of which Wilson had spoken — could be achieved through agencies existing at the time, and he proceeded to mention a few. There was first the open forum, of which Cooper Union in New York and Ford Hall Forum in Boston were the most notable examples, though more than 250 others existed from coast to coast. These combined the best features of the town meeting and the lecture platform: an address by an expert was followed by a question and discussion period. There was also the lyceum and its summer manifestation the Chautauqua, attended by millions of people every year, which, by the introduction of a question and discussion period, could raise the level of lectures and enable audiences once again to establish the habit of public discussion.

Glenn Frank's thoughtful critique of the lecture platform presents a revealing picture of prevailing practice as well as constructive suggestions for the kind of lecture he felt the complicated times required. He is saddened by the fact that lecturing is not a profession in itself but "a medium through which the men of other professions speak." There are no professional standards: anyone may apply. The platform has become a refuge for misfits from other professions; it is dominated by celebrities who have no qualifications as lecturers but are "kept afloat by the swimming bladder of a reputation gained in other fields." A staple of the platform, the "inspirational lecture," is at its worst only "the uninspiring reminiscence of egotistical mediocrity." Frank calls for a lecturer of professional stature, a mediator between the specialist and the layman, an interpreter of changing conditions, one who will do more than deliver a lecture "as a singer might sing a concert." Such modification of platform and lecturer, he is confident, could establish Wilson's parliament of the people: "It is not the strong man with his catch-phrase that democracy needs. The fate of the democratic experiment lies in the hands of Everyman; and Everyman needs to have his judgments tried in the fire of common counsel."[16]

There is little evidence that the 1920s brought any full-scale effort to convert the lecture platform into a parliament of the people. But the development of radio brought numerous attempts to encourage public discussion of serious subjects. In the 1930s and 1940s, educational programs such as *Invitation to Learning* and the University of Chicago *Round Table* presented discussions of high quality on social and political issues as well as literature and art. These, however, were carried on by scholars and recognized experts, with no audience participation. The widely popular *America's Town Meeting of the Air,* on the other hand, included question and answer periods and encouraged local groups formed for the purpose all over the country to continue discussion of the evening's topic after the conclusion of the broadcast.

Political speaking during the 1920s was in general as undistinguished as that of the decades following the Civil War, and for some of the same reasons. Once again, the national attention was fixed on the acquisition of material wealth. In the election of 1920 American citizens — those who took the trouble to vote at all — expressed their willingness to bid farewell to reform and reformers, their weariness with Wilson's entreaties to noble exertion in the cause of world peace, and their desire for normalcy and undisturbed pursuit of eternal prosperity. The priorities, preoccupations, and values of the twenties militated against significant political activity, as well as oratory in behalf of such activity. So exciting were everyday developments in the business world, so beguiling the new opportunities for entertainment and diversion, that politics became unnecessary, except perhaps to do the will of business. Once again, as in the post-Civil War years, the most talented and ambitious turned their attention to the making of money. Once again, the nation's industrialists, rather than her statesmen, were the movers and shakers. Fifty titans of oil, steel, mining, meat packing, and banking were selected by editor B. C. Forbes to be honored in a book entitled *Men Who Are Making America*. "Politics has generally ceased to interest first-rate men," wrote Elmer Davis in 1924, an observation corroborated by James T. Adams in *Our Business Civilization*. There were, thought Adams, few other avenues to distinction: "All other orders in society having been swept away, and a business career being the sole one that leads inevitably to power when successful, the business man's standard of values has become that of our civilization at large."[17]

As business prospered, the stock of the politician sank lower. Foreign visitors were surprised to find that the great men in America seemed to be business leaders rather than leaders of government. The writer of an article on politicians in the *Saturday Evening Post* noted that *politics* had become a term of derision and that "to call a man a politican is to acheive pretty nearly the ultimate in invective." Evidence that these attitudes were being passed on to the next generation was produced by a compiler of data on high school students' views on matters of vital social interest. After visits to ninety-two public and private schools in fourteen states from Massachusetts to California, he reported that of all questions asked, one brought the most derisive laughter: "How many of you are going into politics?" "American youth," he said, "are firmly established in their utter contempt for politicians." If, as Mark Sullivan has suggested, Henry Ford had a more profound influence on the lives of average Americans than Warren Harding, so too the business speaker at Kiwanis or Rotary was probably more listened to, believed, and admired than most political orators. Testing the attitudes of high-school students in Middletown, Robert and Helen Lynd found that 87 percent marked "false" the statement: "Voters can rely upon statements of fact made by candidates in campaign speeches."[18]

Public interest in American politics reached its nadir in the mid-1920s. Disillusionment with Wilson's Great Crusade brought a wave of isolationist sentiment which was to envelop the nation for twenty years; conservatism and indifference marked domestic politics. A people preoccupied with the pursuit of money and pleasure had no need, as had earlier generations, for politics as a means of entertainment and release. There were too many other diversions:

gigantic spectator sports events, the emergence of new entertainment media, the appearance of new national heroes, the excitement of great business transactions. Above all, there was prosperity — that great suppressor of criticism, the impetus to political activity and political oratory. The occupants of the White House and the members of Congress took their cue from the people and directed their efforts toward maintenance of the status quo. Will Rogers's wry comment on President Coolidge, "He didn't do anything, but that's what people wanted done," applied with equal accuracy to a host of public servants.

The three national election campaigns of the twenties were indexes to the current state of politics. The campaign of 1920 was a drab affair, revealing little manifestation of public interest in either major candidate. An electorate accustomed to exciting personalities was presented with Warren Harding and James Cox, evoking the comment from Senator Frank B. Brandegee that "there ain't any first-raters this year." First-raters such as Bryan, Theodore Roosevelt, and Wilson had been removed from the scene: Roosevelt by death, Wilson by illness, and Bryan by diminishing influence. In every presidential election since 1896, as Mark Sullivan has observed, one and sometimes two of these men had been a candidate and even when not candidates they had been prominent participants. By 1920 the spirit of Progressivism was all but dead. The Republican convention was, in the words of delegate William Allen White, "completely dominated by sinister predatory economic forces"; the nomination of Harding was cynically engineered by a Senate cabal. Harding, though he loved to make political speeches, was persuaded by Senate bosses, who feared he would put his foot in his mouth, to remain at home and issue vacuous set pronouncements from his front porch in Marion, Ohio. Cox and Roosevelt in a valiant effort to make the campaign a "solemn referendum" on Wilson's League, stumped the country speaking to listless audiences. In November fewer than half the eligible voters turned out to participate in an election that was less a victory for Harding than a defeat for Wilson's policies.

The election of 1924 brought out 51.1 percent of the voters after another relatively spiritless campaign which pitted two colorless conservative candidates against each other. The Republicans on the first ballot nominated Calvin Coolidge, who had served ten months in the White House after the death of President Harding. The Democrats, in a stormy convention lasting more than two weeks, nominated John W. Davis after 102 ballots. Campaigning on the slogan "Keep Cool with Coolidge," the Republican candidate dealt largely in platitudes, stressed noninterference with business in the interests of continuing prosperity, and made no mention of the scandals of the previous administration. Some vigor was imparted to the campaign by Robert La Follette and Burton K. Wheeler, nominees of a progressive coalition of farmers, laborers, socialists, and middle-class intellectuals. The Progressives campaigned actively for the elimination of public corruption, the return of the naval oil reserves and measures to control monopoly, evoking the inevitable charges of radicalism. Given the enormity of the evidence of corruption in the Harding administration, the voters might have been expected to rise up in a display of righteous indignation to throw the rascals out. Instead, they showed little interest in demonstrated venality and turned their wrath on the exposers of corruption. In a striking illustration of the axiom that prosperity stifles criticism, the electorate returned a majority of Republicans to both House and Senate and gave Calvin Coolidge, the symbol of a prosperous status quo, two million votes more than the combined total of Davis and La Follette.

A year before this election *Bookman* had published another of those by-now-familiar articles on the decline of oratory.[19] Looking back wistfully to a time "not very far gone, when the gift of oratory was the proudest possession of statesmen and politicians," the author pronounced oratory an all but lost art. Directing his fire primarily at legislative speaking, he noted that although the *Congressional Record* was becoming fatter and fatter, it is "a dreary waste of statistics and scraps from newspapers, a journal of partisan bantering and bickering." Debate in the world's greatest deliberative body had, in his estimation, descended to the level of a corner grocery political discussion. This melancholy observer concluded: "In the new and rather turgid democracy which demands 'pep' and 'plain talk' and, above all 'action,' there seems to be no place for the oration."

David Sarnoff, vice president of Radio Corporation of America, concurred in the judgment that oratory was dying out but predicted that radio broadcasting would bring it to life again. Indeed, on all sides the amazing new medium was being hailed as an important social force — one that would not only increase the influence of the speaker but also change the nature of the art. As a dramatic illustration of the range of this medium, it was announced that on March 7, 1924, after-dinner speeches from the Waldorf Astoria in New York City had been broadcast throughout the world, "as far west as Australia and as far east as Constantinople." In 1924 both Republican and Democratic conventions were broadcast to the nation. The *Saturday Evening Post* observed editorially that the greatest service of radio would be its capability of giving events of national importance a national audience.[20] The writer expressed the hope that it might confer another benefit, the setting of higher standards in public speaking. Since radio offers an "uncompromising and literal transmission," which the listener follows with one sense only, there are no distractions, no opportunities for the speaker to conceal a lack of substance with gestures, posturings, or other manifestations of "personality." In the opinion of this writer, "Somehow the spread-eagle sort of thing and all the familiar phrases and resources of the spellbinder sound very flat and stale over the air."

If one may judge from the disgracefully small turnout at the polls in 1924, the entrance of radio into politics does not seem noticeably to have augmented public interest in the opinions or activities of politicians. Americans in the 1920s apparently had other things to do than listening to political speeches. One observer at the Democratic convention recorded his surprise at the lack of interest in speakers. Even when the few really able speakers were performing, he reports, the crowd was downstairs eating hot dogs and discussing baseball. Even William Jennings Bryan was unable to hold their attention, a fact that this observer attributes less to Bryan's decline as a speaker than to the decline of his audience as listeners. "The command of the minute," he says, "is 'Make it snappy.'" "'The less said, the better' has become a national policy."[21]

Whatever else might be said of the campaign of 1928, it was not dull. In November, 67.5 percent of the electorate cast their ballots; it was the largest national vote up to that time. Much popular interest was generated by two issues: prohibition and the religion of the Democratic candidate. Alfred E. Smith, the efficient and popular governor of New York, was a colorful figure, a rousing if not particularly cultivated speaker, and the first Roman Catholic to be nominated for the presidencey. Smith drew enthusiastic crowds and tried to engage his Republican opponent in debate, but the magisterial Herbert Hoover refused to acknowledge his rival's existence. Hoover's celebrated "Rugged Individualism" speech of October 22 epitomized the tone of his campaign, which lauded "the American Way" of free competition and private initiative and denounced the Democratic platform as state socialism. Smith's personality generated both loyalty and hatred; the Catholics and the anti-Catholics, the "wets" and the "drys" exchanged insults. These elements of conflict made it an exciting campaign, but it was far from being a serious debate on important national issues. Nor was the outcome ever seriously in doubt. Smith's association with Tammany Hall, his religion, and his stand on prohibition which made him anathema in certain Democratic strongholds of the South and West were liabilities too great to be overcome. And the Republicans again found their greatest asset to be prosperity, or the illusion of prosperity. Hoover won by more than six million votes.

In 1928 radio was for the first time important in a presidential campaign; speeches by both major candidates were carried on national hookups. It is difficult to judge whether the new medium worked to the advantage of either candidate. Hoover's ponderous generalizations delivered in a rumbling monotone were not calculated to hold attention at a high peak. Smith's lively, colloquial style was far more attractive, but his voice had a harsh, unpleasant quality, and his New York dialect grated on the ears of those to whom it was unfamiliar; fastidious listeners thought his diction uncouth in one being considered for the nation's highest office. But whatever its influence in this election, it was apparent to all that radio was destined to affect the techniques of political campaigning. Those astute observers of the American scene in the twenties, Robert and Helen Lynd, noted that radio was bringing families together in the evenings, and that "it is beginning to take over that function of the great political rallies or the trips by the trainload to the state capitol to hear a noted speaker or to see a monument dedicated that a generation ago helped to set the average man in a wide place."[22]

Al Smith, in an autobiography published after the 1928 campaign, spoke of the way in which radio had extended the range of a speaker's voice.[23] Before radio, in his first campaign for governor of New York, Smith depended upon speeches to a comparative few and newspaper accounts of these speeches. In a third campaign for the governorship in 1922, he was able to make use of amplifiers in large halls, supplemented by additional amplifiers for overflow audiences in the street. In 1924 a limited use of radio increased still more the size of the audience, though the "pie plate" microphones suspended before them annoyed the speakers, and the amplifiers distorted their voices, giving a metallic sound. By 1928 millions of voters were able to hear the candidates, acquiring familiarity with them on the basis of their voices and manner of speaking as well as on what they said. Smith contrasts this with an earlier day when a person speaking every night for a month could reach only about 30,000 people, or less than 1 percent of the electorate of New York State. Radio, he said, had also rendered obsolete the practice of sending large numbers of printed speeches through the mails, most of which had been wasted.

Later, in the pages of the *Saturday Evening Post,* Al Smith blunted this testimonial to the power of radio by stressing the importance of the living presence of the speaker. The microphone, he said, is a piece of cold metal suspended on a string. It never nods approval, expresses dissatisfaction, or recognizes sarcasm. Conceding the increasing influence of radio, he insisted that "there must always be some reasonable degree of public speaking to actual audiences, because otherwise the candidate himself might as well rest at home and have somebody say his speeches for him." Under the title "Spellbinding"[24] Smith wrote an article of the kind common early in the century, but something of an oddity at the end of the 1920s. He extolled the power of the spoken word: "Oratory — the power to debate, the ability to hold an audience — will always have a prominent place in our national life." He related anecdotes of "happy hits" of oratory, courageous handling of embarrassing interruptions, rough tough debaters, masters of wit and sarcasm, virtuosos of the purple passage. He pleaded for renewed cultivation of oratory as an art, for training in the public schools, and gave testimony to the importance of such training and of oratorical contests in his own career. Throughout he revealed his admiration for the old-time speakers. They spoke without benefit of amplification in the open air. They did not read their speeches; they had extemporaneous facility. They could hold an audience; could handle unruly crowds, noisy small boys, and hecklers; could engage in genuine political debate. Al Smith was himself such a speaker, one of a rapidly disappearing breed. Though he had no way of knowing it, oratory as he defined it — the power to debate, the ability to hold an audience by extemporaneous speech — was in the future to be the remarkable exception rather than the rule.

In attempting to explain the lack of interest in political speaking in the twenties, I have cited the national preoccupation with business, the general satisfaction with a prosperous status quo, and a suspicion of those who rocked the boat or were seen as critics of the American way. It is worth noting that the occupants of the White House during this decade were all men who lacked the gift for demonstrating the potentialities of the spoken word for inspiration, education, and leadership. Warren Harding had established a reputation as an effective public speaker in the unsavory world of Ohio politics, but as a member of a Senate which included William E. Borah, Robert M. La Follette, and Henry Cabot Lodge he was hopelessly out of his depth. And as principal spokesman for a great nation he was a ludicrous burlesque. His inaugural address was an incredible mélange of banality and tortured syntax. Few of our presidents would have been capable of such sentences as these: "Since freedom impelled, and independence inspired, and nationality exalted, a world supergovernment is contrary to everything we cherish and can have no sanction by our Republic. This is not selfishness, it is sanctity." The cruel appraisal of his style by William Gibbs McAdoo has been frequently quoted only because it is so apt: "His speeches leave the impression of an army of pompous phrases moving over the landscape in search of an idea; sometimes these meandering words would actually capture a straggling thought and bear it triumphantly, a prisoner in their midst, until it died of servitude and overwork."

Still, Harding considered himself a good speaker. Mark Sullivan's observation that he found spiritual restoration in making speeches is surely an accurate one. He much preferred "bloviating" (his word) on the campaign trail to the arduous duties of office. He was proudest of his delivery and seemed unaware that any other aspect of speaking was of much importance. The fact that audiences too thought him a good speaker may be indicative of public expectations, of the level of public taste. His political cronies were quick to recognize him as an asset. They used him frequently in Ohio campaigns; they chose him to nominate Taft in the Republican National Convention of 1912; he blistered Theodore Roosevelt in a keynote speech in the 1916 convention. Crowds liked him, responded sympathetically to him. Here was no wrestling with difficult problems, no complexities or subtleties — simply a handsome man uttering platitudes in an orotund voice and an ingratiating manner. This, for the time, would serve.

Calvin Coolidge, Harding's successor in the White House, though cultivating a reputation for taciturnity, was a tireless public speaker. A selection of his addresses as state senator and governor of Massachusetts was considered worthy of publication in a volume entitled *Have Faith in Massachusetts.* As vice president he had plenty of time for speeches, and he gave many, writing them out in longhand in his office while someone else presided over the Senate. As president, Silent Cal was far from silent. Though he lacked Harding's affability and talent for crowd-pleasing, he managed to create an impression of dignity and substance through his solemn, undemonstrative manner. "It is not difficult for me to deliver an address," he once said, "the difficulty lies in its preparation." This is understandable, since delivery was for him simply the act of reading aloud from a manuscript in a flat, nasal voice. Like Harding, he dealt generously in abstractions and clichés, but in contrast to Harding's "army of pompous phrases," they had at least the saving quality of brevity. The Coolidge style was marked by short, simple sentences, aphorisms, frequent and often wooden use of antithesis and parallel structure, and an all-pervasive moral tone. A brief excerpt will suggest the flavor of a typical political sermon: "We do not need more material development, we need more spiritual development. We do not need more intellectual power, we need more moral power. We do not need more knowledge, we need more culture. We do not need more laws, we need more religion." The sentiment expressed in one of his most famous aphorisms explains why Coolidge's messages found a willing audience in the 1920s: "The man who builds a factory, builds a temple; the man who works there, worships there." His favorite themes were the dignity of hard work, obedience to law, economy in government and private life, noninterference with business, individual initiative, and self-reliance. William Allen White, after witnessing his inaugural address to an undemonstrative crowd, sized him up in this way: "a sentimentally aspiring man, full of goodwill, a man not without an eye to the political main chance, a man always considering the vote-giving group, shrewdly eloquent about accepted beliefs, never raising debatable issues, a good man honestly proclaiming his faith in a moral government of the universe."[25]

President Coolidge's inaugural address was the first to be broadcast by radio. For the first time a president had at his disposal an instrument for instant communication with the entire nation. The potentialities for personal influence were enormous. Calvin Coolidge's voice now reached more listeners than had that of any previous American president — perhaps more than any speaker's in history. Millions who had never heard a presidential address could now do so. A reviewer of a volume of Coolidge speeches ventured the opinion that "more than any other speaker, he is moulding the popular concept of public address."[26] This, if true, was a sobering thought.

The third and last chief executive to preside over the era of the Golden Twenties was Herbert Clark Hoover, secretary of commerce under Harding and Coolidge. Hoover followed his predecessors in glorification of the American System. In an address accepting his party's nomination he announced: "We in America are nearer to the final triumph over poverty than ever before in the history of any land. The poorhouse is vanishing from among us." In his inaugural he spoke of a future bright with hope. "We have reached a higher degree of comfort and security than ever existed before in the history of the world." For wise guidance in achieving this happy condition he acknowledged the nation's indebtedness to Calvin Coolidge. Despite the triumphant spirit of such words, little exhilaration was imparted by the speeches of Herbert Hoover. Austere, unsmiling, he read monotonously from his manuscript, pausing for breath so infrequently that the diaphragms of his listeners were often tense with anxiety before he reached the end of a phrase. Apparently unaware of the presence of his audience, he showed no sign that he desired, or recognized, reactions from those to whom his words were being read. Perhaps because of this deficiency of audience-consciousness, Hoover's speeches were not notable for their lucidity or interest value. "No ray could disclose, no key unlock the secret of those sentences," wrote one unfriendly critic. This was not altogether fair; a more accurate appraisal was the observation that his speeches read as if he had been brought up on a steady diet of corporation reports as printed in the *London Times.*

Such inattention to even the rudiments of the rhetorical art was no particular liability so long as presidential utterances were largely ceremonial in nature. While times were good, Americans could afford to be indulgent — even pleased — with ritual declarations of the greatness of America and the blessings of a business civilization, as they had been with the vacuous generalities of a Harding and the moralizing of a Puritan in Babylon. But it was Hoover's tragedy that he was not to have prosperity as an ally for long. Less than a year after that confident inaugural, the end came suddenly to the dream of eternal affluence, and everything was changed. Everything, that is, but the presidential oratory. Hoover continued to issue optimistic statements intended to inspire confidence. The depression, he confidently asserted, is due to no fault in the American System, but attributable to international causes. The dislocation is temporary; the end is in sight.

But as the months passed and conditions worsened, people found it impossible to take comfort in optimistic predictions of the imminent return of prosperity. Helpless citizens were enraged by exhortations to help themselves, to rely upon local agencies for relief. The president reminded them of a basic tenet of the American System that the federal government is not a bountiful father to be turned to for a handout whenever things go badly. "Prosperity," he admonished, "cannot be restored by raids on the public treasury." Soon the Great Engineer, the cool, efficient administrator whom they had elevated to leadership, in 1928, became in the eyes of troubled people a cold, aloof figure, indifferent to human suffering. His appearance on the platform in his high stiff collars, his severe countenance, his heavy, emotionless voice — all contributed to the image of a man who had lost touch with people, and with reality.

It is not suggested that Herbert Hoover's downfall was the result of his dull, unimaginative presidential speeches. Hoover was a devout believer in, a principal spokesman for, laissez-faire individualism. When the crash of 1929 and the ensuing depression brought his world down in ruins, his ideas (ideas which in the times of McKinley, Harding, and Coolidge had been indisputable truth) seemed outmoded. It was inevitable that Hoover, the most visible symbol of a discredited system. should have been the scapegoat. Still, his persistent reiteration of the same appeals in the face of drastically altered conditions, his inability (or his steadfast refusal) to dramatize himself or his policies, did little to help lift the country out of despair or to impart courage to face its difficulties. The contrast in the campaign of 1932 between the president and his opponent offered vivid illustration of the efficacy of a vital new spirit skillfully projected from the platform, as well as of a new political philosophy.

Such, then, was the nature of presidential rhetoric during the decade of the twenties. Undistinguished by most standards of excellence, it served well the desires (if not the needs) of a nation well pleased with itself and eager to be free of the meddling of politicians. Oratory (whatever that might be) was proscribed by a modern taste for what was businesslike, and — until October 1929, at least — clarion calls from the White House for noble exertion would have been unwelcome in the extreme. But times of crisis make different demands upon public servants, as the decades of the thirties and the forties would demonstrate.

In the twenties, as in earlier times, the detractors of oratory (or now, of "public speaking") were active. The antics of speakers have always been irresistible targets for iconoclasts and sundry humorists, whose comments have ranged from good humored ridicule to savage derision. One of the gentlest, but at the same time one of the most effective, critics was Will Rogers, the Oklahoma cowboy, who came closest to taking over the mantle of Finley Peter Dunne's Mr. Dooley as a political satirist. As a monologuist in the Ziegfeld Follies, as radio speaker, syndicated newspaper columnist, and lecturer on the banquet circuit, Rogers delighted the nation with his irreverent comments on public men and events. Among his favorite topics were prohibition, taxes, the protective tariff, Congress, business corruption, and political conventions. He was fond of saying that all he knew was what he read in the papers; his columns, lectures, and Follies routines often took as a point of departure some item from the current newspaper. He admitted to scanning published speeches for subject matter for his jokes. "If a man makes a speech he takes a chance on saying a damfool thing, and the longer his speech the greater the thing." He commented freely on presidents and presidential aspirants. At the 1924 Democratic National Convention he reflected upon the speaking career of William Jennings Bryan: "He hibernates for four years, and then emerges, and has a celebration at every Democratic Convention. In the meantime, he lectures in tents, shooting galleries, grain elevators, snow sheds or any place he can find a bunch of people that haven't got a radio." Of Bryan's power to influence a convention's choice, he said: "He can take a batch of words and scramble them together and leaven them properly with a hunk of Oratory and knock the White House door knob right out of a Candidate's hand." When Calvin Coolidge issued his cryptic "I do not choose to run" statement, Rogers labeled it "the best-worded acceptance of a nomination ever uttered by a candidate . . . . He spent a long time in the dictionary looking for that word 'choose' instead of 'I will not.'" Of President Hoover's laborious attempt in his 1930 State of the Union message to explain the causes of the depression, Rogers said, "If a snake bites you you ain't going to stop and study out where he comes from and why he was there at the time . . . . You want to figure out what to do with yourself there and then."[27]

While Will Rogers sought mainly to evoke laughter by holding up to ridicule some of the "damfool things" uttered by politicians, Henry Mencken was infuriated by the mere sight of a speaker addressing an audience. In a brief note on "The Alchemy of the Platform" he once wrote: "All that is necessary to raise a piece of imbecility into what the mob regards as a piece of profundity is to lift it off the floor and put it on a platform. Half the things that are said from a pulpit or rostrum or stage would get their spokesmen the bum's rush if they enunciated them five feet nearer the sea level." Mencken clearly regarded all political orators as idiots and demagogues, bent only on flattering the foul breath of the multitude. He found in Warren Harding the perfect victim, and his characterization of Harding's speeches has become a classic lampoon. He thought Harding's English the worst he had ever encountered. It reminded him, he said, of a string of wet sponges, of tattered washing on the line, of stale bean soup, and college yells. "It is so bad that a sort of grandeur creeps into it."[28] But it should not be forgotten that Mencken was nearly as contemptuous of the speaking of Bryan (whom he accused of inflaming half-wits with a roaring voice) and of Woodrow Wilson, perhaps the most eloquent of American presidents. Mencken's denunciation of orators and the "booboisie" who heeded them was a part of his distaste for majority values and the processes of political democracy. One is reminded of Senator Jonathan Dolliver's response to Carlyle's attack on the stump orator. Such criticism, he said, is aimed "at our form of government, at the management of their own affairs by the people themselves." Very possibly Mencken, like Carlyle, was as much disturbed at "the count of heads" as at "the clack of tongues."

Mencken was chief spokesman for an element in society whom Frederick Lewis Allen has called "embattled highbrows," who in the pages of the *American Mercury*, the *New Yorker*, and occasionally in *Harper's, Atlantic,* and *Scribner's,* expressed their disdain for the unlovely aspects of democracy and the crassness of the new business culture. Since public speaking was becoming more and more identified with salesmanship and public relations, it came in for its share of condescending criticism. Mencken used the "Americana" section of his *American Mercury* to display absurdities from here and there. One of his numerous thrusts at the fatuity of much business speaking was his inclusion of excerpts from a circular issued by a Harrisburg, Pennsylvania, firm which advertised for sale speeches for use at lodges, political meetings, and luncheon clubs. For only three dollars one could select any ten speeches from a list including "Rotary, the Applied Science of Living," "The Influence of Highway Transportation upon Religious Life," and "Speech at the Presentation of an Automobile to a Pastor."

No one did more to expose the gaucheries, the juvenile attempts at slangy humor, and the depressing banality of service club rhetoric than novelist Sinclair Lewis. In his parodies of a business civilization, particularly in *Babbitt, Main Street, Gideon Planish,* and *The Man Who Knew Coolidge,* Lewis pilloried what passed for eloquence in the hotel dining rooms of the 1920s. In George Babbitt's speech to the Zenith Real Estate Board,[29] Lewis displayed the hackneyed themes of the standard business pep talk. They are all there, magnified to the tenth power: distrust of foreigners, effusive praise of things American, statistics on material accomplishments, disparagement of intellectuals, exhortations to have pep, to boost, and to crack down hard on knockers and socialists. Beginning with a gratuitous anecdote of the two Irishmen, Pat and Mike, and the predictable local compliment, "standing together eye to eye and shoulder to shoulder as fellow-citizens of the best city in the world," Babbitt moves enthusiastically from subject to subject and closes with a salute to the "God-fearing, hustling, successful, two-fisted Regular Guy, who belongs to some church with pep and piety to it, who belongs to the Boosters or the Rotarians or the Kiwanis . . . or any one of a score of organizations of good, jolly, kidding, laughing, sweating, upstanding, lend-a-handing Royal Good Fellows, who plays hard and works hard." Babbitt's friend Vergil Gunch, after this speech and others like it, tells him admiringly, "You're getting to be one of the classiest spellbinders in town."

Even the serious lecture designed to disseminate "culture" was not immune to criticism. One commentator, distressed by the increasing quantity and the diminishing quality of public lectures and by the fact that lecturers were being paid more than doctors, dentists, and clergymen, noted, "Demand creates supply and even rhetoric must submit to economic law." "We are witnessing," he wrote, "the avatar of the Great God Gab." British philosopher C. E. M. Joad, in a virulent little book, *The Babbitt Warren*, wrote disdainfully of the American businessman's attempt to "imbibe concentrated culture and uplift in tabloid form" on his lunch hour. He buys culture at the lecture shop and is rich enough to buy the best. The more celebrated the lecturer, the better (and more expensive) the culture. According to Joad, who was probably not in a position to speak so authoritatively for all foreign lecturers, European celebrities regard lecture tours in America as a standing joke. They settle for the highest offer, are marketed like dentifrice or chewing gum, provide pep and uplift several times a day, and return home exhausted by travel and considerably enriched. American business, says Joad, is "a gigantic milch cow, whose udders could be milked indefinitely by the supple fingers of the famous."[30]

Manifest in much censure of public speakers and speaking were two principal lines of attack, both employed by Carlyle, but both familiar long before Carlyle wrote. The first was the charge, or the unspoken assumption, that the wise man is silent, but the fool is given to much talk. Professional writers (often deficient in platform skills) have been fond of pointing out that orators elevate sound over sense, manner over matter. From this it is only a step to the argument that the more successful the speaker in meeting the demands of the platform, the less substance to his utterance. There is a willing acceptance of the proposition that skillful speakers invariably talk nonsense, while bumbling inarticulateness inevitably conceals wisdom. One frequently encounters variations of the argument that because a certain celebrated orator is empty-headed, and because a man of great intellectual attainments such as James Bryce habitually leans on the lectern with his legs in an awkward position while delivering substantial speeches, one should therefore cultivate awkwardness because grace in delivery always accompanies senseless sound.

A second line of attack upon the orator stemmed from the familiar dichotomy between talk and action. Speakers, so the argument went, are seldom doers. Action is preferable to talk. Public speakers talk because they are incapable of action. In the America of the twenties, the businessman was regarded as the principal man of action; the politican was the talker. In introducing *Men Who Are Making America* (all, it will be remembered, captains of industry), B. C. Forbes expressed the spirit of the times: "Our greatest distinction has been won by actions, not words, by deeds, not dreams, by concrete accomplishment, not airy theorizing. The world can match our statesmen and philosophers and poets and artists and composers and authors. But no nation can match our galaxy of doers, our giants of industry, transportation, commerce, finance, and invention."[31] There was irony, however, in this constant elevation of action over talk. It was clear that action from politicians was not wanted, while talk from businessmen was welcomed. Apologists for the business community were fond of declaring that politicians were all talk and no action. At the same time, they opposed positive political action, while exhorting businessmen to do their own talking, to tell their story, and thus counteract the harmful talk of hostile groups.

The national rejection of "oratory" and the turn toward relatively unadorned, utilitarian public speaking was reflected in — and subsequently influenced by — the kind of formal training made available to aspiring speakers. During the "Golden Age" of the early nineteenth century, studies in rhetoric (the art of effective discourse) were part of the curricula of major American colleges. In 1805 John Quincy Adams was appointed to the Boylston Professorship of Rhetoric and Oratory at Harvard, the first such chair in an American university. His lectures, published in 1810, were largely a restatement of the classical doctrines of Aristotle, Cicero, and Quintilian. Though the terms of Adams's appointment focused his attention primarily upon spoken discourse, most early nineteenth-century courses in rhetoric were devoted to training both writers and speakers, primarily in the art of composition. In response to popular demand for more attention to delivery, the Elocutionary Movement, influential in England during the preceding century, gained ground in this country, receiving initial impetus from the publication in 1829 of Dr. James Rush's scientific treatise on vocal production, *Philosophy of the Human Voice.* In 1830 professors of elocution were appointed at Harvard and Yale. In time, training in elocution (the mechanics of voice, articulation, and gesture) became in many institutions separate from rhetorical training. "Rhetoric and Oratory" tended to become "Rhetoric and Belles Lettres," as the emphasis changed from the spoken word to literature and literary criticism. Elocution remained in vogue through the 1870s, through the study of classical rhetoric continued, usually in departments of English. During the later years of the century, however, the excesses of the elocutionists — their preoccupation with technique and the often ridiculous artificiality and ostentation of their performances — brought them into disrepute. Eliminated from the curricula of many of the better colleges, training in elocution was taken over by itinerant teachers and by private schools specializing in the subject.

The early decades of the twentieth century saw the fruition of efforts by academicians to bring together in one department all aspects of the study of oral discourse — substance as well as form and technique, theory and history as well as practical training. In 1914 a group of college teachers, in protest against the neglect of the spoken word by departments of English, seceded from the National Council of English Teachers and established their own professional organization. In order to distinguish themselves from the private teachers of elocution, they called the new organization the National Association of Academic Teachers of Public Speaking. In 1916 they established their own professional journal, the *Quarterly Journal of Public Speaking*. The early issues of this journal reflected a reaction against both "elocution" and "oratory." "Oratorical style," it seemed, was passé; the emphasis was henceforth to be on informality and communicativeness. This emphasis was apparent in the most influential of the new textbooks, *Public Speaking,* by James Winans of Cornell University. Winans, one of the founders of the new association, stressed the importance of the "conversational mode" of public speaking, and his ideas found their way into subsequent textbooks on the subject. Rejection of old emphases was seen also in modified academic nomenclature. Winans, who in 1899 had been an instructor in elocution and oratory at Cornell, was appointed professor of public speaking by that institution in 1914; the School of Oratory at Northwestern University became in 1921 the School of Speech.

There were, of course, voices of protest against the new era. The president of Emerson College of Oratory in Boston deplored the utilitarian trend. He expressed sadness that the new generation had ceased to value oratory, that national energies had been directed to other things, and that the creators of great art were no longer venerated.[32] A member of his faculty was more conciliatory. Noting that the fine art of oratory (whose purpose was to bring beauty into the world, to inspire and uplift mankind through the human voice) had become a practical art (whose purpose was to make money and to bring material rewards), he suggested an accommodation. "Our job," he said, is "to add to this practical art something of the beauty and the uplift and the inspiration of the fine art." He was hopeful that if such a combination could be achieved, "oratory again will come back to its high estate and it will not be an insult to a man to call him an orator."[33]

Such concern was to be expected from old-time schools of oratory, but signs of uneasiness were evident even in university departments of public speaking. Professor Edward Rowell of the University of California expressed alarm that instruction in public speaking was perceived by many as salesmanship training. The salesman image was everywhere familiar: ministers were urged to "sell" the gospel, writers and speakers to "sell" ideas, young men to "sell" themselves. To Rowell, salesmanship implied manipulation, overcoming sales resistance in order to put something over on someone, caring more about "selling" than about the quality of the goods offered — traits that any teacher of integrity and good taste discouraged in his students. "To use the image of salesmanship in referring to the nature of public speech," said Rowell, "is a vagrant and shabby practice unworthy of the intelligence of men of culture, unnecessary as a pedagogical device, and unwholesome as an influence on a human activity which has possessed associations of decidedly nobler quality."[34]

One further development on the academic scene deserves mention. With the growing preoccupation with literature and criticism in departments of English and with the decline of interest in oratory as literature, publication of works dealing with speechmaking was taken over by representatives of the Department of Speech, as the new discipline was soon to be called. Textbooks on public speaking, argumentation, group discussion, and debate appeared in unprecedented numbers. Compact volumes of speeches, often classified as to purpose or occasion and intended as classroom models, replaced the compendious anthologies of orations of an earlier period. Among the best and most widely used of the new collections were two volumes, *Classified Models of Speech Composition* (1921) and *Modern Short Speeches* (1923), edited by James M. O'Neill, chairman of the Department of Speech at the University of Wisconsin and leader of the revolt which had resulted in the formation of an independent association of teachers of public speaking. O'Neill's dedication to *Modern Short Speeches* is a quotation from Longinus denouncing bombast, puerility, and false sentiment. The editor ventures the hope that "these modern examples of simple, fitting and gracious speech" may help put an end to these vices. In his preface, he makes explicit his break with the past: "This is distinctly not a book of great oratory. It is offered as a collection of fine examples of how intelligent men and women have served certain social, professional, and political occasions through speech."

But oratory was not completely forgotten, in retrospect at least. This decade witnessed the publication of the first history of American oratory, the work of Warren Choate Shaw, professor of public speaking at Knox College.[35] While sensitive to the literary qualities of great oratory, Shaw was aware also of its instrumental aspects and of the importance of historical and biographical setting. His book, he says, "has been written to give the full setting for each masterpiece of oratory, to bring back to life all the contending forces with which the orator had to grapple, and to introduce the effective portions of each speech as a fitting climax for the action of the plot." Significantly, this history, published in 1928, concludes with Wilson's speech on the League of Nations in September 1919. Apparently during the 1920s there was no "oratory" worthy of mention.

ঙ৬ঙ
THE ROOSEVELT ERA
Tumultuous Polemics

> More than any other president — perhaps more than
> any other political figure in history — Franklin D.
> Roosevelt used the spoken and written word to
> exercise leadership and to carry out policies.
> — SAMUEL T. ROSENMAN

> Government includes the art of formulating a policy
> and using the political techniques to attain so much
> of that policy as will receive general support; per-
> suading, leading, sacrificing, teaching always, be-
> cause the greatest duty of a statesman is to educate.
> FRANKLIN D. ROOSEVELT

In the 1930s the combination of an economic crisis in which all
Americans were deeply and tragically involved, a new medium of
mass communication, and a charming, articulate speaker who made
that medium his personal instrument for reaching the people
brought about a dramatic renaissance of political speaking.

The most auspicious harbinger of this renaissance was the inaugural address of the new president on March 4, 1933. On this
dreary day under a leaden sky, Franklin Delano Roosevelt raised
his hand on the steps before the Capitol to take the oath of office.
Before him in the square stood 100,000 of his countrymen; half a
million more were to line the route of the inaugural parade. All
across the nation millions leaned anxiously toward their radios to
hear his first words. His face grim but in a voice vibrant with
confidence, the president spoke the ringing words of assurance that
will forever be associated with his name: "This great Nation will
endure as it has endured, will revive and will prosper. So, first of
all, let me assert my firm belief that the only thing we have to fear is
fear itself — nameless, unreasoning, unjustified terror which
paralyzes needed efforts to convert retreat into advance." The
voice, the manner, the long-awaited proclamation that "this Nation
asks for action, and action now," constituted such a startling con-

trast to the plaintive pronouncements of the retiring president that the response was overwhelming. Four hundred and fifty thousand letters poured into the White House. "Millions will say as they read the inaugural this morning," said the *Cleveland Plain Dealer*, "Here is the man we have been waiting for." The *Atlantic Constitution* paid the speech the ultimate compliment of comparing it with Lincoln's Gettysburg Address. "It was not an inaugural address in the usual meaning of the expression," wrote the Republican *Boston Herald*. "It was more like a manifesto of a man who knows what he wants and intends to get it." "America has found a man," said the London *Observer*. "Mr Roosevelt has made a splendid beginning. . . . In accent and action his beginnings suggest success."

Roosevelt's first inaugural heralded an era in which oratory would once again be a prime instrument for the conduct of public affairs. In the years ahead the president was to use public speeches to propose new social and economic reform programs and to enlist in their support the forces of public opinion. Rexford Tugwell mentions several events immediately following the inauguration which spread good feeling "like a wave of sunlight over the whole country." These were Roosevelt's appeal for cooperation at a conference of state governors, his first news conference which did away with the established practice of written questions and established an atmosphere of openness and candor, and his first "fireside chat" on the banking crisis. "Thus," said Tugwell, "the first battle with fear was won with talk."[1] Immediately following pledges of action came action itself. And further actions were facilitated by more talk — words of assurance and explanation to the people, words of instruction and exhortation to the Congress. The months of feverish activity following the inauguration were characterized by words and action in tandem: messages to Congress outlining needed measures for recovery, and after their passage informal progress reports via radio to the nation, together with announcements of more action to come. During the now-famous "first hundred days," Roosevelt issued two proclamations, one calling a special session of Congress, the other declaring a national bank holiday; made ten public speeches; sent fifteen messages to Congress; and successfully sponsored fifteen pieces of major legislation.

Actually, of course, the beginnings of the new era may be detected much earlier, before the inauguration and even before the election of the new president. On the second day of July 1932, the nominee of the Democratic party had flown from Albany to Chicago to deliver his acceptance address before the national convention. The speech was a clear signal to the nation that the nominee was to be a breaker of precedents. Scorning the tradition of waiting several weeks for a formal notification before issuing an equally formal acceptance, Roosevelt chose to deliver his acceptance speech to the convention which had named him their standard-bearer. His means of transportation to Chicago was also symbolic; never before had a presidential candidate used an airplane to take him to the scene of a campaign speech. Explicitly calling attention to the symbolism of his actions, the nominee went on to promise future innovation: "Let it be from now on the task of our Party to break foolish traditions . . . . Ours must be a party of liberal thought, of planned action, of enlightened international outlook; and of the greatest good to the greatest number of our citizens . . . . I pledge you, I pledge myself, to a new deal for the American people."

The presidential campaign that followed was, according to Judge Rosenman, more like a triumphant tour than a campaign. A dynamic new personality brought fresh resolve to a nation which had all but given up hope. James Farley, chairman of the Democratic National Committee, tells about his conversations with party leaders during the summer of 1932 concerning the kind of campaign their nominee should conduct. He remembers that they were almost unanimous in their conviction that Governor Roosevelt should stay home, give a few radio talks and perhaps a few major addresses at carefully planned rallies in nearby cities. Since the election was a sure thing, they reasoned, why take chances? Why risk a disatrous incident or an ill-advised statement which might backfire? The arguments for a front-porch campaign were impressive: Bryan had stumped the country while McKinley stayed home and won the election. Cox, Hughes, and Davis had conducted vigorous speaking campaigns, only to lose to Harding, Wilson, and Coolidge, who had not. After Farley recounted these arguments to the candidate he was asked for his own opinion. "I think you ought to go and I know you are going anyway," was the answer. "That's right," Roosevelt replied, "I'm going campaigning to the Pacific

Coast and discuss every important issue of the campaign in a series of speeches."[2]

Roosevelt, of course, did just that. His travels took him 17,000 miles, to the Pacific Coast and back, and even into the Solid South where Democratic support was certain, not to win votes but to create good feeling which might be useful later on. He visited forty-one of the forty-eight states, making hundreds of speeches, among them a series of policy statements each addressed to an important interest group, and each dealing specifically with a major problem — banking, agricultural relief, unemployment, housing, health, supervision of public utilities. In his account of this campaign, Raymond Moley later recalled: "We had, half-unconsciously, created a new kind of political oratory. Each major speech contained a well-matured exposition of policy. And if those sections of each speech were put together, they formed, in combination, a sweeping program of reform and experiment."[3]

Campaign promises are often conveniently forgotten once they have accomplished their function of converting candidates into officeholders. In this case, however, the new administration set about immediately to enact the "sweeping program" outlined prior to the election. Each of the major bills acted upon by the Congress during the Hundred Days and in the months that followed — the Emergency Banking Act, the Federal Home Owners' Loan Act, the Agricultural Adjustment Act, and acts establishing the Civilian Conservation Corps, the Tennessee Valley Authority, and the Farm Credit Administration — had been foreshadowed in the remarkable series of policy speeches delivered by Roosevelt during the presidential campaign. By the end of February 1934, Walter Lippmann, whose initial response to Roosevelt's candidacy had been lukewarm, could write: "A year ago men were living from hour to hour, in the midst of a crisis of enormous proportions, and all they could think about was how they could survive it. Today they are debating the problems of long term reconstruction." The people, he said, have recovered courage and hope. No longer hysterically anxious about the immediate present, "they have recovered not only some small part of their standard of life, but also their self-possession."[4] This change had been wrought not only by courageous, innovative actions but also by inspiring words, uttered by a strong man in tones of confidence and optimism.

Any discussion of speechmaking during the Roosevelt era must begin with Franklin Roosevelt himself. The president was the central figure, the dominant voice, the principal actor to whom others reacted. During the twelve years of his administration the nation faced two of its gravest crises: an economic depression of unprecedented severity and a world war. Both crises demanded in addition to vigorous action, words of clarification, persuasion, and inspiration. Roosevelt provided both action and words. His speeches, as his friend Harry Hopkins said, were "the vehicle by which he set in motion tremendous social and moral forces to combat fear and evil." During the Great Depression the president's voice was the voice of their government to the people; after the war began he was the voice of America to the world. "More people," said Hopkins, "listened to Franklin Roosevelt's speeches than ever before heard the voice of any man."

Roosevelt was fully aware of the importance of oratory in democratic leadership. He regarded the preparation and delivery of his speeches a vital part of his presidential responsibilities, deserving a large measure of his time and energies. Some presidents, regarding speech preparation as onerous, have been content to delegate such work largely to others. This Roosevelt never did, although such immensely talented men as Raymond Moley, Adolph Berle, Rexford Tugwell, Benjamin Cohen, Samuel Rosenman, Archibald MacLeish, and Robert Sherwood worked with him on speeches at different times during his long tenure of office. The detailed accounts by Rosenman and Sherwood of speech-writing sessions in the White House reveal the prodigious efforts expended in the production of presidential addresses.[5] Even with the aid of two or three assistants, important speeches often required a week or more of sustained labor following a period of preliminary planning.

In the years of Roosevelt's occupancy of the White House, when crises followed one another in relentless procession, the presidential schedule left little time during the day for attending to the myriad details involved in preparing a major address. But after dinner the president was often able to give full attention to the task of getting the speech down on paper. Playwright Robert Sherwood, one of the chief speech writers during the war years, has recorded the proceedings in absorbing detail.[6] After a full day's work at the White House, the president would join his writers (most frequently in the early forties Sherwood, Rosenman, and Hopkins) at 7:15 in the Oval Office for cocktails. Roosevelt found relaxation in the ceremony of mixing the drinks himself on a tray before him on his desk, while presiding over a half-hour of small talk. Dinner was served in the office about 7:45. After dinner the president sat on a couch near the fireplace and read aloud the most recent speech draft while a secretary sat ready nearby to take his dictated revisions and addenda. The evening would be spent discussing the occasion, the audience, the purpose of the speech, the probable impact of individual passages on various elements of the national and international audience. Phraseology would be tightened up and simplified; sentences, paragraphs, often whole pages would be eliminated, and fresh passages dictated to take their place. Material would be drawn from the Speech File, a miscellaneous collection of items from the president's correspondence, notes from his reading, memoranda, clippings, telegrams, as well as suggestions submitted by senators, cabinet members, foreign statesmen, and private citizens who wished to be helpful. Sometimes a call would go out to Archibald MacLeish, Librarian of Congress, or some other close confidant to come in and lend a hand. At eleven o'clock, the president would go to bed, and the writers would move to the Cabinet Room, where they often worked most of the night producing another draft to be placed on the presidential breakfast tray in the morning. If there was time during the day, they would confer again and receive further reactions and instructions from the president. Then, in the evening, there would be another after-dinner session in the Oval Office. This process would continue day and night until a final reading copy was produced. Some speeches went through as many as twelve drafts, each of which had been studied, read aloud, and subjected to searching criticism. By the time Roosevelt was to deliver the speech he knew it practically by heart and needed only occasional glances at the manuscript during presentation.

Sherwood has observed that although Roosevelt seemed to take his speeches lightly, he really attached great importance to his public utterances and exercised meticulous care in their preparation. "Roosevelt," said Sherwood, "with his acute sense of history knew that all of those words would constitute the bulk of the estate that he would leave to posterity and that his ultimate measurement would depend on the reconciliation of what he said with what he did." He knew that when he spoke into the microphone his words were, in Carl Sandburg's evocative phrase, "throwing long shadows."

The Roosevelt presidency was distinguished by the variety of ways in which speechmaking was effectively employed. Speeches were used to inform, to persuade, to motivate, and to inspire. Traditionally, political oratory has flourished in election years, when appeals must be made for tangible support at the polls. Roosevelt was an effective campaigner; his speeches were essential to his success in winning elections and maintaining himself in office. But they were also essential instruments in the conduct of his office. Through messages to Congress designed to instruct and activate, through periodic progress reports to the people, through messages of affirmation and inspiration in moments of great national apprehension and despair, he exercised leadership.

The fireside chat, which had its beginnings in Albany while he was governor of New York, was probably his greatest innovation, and one of his greatest triumphs. It was great oratory precisely because it didn't sound like "oratory." If eloquence be, as rhetorician George Campbell has asserted, the art by which a discourse is adapted to its end, then Franklin Roosevelt's fireside chats during the depression and later through World War II were unquestionably eloquent. Here was form perfectly fitted to its desired end, and to the need of the times — a need for the people of the nation to draw together and in unity to find the strength and the will to meet adversity. As troubled citizens gathered before their radios all over the nation, they heard their president reporting as if in a person-to-person telephone call on how things were coming along in Washington, what was being done, what had already been accomplished, and what actions lay ahead. Frances Perkins, his secretary of labor, described him seated before the microphone: As he spoke, visualizing the people he was talking to not as an audience, certainly not as "the masses," but as individuals in their own homes, perhaps seated around the dinner table, "his head would nod and his hands would move in simple, natural, comfortable gestures. His face would smile and light up as though he were actually sitting on the front porch or in the parlor with them."[7] And his listeners would nod and smile and laugh with him.

If he enjoyed these intimate chats from behind his desk at the White House or from his Hyde Park home — and it is certain that he did — he also enjoyed addressing huge crowds from the public platform. Roosevelt loved political campaigning; he loved travel, enjoyed riding on trains, even endured graciously the painful trips to the rear platform to greet a new audience at every stop. Campaigning was for him a source of relaxation and renewal. Confined as he was to a wheelchair, he was more than most presidents a prisoner in the White House. He enjoyed being among people, and these long trips by train and shorter trips by automobile offered welcome opportunities to see the country and sample public opinion. His speeches on these occasions, though raised a step or two above ordinary conversation to meet the physical demands of the situation, were not markedly different in tone from his informal chats from his office or home. More than any other American president he had the faculty of creating a warm personal bond with an audience, even under the most difficult conditions. During the campaign of 1944, when it had become excruciatingly painful for him to stand for public speeches, even with the aid of locked steel leg braces, he addressed an immense audience in an outdoor ball park in Philadelphia. He sat in his automobile, parked near second base, and spoke to listeners all but invisible to him in the remote darkness of the grandstand and bleachers. To this audience, the speaker was a tiny speck in the distance, yet he managed to bridge this formidable gap and create the illusion of intimacy. The communicative bond, according to one witness, was particularly close when he talked to his listeners, many of whom had sons and daughters in military service, of his own sons overseas.

This gift for "conversational oratory" was one of Roosevelt's greatest assets. Yet there was no contrived folksiness, no anxiety to be perceived as just one of the "people." The cultivated voice affected no barbarisms. The manner suggested dignity without pretentiousness. His was no sweaty, shirt-sleeved harangue. He never shouted or battered the ears of the multitude; instead, he managed to convince each individual that he was speaking directly to him. Like Wendell Phillips, the Boston patrician who a century earlier had championed the cause of the dispossessed and had been branded a traitor to his class, Franklin Roosevelt maintained on the platform the speech and manner of an aristocrat. He was the supreme twentieth-century practitioner of that genuinely communicative style of delivery which had caused Phillips to stand out amidst the rhetorical display of his time. He was as that earlier rebel against the respectable establishment had been, "a gentleman conversing."

The close communicative bond with his listeners was forged not only at the time of delivery but also during the entire process of speech preparation and composition. The Roosevelt speeches were written with the listener constantly in mind. Roosevelt was a speaker who listened, and to this can be attributed much of his success as a communicator. He had a better grasp of public opinion, public attitudes, problems, needs, and feelings than any American president before or since. He read a variety of newspapers, hostile as well as friendly, every day. He was provided with a digest of editorials prepared by the Commerce Department. He carried on an immense correspondence. He studied the public opinion polls and read a representative sampling of letters and telegrams in response to his speeches. He sent Mrs. Roosevelt to places he could not go himself, and placed great faith in her expert reports. He loved conversation and knew how to extract a maximum of information from each of the scores of experts who visited him. Moley marveled at the "intellectual ransacking" to which FDR subjected his frequent guests. His Oval Office in the Executive Wing was, as Grace Tully observed, "a crossroads of the globe." And this habit of listening to people was cultivated not as a means of holding a wetted finger to the wind in order to decide which way to veer but rather to see how much and what kind of persuasion was necessary. This genuine concern for what people were thinking about, worried about, puzzled about — and the desire to communicate his message in language which would be most meaningful and persuasive to them — conditioned the subjects emphasized, the arguments used, and the language and illustrative material selected. H. G. Wells visited Roosevelt during his first term in office and was impressed by his ability to speak plainly and convincingly to the ordinary voter. He wrote of the president: "He is, as it were, a ganglion for reception, expression, transmission, combination and realization, which I take it, is exactly what a modern government ought to be."[8]

That the president regarded speechmaking as an indispensable tool for leadership there can be no doubt; that his speeches had tremendous impact is equally certain. In 1936 and 1940 he entered the campaigns much later than his Republican opponents, and in each case the influence of his presence on the stump was immediately felt. The enthusiastic response to his campaign tour of October 1936 soon made it apparent to all but the conductors of the *Literary Digest* poll that Landon's chances were negligible. In 1940, seeking an unprecedented third term, Roosevelt announced to the nominating convention in July that in view of the international crisis he would not "have the time or the inclination to engage in purely political debate." But when it appeared that Willkie's campaign was proving much more effective than expected, Roosevelt was persuaded by apprehensive party leaders to enter the contest. He succeeded in wresting the offensive from his opponent; Willkie carried only ten states.

The president had established the practice of addressing the nation by radio on Sunday evenings, when the audience was largest. But in 1942 he abandoned this practice in defense to churchmen who complained of reduced attendance at evening services. He also had to abandon the practice of announcing speeches more than two or three days in advance. The Axis powers, aware of the impact of Roosevelt's speeches on his countrymen and on the world, took extraordinary measures to create competing headlines — alarming bulletins to negate the president's confident words of encouragement. On the night of the delivery of the "Arsenal of Democracy" speech, the Germans subjected London to unusually ferocious firebombing which destroyed a large section of the city.[9] Shortly thereafter a Japanese submarine fired on the California coast near Santa Barbara during the delivery of a fireside chat.

Conclusive evidence that the people were listening and responding to Roosevelt's speeches is to be found in the president's mail. During Hoover's administration the White House mail averaged 500-600 letters per day. Estimates of the daily mail under the New Deal vary from six thousand to eight thousand pieces. Ira R. T. Smith, chief of mail in the White House, reports that they ultimately had to give up attempts to count the letters; they simply lined them up and measured the length of each row. Smith, who for thirty-six years had handled the presidential mail himself, asked for fifty assistants to help with the half-million unopened letters accumulated during the week following the first inaugural address. He ultimately assembled a staff of twenty-two regulars and seventy emergency assistants.[10]

The mail always increased dramatically after a radio address, occasionally reaching as many as 150,000 letters and parcels in a single day. Seventy thousand letters were received after a radio talk on administration efforts to prevent home foreclosures. In one of his fireside chats the president invited his listeners to "tell me your troubles." Convinced that he was speaking directly and personally to them, hundreds of thousands of troubled Americans did just that. "It was months," says Ira Smith, "before we managed to swim out of *that* flood of mail." Leila Sussman, a student of FDR's mail, notes two chief recurring themes in letters written to the president: references to his personal warmth, which elicited genuine — often effusive — affection, and to his strength of leadership, which gave the writers a feeling of security. These impressions were gained from listening to Roosevelt's speeches — in the newsreels, over the radio, or in mass meetings. Listeners were moved to respond immediately after turning off the radio: "Your speech tonight made me very happy. You know somehow you seem very close to me like a very old friend." "I heard your wonderful speech this morning." The letters were often intensely personal. One begins, "My dearest and best Friend on Earth." And in another, "Words are not enough to express my love for you. You are the most wonderful President America has ever had." The correspondence makes clear that presidential speeches were listened to regularly and anticipated with excitement: "I am taking the liberty of addressing you just because I must express my admiration for your speeches, to which we all (Mother, Father, sisters, brothers and even my little 8 year old daughter) look forward with great delight. Your sincerity, truthfulness and convincing manner must reach the masses, who we are hoping will show their belief in you by keeping you in the White House for the next four years."[11] Listeners begged him to speak more often, and at greater length. "What a privilege to listen to our President talk to the nation in his radio broadcasts!" one listener wrote to the *New York Times*. "No one can help but be thrilled and feel that he is sitting face to face with the greatest leader of our times. Although present financial and economic problems may be too complex for the average citizen to fathom, we must at least have confidence that the man at the helm is steering a true course."[12]

The importance of the radio as an influence on the speaking of this period cannot be overestimated. This new medium of communication greatly increased the prominence and power of the president, while tending to diminish that of the Congress. While theoretically the airwaves were open to all, it was impossible for Congress to speak with one voice, and the microphone was less available to five hundred legislators than to one executive. Before the age of radio, the president of the United States was to most citizens nearly as remote a figure as a foreign monarch; by the 1930s that relationship was to be profoundly changed. Woodrow Wilson was the first chief executive to broadcast, but his distorted voice could be heard indistinctly by only a handful of his countrymen.[13] Harding was the first to be heard on a "network," if a linkage of three stations in Washington, New York, and Saint Louis could be dignified by such a term. He was bothered by the presence of a fixed microphone and did not find radio an appropriate medium for his "bloviating" style of oratory. Coolidge's flat, nasal voice carried well over the air, and he was regarded (and regarded himself) as an effective radio speaker. However, since he presided over a period of national self-satisfaction during which he felt no need to advocate new legislation or to champion an active "program," he was either unable or unwilling to exploit radio's potentialities for leadership. Herbert Hoover, as secretary of commerce, played an important role in dealing with the vexing problem of public versus private control of the airwaves and in setting the pattern for future governmental regulation. During his administration hundreds of hours of broadcasting time were devoted to reports of government activities and discussions of pending legislation; in 1932, over one thousand radio speeches were delivered by several hundred government officials.[14] President Hoover himself made frequent use of the medium but lacked the skills to use it to its greatest advantage.

Radio came to maturity at precisely the right time for Franklin D. Roosevelt. It proved to be the perfect instrument to meet the national need for unity, and Roosevelt was admirably equipped to use it as a means of effective personal leadership. A week after the first fireside chat a writer in the *New York Times* noted that "already Mr. Roosevelt is being called 'the Radio President.'" "Radio looms as President Roosevelt's modernized Big Stick." An official of the Columbia Broadcasting System was quoted as saying: "We believe that, during this critical period, radio can and will play a great part in creating a new confidence in our government and our institutions, and that the creation of such confidence is radio's most important function at this time."[15]

Even before attaining the presidency, Roosevelt had become aware of the usefulness of radio and its potential for facilitating genuinely democratic government. During the 1932 campaign he referred in a letter to a supporter to his experience as governor of New York: "I was particularly interested in your comment on the importance of the radio. Time after time, in meeting legislative opposition in my own state, I have taken an issue directly to the voters by radio, and invariably I have met a most heartening response. Amid many developments of civilization which lead away from direct government by the people, the radio is one which tends on the other hand to restore direct contact between the masses and their chosen leaders."[16] As in New York he had used radio to go over the heads of the legislature, so as president he went over the heads of Congress and a hostile press to appeal directly to the voters.

Radio was also the principal medium for creating and conveying the presidential image to the nation, and eventually to the world. FDR's public image was not contrived by advertising agencies and public relations men; he made it himself. The American people met him through his speeches, and since for millions those speeches were heard only, rather than being attended in person or made visible by television, the initial impression was made, the "image" created, through the voice alone. Subsequently, the smiling, confident presence pictured in newsreels in movie theaters throughout the land reinforced the earlier impression — that of a friend in Washington, reporting on how he was transacting the people's business. Nor did Roosevelt need to devote much attention to "projecting a favorable image." The warmth, the concern, the supreme confidence were genuine. Not only was it unnecessary to simulate them, they were irrepressible; they could not be concealed. They were qualities of the private, as well as the public, man; they were no mere accoutrements to be donned for public-speaking occasions.

There were many, of course, who sought to create a vastly different image of the president. He was, it was affirmed, a power-mad dictator, a crack-brained experimentor, a demagogue who set class against class. Opposed by a substantial majority of the nation's newspapers, he was assailed regularly by syndicated columnists and in the editorial pages. But, as he once observed to a reporter, he was not greatly concerned about editorial opposition as long as the papers reported accurately what he said and did. And, he might have added, as long as he could speak for himself via radio. Despite the attempts of articulate Roosevelt-haters to picture him as a devious and potentially dangerous subverter of cherished American values, the image that prevailed among the majority of voters (as evidenced periodically in the election returns) was the image projected by the man himself from the public platform and through radio receivers in millions of homes. Arthur Schlesinger has written of Roosevelt's "brilliant dramatization of politics as the medium for education and leadership." His popular strength, according to Schlesinger, was attributable to "that union of personality and public idealism which he joined so irresistibly to create so profoundly compelling a national image."[17]

Though the presidential oratory was dominant during the early months of his administration, the 1930s were not to be characterized by an uninterrupted monologue from the White House. Rather, the New Deal era is remembered for its turbulent, vigorous, occasionally vicious polemics. H. G. Wells, visiting the United States in the spring of 1935, was impressed by the "atmosphere of unbridled public discussion — brawling public discussion," which he found here. Anyone, it seemed to him, was permitted to say anything. He noted a "tornado of angry voices," raucous voices which were carried by radio from coast to coast and influenced the thinking of vast audiences. He learned, for example, that great pressure had been brought to bear upon the United States Senate to reject membership in the world court by a flood of telegrams, inspired by the radio addresses of Father Charles Coughlin and Will Rogers.[18]

The raucous voices that first reached Wells's ears in March of

1935 were those of General Hugh Johnson and Senator Huey Long, whose ill-tempered exchange of views was broadcast over the national networks. General Johnson, former head of the National Recovery Administration (NRA), speaking on March 4, at a dinner in his honor in New York's Waldorf-Astoria Hotel, delivered a blistering attack on the "Pied Pipers," Huey Long and Father Coughlin, whose demagogic appeals were causing concern in New Deal councils.[19] After reviewing the accomplishments of the New Deal, Johnson noted signs that the early impetus, the enthusiasm and solidarity of 1933, were waning. He attributed much of the blame to a resurgence of the Old Guard and to a "fringe" led at the moment by Coughlin and Long, which substituted emotions for beliefs and attracted into its ranks malcontents of all sorts. "Two Pied Pipers have come to Hamelin Town," said Johnson. "You can laugh at Father Coughlin — you can snort at Huey Long — but this country was never under a greater menace than from the breakup of spontaneous popular cooperation being engineered by the combination of this dangerous demagogy with the assault of the old social Neanderthalers." Warming to his task, the general branded the Louisiana senator a dictator, "the Hitler of one of our sovereign states," and accused Coughlin of using his priestly office for political purposes — "in the name of Jesus Christ, demanding that we ditch the President for Huey Long." The promise of one to divide up the nation's wealth and make every man a king, and of the other to make money out of nothing, he dismissed as a cruel hoax.

Admitting his own differences with Roosevelt, Johnson affirmed his belief that the national hope rested in the president and called for a restoration of that "spontaneous cooperation of a free people" which Woodrow Wilson had called the highest form of efficiency. "I regard as traitors to our common cause," he proclaimed in conclusion, "all those who . . . after urging their opinion as vehemently and as vigorously as they will, fail to accept the verdict of the polls, but jog, or try to break, the elbow of our pilot in this Sea of Shoals."

Huey Long was understandably furious. The following day he subjected his colleagues in the Senate to an angry tirade against General Johnson and President Roosevelt, accusing them of doing the bidding of the financial interests and singling out for special attack Bernard Baruch.

Long was answered immediately by Joseph Robinson, the majority leader, who accused him of trying to bulldoze his fellow senators, describing his outburst as a demonstration of "egotism, of arrogance, of ignorance." Robinson denounced Long for his gratuitous attack on Baruch, his ridicule of the president's policies, and his failure to answer Johnson's charges. The majority leader's closing words were a tacit apology for having expended time and energy in a reply. "I realize," he said, "that there are those who are listening to me who will say, 'Why pay attention to the ravings of one who anywhere else than in the Senate would be called a madman?'" Long was soon on his feet again, this time with a personal attack on Senator Robinson, who was goaded to respond. The unseemly fracas had occupied a large part of the Senate's working day.

On March 7, assured of a huge national audience by newspaper coverage of his antics in the Senate, Huey replied to Johnson in a radio address on "Our Blundering Government and Its Spokesman — Hugh Johnson."[20] Announcing at the outset that the Roosevelt administration had declared war on him, Long presented himself as an intrepid champion of the people, suffering the vicious attacks of representatives of the special interests like General Johnson. Pausing only briefly to blame the administration for the deplorable state of the country and to satirize the NRA and "the other funny alphabetical combinations," he shrewdly took advantage of this opportunity to explain to an audience of millions the details of his share-the-wealth program. After presenting a beguiling six-point plan to redistribute the wealth, extend educational opportunities, shorten hours of labor, increase agricultural production, provide old-age pensions after the age of sixty, and pay veterans' bonuses, he closed with an appeal to establish share-the-wealth societies in local communities.

But the second Pied Piper was yet to be heard from. On March 11, the National Broadcasting Company made its facilities available to the Reverend Charles E. Coughlin for a reply to his accuser.[21] In polished prose that offered a striking contrast to Huey's bare-fisted verbal assault, Coughlin skillfully parried General Johnson's personal attacks. Johnson, he charged, a mere tool of the "Tories of high finance," was more to be pitied than condemned. "The money changers whom the priest of priests drove from the temple of

Jerusalem both by word and by physical force have marshalled their forces behind the leadership of a chocolate soldier for the purpose of driving the priest out of public affairs." The bulk of the address was devoted to a denunciation of this gang of international bankers led by the archvillain "Bernard Manasses Baruch," who had brought the nation to the brink of ruin, and to a defense of Coughlin's National Union for Social Justice. Reaffirming his faith in "our beloved President," Franklin D. Roosevelt, the priest placed the blame for frustrating the president's efforts at reform squarely on the "Wall Streeters" and international bankers, "who whispered into his perturbed ears the philosophy of destruction."

Thus ended, for the moment at least, what H. G. Wells described as "a great slanging match." It has been a busy week for radio speakers, and for their listeners.

The altercation between the general and the Pied Pipers, though among the most dramatic, was by no means the only spirited exchange between the critics and the defenders of the New Deal. As Roosevelt's first term neared its close and attention turned toward another election year, the polemic spirit intensified. On February 2, 1936, Norman Thomas opened a speech to a national audience over the Columbia Broadcasting System with these words: "The air rings, the newspapers are filled with the politics of bedlam."[22] Thomas then proceeded to particularize by specific mention of some of the principal speeches with which the air had rung during the past few days. The catalog included: President Roosevelt's annual address to the Congress and the nation, Al Smith's criticism of New Deal policies before the American Liberty League, Senator Robinson's response to Smith, Governor Eugene Talmage's repudiation of Roosevelt's leadership in Macon, Georgia, former President Hoover's denunciation of his successor's administration, Senator Borah's speech to Brooklyn Republicans, and an address by Governor Alfred Landon outlining his political philosophy. Thomas could speak with some confidence that at least part of his audience would understand and respond to these references, for the complete texts of all seven had appeared in the *New York Times,* and five had been carried coast to coast by the radio networks.

The American citizen of the 1970s, who may quite possibly never have heard an entire political speech — whose familiarity with the utterances of statesmen is limited to thirty-second excerpts, incorporated into the evening television news broadcast, will have difficulty appreciating the fact that Americans of the 1930s and 1940s listened frequently and responsively to speeches with a beginning, a middle, and an end — whole speeches, which more often than not dealt specifically with vital national issues. Radio made possible a great national town meeting. Individual concern about bread-and-butter issues, plus the novelty of being able to hear the voices of political leaders in one's living room or dining room, insured a large, attentive audience. Never before had so large a segment of the population experienced such an intimate sense of participation in the affairs of their government.

No political campaign in which Franklin Roosevelt was involved was completely without interest, but the presidential campaign of 1936 was perhaps the most remarkable demonstration of the power of oratory as a means to individual triumph. The president did not begin actively to campaign until the end of September. By late summer anxiety had become apparent among Democratic leaders; some feared a Landon victory unless their leader showed an immediate disposition to lead. But Roosevelt continued his unhurried "nonpolitical" tour of the flooded areas of Pennsylvania and Ohio and the drought-stricken plains of the Middle West. At last, with only a month remaining until election day, he opened his campaign with a speech to the New York Democratic Convention at Syracuse. According to James Farley (who as head of the Democratic National Committee cannot be regarded as a completely unbiased observer) Roosevelt's one month on the stump deserves to be recorded as "the greatest piece of personal campaigning in American history."[23]

The president himself was astonished at the size of the crowds and the intensity of their emotion. He drew huge audiences in Kansas, his opponent's home state; more than 100,000 people jammed Cadillac Square in Detroit; his visit to New England in late October brought out what Roosevelt described as "the most amazing tidal wave of humanity I have ever seen"; his final address in Madison Square Garden evoked an orgy of hero-worship from a capacity crowd who again and again rose to their feet in thunderous applause.

Farley was at a loss to explain "the magical effect of his presence and his voice upon the crowds." He concluded that people seem to have confidence in some politicians as they do in their doctors, without quite knowing why. Whatever the quality capable of eliciting this response, it is felt rather than understood. Roosevelt had it. It was projected through his voice alone over the radio, and even more powerfully by his physical presence before an audience. In the face of the unquestionable persuasiveness of the president's speeches, and his ability to evoke public confidence in his sincerity and courage, his opponents had no recourse but to attempt to convert speaking skill into a political liability. Late in October, *Newsweek,* noting that Roosevelt was attracting the greatest gatherings in history, added pointedly: "But old-line observers declined to predict that the President's crowd-appeal would necessarily win more votes than the Governor's quiet simplicity."[24] Governor Landon, acknowledging the obvious fact that he was an indifferent speaker, decided to capitalize on "quiet simplicity." Identifying himself in his acceptance speech as "the everyday American," he determined to offer the voters a choice between a plain, sincere, blunt purveyor of common sense and a smooth, urbane, "eloquent" (and hence dangerously deceitful) rascal. In short, he fell back upon the oldest known method of dealing with an articulate opponent. Like Shakespeare's Anthony ("I am no orator, as Brutus is"), he sought to identify effective oratory with deceit, and inarticulateness (genuine or feigned) with honest competence. In this he found willing allies: he was introduced to a Minneapolis audience as the candidate who was not a "radio crooner"; friends cautioned against any attempt to improve his delivery; and the press repeatedly pointed up the striking contrast between his plain, honest talk and the president's beguiling "eloquence."[25] Two years after the election, Landon was still playing upon the age-old mistrust of "oratory": "I had not thought of myself as an orator. There is a certain deceit in oratory in that it may appeal to the emotions more than to reason. The important thing to me in what I had to say was the idea I would convey and what I stood for. The Presidency is primarily an elective office, not a broadcasting station." Admitting that after his nomination he had been provided with recording equipment and an instructor to teach him techniques of radio delivery, he explained that he had had little time for practice. Of his Democratic opponent he said: "The spell of his personal charm and his facile words were the cover for his inconsistencies and his experiments which had failed." "What chance had a simple Governor of Kansas . . . against this matter of political magic?"[26]

Though many vital issues of domestic policy were debated during the 1936 campaign, the principal issue was by common consent the president himself. Should the New Deal, under his very personal brand of leadership, be continued, or did the voters prefer to return to the Old Deal? Landon centered his attack on the extravagant spenders in Washington, the waste and excessive centralization brought about by "that man" who threatened individual freedoms and the American Way of Life. Roosevelt hammered away on the contrast between recovery under the New Deal and depression under the Old, and proposed a pragmatic test: Are you better off than you were? What freedoms have you lost? The results of the election (a plurality of eleven million votes, an electoral vote of 523-8, huge majorities in the House and Senate) constituted an unmistakable popular endorsement of the president and his policies. Though it would be too much to attribute this victory at the polls to superlative political oratory, there can be little doubt that the president's skill on the platform was an important contributing factor. At the very least, Roosevelt's mastery of the art of public speaking had not been deterrent to success. Nearly twenty-eight million Americans had apparently refused to accept Alf Landon's implication that oratory is inevitably deceitful and had conceded that truth and common sense may sometimes be eloquent.

It is noteworthy that the polemic spirit of the 1930's was manifested not only by the voices (raucous and otherwise) of political leaders from the platform and over the radio. Unprecedented opportunities were provided for the voice of Everyman to join the chorus. In the winter of 1934, George V. Denny, associate director of New York's Town Hall, was talking with a friend after listening to a radio speech by President Roosevelt. The friend told him of a neighbor who would rather be shot than be caught listening to Roosevelt on the radio.[27] Appalled by this unwillingness even to listen to opposing views, Denny sought a way of inducing people to hear "the other side." He conceived the idea of a nationally broadcast radio forum through which the whole country might hear the kind of informal debates which citizens in local town halls had heard in the past. It was one thing, he thought, to attend a political rally and applaud views already firmly held; it was quite another to hear a variety of views expressed from the same platform, and then to have a chance to respond to the speakers. Denny secured the cooperation of the National Broadcasting Company, and beginning in May 1935, America's Town Meeting of the Air was broadcast weekly from Town Hall in New York City. The format never varied: following the ringing of the town crier's bell and his intoned announcement, "Town Meetin' tonight," Denny (who proved to be a remarkably fair and skilled moderator) introduced the subject and the speakers. After uncensored presentations by three or four qualified speakers, often resulting in a most uninhibited clash of opposing ideas, the microphone was made available to members of the audience for equally uninhibited questions. Town meetings were soon organized through the country, where audiences listened to the speakers by radio and then held their own open forums. Sometimes provisions were made for members of these distant audiences to question the speakers in New York directly and receive immediate answers by radio. Transcripts of the programs, including questions and answers and correspondence from listeners, were available for ten cents a copy. Schools used the program to enhance students' political interest; miniature reproductions of Town Meeting were mounted in high schools and colleges. Denny's efforts to build a sense of community by making America one great town meeting were phenomenally successful. In 1936 America's Town Meeting of the Air was voted the nation's most popular educational program. Offers of commercial sponsorship from firms wishing to cash in on its popularity were rejected; Town Meeting remained untainted by even the appearance of control of any kind.

Less dramatic but also influential were the public forums sponsored by the United States Office of Education. J. W. Studebaker, commissioner of education, noted in 1936 that "one of the most encouraging indications of a renaissance of democratic sentiment is to be found in the nation wide growth of public discussion of national affairs."[28] Noting the existence of 350 public forums reporting their activities to the Office of Education, Studebaker pledged the support of his office in extending such forums. Federally funded demonstration forums were to be established in ten different states — "beacon lights of democracy," advancing the tradition of public discussion begun in colonial town meetings and carried forward in Lyceum and Chautauqua. "For the annual outlay required to keep one battleship afloat for national defense," said the commissioner, "we could make a good beginning on a nation wide program of adult civic education to keep democracy afloat in the angry seas of world confusion and economic chaos."

It should be apparent even from this fragmentary review of the polemics of the New Deal that the freedom and the opportunity for almost everyone to speak his mind which had earlier impressed H. G. Wells obtained throughout the campaign of 1936, and indeed characterized the entire New Deal era. Opponents sometimes spoke ominously of dictatorship, a charge that elicited from another foreign visitor to this country the sharp rejoinder that if Roosevelt was a dictator, he was surely the strangest dictator yet seen in the world to tolerate the savage criticism to which he was constantly subjected. "When your dictator comes, if he comes," said this visiting lecturer, a Frenchman, "I think you will not find him so tolerant."[29] On the eve of the 1936 election the *New York Times* paused to reflect upon the campaign. There had been a deplorable lack of truly great speeches. There had been no great, clear-cut issues between the two parties. But free rein had been given to democratic activities. "There has been entire liberty of speech and criticism even if much of both has seemed pointless and foolish. The choice of the American people on November 3 will not be dictated." The "unbridled discussion" which Wells has found so refreshing in early 1935 was still unrestrained.

As national attention turned from domestic to international crisis, public discussion continued, with no diminution in the number or impact of speeches by public men. Headlines reporting the shocking exploits of aggressors in Asia and dictators in Europe were alarming, but Americans cherishing the isolationism of twenty years tried to assure themselves that they could continue to remain aloof from the troubles of the rest of the world. The president, passionately convinced of the folly of this view, set himself to the task of educating his countrymen to the realities of a world that was rapidly becoming smaller and more dangerous. Looking back on this battle against isolationism, Harry Hopkins would say much later: "Roosevelt had more to do than any man of his time in arousing the conscience of the civilized world to the menace of Fascism and Nazism. And he did it by making speeches."

The campaign to combat the spirit of isolationism was launched in October 1937, when the president journeyed to Chicago, heart of isolationist country, to dedicate the Outer Drive Bridge. In his address he called attention to the existence of "a state of international anarchy and instability from which there is no escape through mere isolation or neutrality," and to the urgent necessity for "positive endeavors to preserve peace." Employing a homely figure of speech, a favorite device for making his point, he spoke of the spread of "an epidemic of world lawlessness" and added: "When an epidemic of physical disease starts to spread, the community approves and joins in a quarantine of the patients in order to protect the health of the community against the spread of the disease." Despite his concluding assertion that "America actively engages in the search for peace," the president was attacked as a meddler and a warmonger. Roosevelt had made the mistake of which he was seldom guilty; he had misjudged the readiness of the public to go along with him. "It is a terrible thing," he later observed ruefully to Rosenman, "to look over your shoulder when you are trying to lead and to find no one there." Later there would be someone there; ultimately the pressure of world events and the president's unceasing efforts in behalf of collective security would reveal the obsolescence of isolationism, but it was to be a slow and painful process.

The presidential election year of 1940 was marked by intense isolationist sentiment. The efforts of William Allen White's Committee to Defend America by Aiding the Allies were countered by the formation of a Committee to Defend America First. Isolationist orators Burton K. Wheeler, Charles Lindbergh, Hamilton Fish, Gerald Nye, Robert Taft, Arthur Vandenberg, and Charles Coughlin stumped the country. Wendell Willkie, the Republican candidate, no isolationist himself, was impelled in the heat of the campaign to verbal excesses which he was later to regret. In June, news of Italy's sudden entrance into the war motivated Roosevelt to insert in the text of an otherwise undistinguished address at the University of Virginia the startling sentence, "the hand that held the dagger has struck it into the back of its neighbor," thus dramatizing the event and immortalizing the speech as the "stabin-the-back" speech. Isolationists protested, but public opinion was moving the president's way. In a press conference in December, as Nazi firebombs were incinerating huge sections of London, Roosevelt paved the way to Lend-Lease with his irresistible analogy of the garden hose: "Suppose my neighbor's home catches fire, and I have a length of garden hose . . . . If he can take my garden hose and connect it up with his hydrant, I may help him to put out his fire." Later that month President Roosevelt delivered to the nation and to the world what he considered his most important fireside chat since the one dealing with the banking crisis in 1933. Referring to that earlier domestic crisis and his attempt to convey to the American people its meaning in their individual lives, he expressed a desire to do the same thing in this new international crisis, in order that it might be met with the same courage and realism. He spoke of the impossibility of appeasing Hitler, of the importance to America of an allied victory, of the dangers ahead if Britain were to fall. The Atlantic and Pacific oceans could no longer be regarded as defensive barriers, he said; the airplane had rendered them obsolete. Aware of the fervent desire to keep out of war, Roosevelt justified aid to Great Britain on the ground of self-interest: "I make the direct statement to the American people that there is far less chance of the United States getting into war if we do all we can now to support the nations defending themselves against attack by the Axis than if we acquiesce in their defeat, submit tamely to an Axis victory and wait our turn to be the object of attack in another war later on." This speech, which like so many other Roosevelt addresses, was subsequently identified by one striking phrase from its text (in this case, "the arsenal of democracy") brought the greatest mail response since the first inaugural. But the president's battle was far from won; isolationist spokesmen within and outside his own party were to fight him every step of the way. The following evening Senator Burton K. Wheeler was on the radio coast to coast with his rebuttal. The idea that America was in danger he branded as fantastic. Hitler could not possibly convoy an invasion force across the Atlantic. "If Hitler's army can't cross the narrow English Channel in 7 months, his bombers won't fly across the Rockies to bomb Denver tomorrow." The only danger lay in our joining some so-called union of free nations, which would inevitably involve us in war. "I say now and intend to continue to say, even if at the end I stand alone: Americans! Do not let yourselves be swayed by mass hysteria. Do not travel again the road that you took in 1917 . . . . Let your Representatives in Washington know that you have not surrendered the independence of America to warmongers and interventionists."

The Japanese attack on Pearl Harbor brought an abrupt end to the isolationist-interventionist debate, but it did not end the need for presidential oratory. Behind was the preoccupation with domestic recovery and reform; mobilization of the nation's industrial plant for war brought about the full employment which the New Deal had never been able to achieve. As the president later told a reporter, on December 7, 1941, "Dr. New Deal" turned his practice over to a new physician, "Dr. Win-the-War." In this new role Roosevelt was to become the principal leader of the free world in the death struggle with the Axis powers. And exercise of this leadership involved, as it did for that other great war leader Winston Churchill, the making of speeches. Especially important in the months following Pearl Harbor was the maintenance of civilian morale during the dark year of 1942 when everything seemed to be going wrong.

The swift advance of the Japanese in the Pacific, the success of the Nazis in the battle of the Atlantic, the shocking losses to Allied shipping as a result of submarine warfare, all threatened to accelerate a wave of defeatism and panic. Roosevelt, confident that people could be reassured if they could be made to understand the situation and the strategy and to feel that their leaders knew what they were doing, initiated elaborate preparations for a fireside chat. Starting with a thirteen-page draft dictated by the president, speech assistants Rosenman, Sherwood, and Hopkins set about the arduous process of revision. The newspapers were asked to publish maps of the war theaters for reference by the national audience during the speech. After seven drafts, the address was ready for delivery on the Washington's Birthday holiday, February 23, 1942. The president acknowledged at the outset the existence of "formidable odds and recurring defeats," drawing a comparison with similar difficulties faced by General Washington during the Revolution. He then explained to his listeners the disastrous results of following a "turtle policy" of pulling all their warships and planes into home waters for a last ditch defense and the advantages of carrying the war to the enemy in distant lands and waters. It was a masterful speech setting forth in broad strokes the global strategy to be followed, and it had the desired effect of reassurance through explanation, of allaying fear and counseling patience until decisive action would at last be possible. The Japanese act of lobbing a few shells ashore on the California coast during the broadcast proved a futile gesture which failed to counteract the impact of the president's words.

From the terrifying winter of 1942, through better times after the tide of war had turned in the allies' favor, to the day of his death when victory was at last in sight, Franklin Roosevelt continued to find time despite his crushing duties as commander-in-chief for periodic progress reports to the nation and messages of inspiration and encouragement which were carried throughout the free world. It was not always so much what he said, as his friend Frances Perkins observed, as the spirit he conveyed. Like Churchill in England, he was a symbol of hope and determination. General Dwight D. Eisenhower said of Roosevelt after the victory in Europe, "From his strength and indomitable spirit I drew constant support and confidence in the solution of my own problems."[30] The same could be said by millions of ordinary citizens, to whom these qualities of leadership were made manifest primarily through public speeches which seemed to each listener very private and personal communications.

In retrospect the era of Franklin D. Roosevelt seems a period of tumultuous polemics. At a time when great revolutionary forces were at work in the world, when strong men in other lands were affecting change by dictatorial fiat and force of arms, America's revolution, if revolution it was, came about through persuasion, public discussion, and the friction of competing ideas. The president, aware of the necessity of education and persuasion to truly democratic government, used his remarkable talents and the miraculous new medium of radio to become the nation's most effective persuader. But since persuasion involves the possibility of choice, other persuaders were always in the field with simultaneous access to the ear of the electorate. It was Roosevelt's triumph that despite the power of dissenting, often hostile, voices he was able for twelve eventful years to convince a majority of his countrymen of the essential rightness of his policies and the trustworthiness of his leadership through the nation's most devastating depression and the world's most horrible war. The Roosevelt years were years of perpetual talk — talk that sometimes became tiresome, ill-tempered, and irresponsible. To those who were scornful of this ceaseless public dialogue, Walter Lippmann had the perfect answer. "This endless talking," he said, "marks a very great advance in civilization. It required about five hundred years of constitutional development among the English-speaking peoples to turn the pugnacity and the predatory impulses of men into the channels of talk, rhetoric, bombast, reason and persuasion. Deride the talk as much as you like; it is the civilized substitute for street brawls, gangs, conspiracies, assassination, private armies. No other substitute has as yet been discovered."[31]

But these were years also of decisive, epoch-making action. During the preceding administration someone had published a book entitled *What This Country Needs*. America's need, in the opinion of this writer, was for statesmen, not spokesmen. "Action — the test of statesmanship, the only test. What our leaders say does not matter in the least . . . . What our leaders *do* is of the utmost importance." "We need action and men of action . . . . We don't need any more of these strong loquacious men who fill columns of type and who do nothing but shake hands."[32] This is a familiar refrain. For centuries there have been those who have sought to perpetuate the myth that talk necessarily precludes action ("speakers are never doers"), and that wisdom and eloquence are incompatible ("He who knows does not speak; and he who speaks does not know"). Roosevelt demonstrated — as did Churchill — and as had been convincingly demonstrated by others before them, that talkers may also be doers, and that words may pave the way to action, may make corresponding deeds possible. Moreover, as those who heard the wartime speeches of Roosevelt and Churchill will testify, words themselves may be a kind of action. These speeches were acts of affirmation and example which lifted spirits and helped to transform defeat into victory. Roosevelt knew that as the leader of a democracy he could move only as far and as fast as the people would let him. Popular understanding and support were prerequisite to action; understanding and support were achieved by talking to the people. While it is undoubtedly true that talk without action brings antipathy and frustration, it is also true that action without preliminary discussion, explanation, and consultation smacks more of tyranny than of democratic government.

If the stimulating oratorical crossfire of the Roosevelt years helped to moderate the assumption that "mere" is the indispensable modifier of "rhetoric," this period also witnessed the melioration of some of the connotations surrounding the terms *politics* and *politician*. Franklin Roosevelt, like his cousin Theodore, regarded politics as an honorable profession. This patrician president was proud to be known as a politician and was an uncommonly successful one. "Politics, after all," he once said, "is only an instrument through which to achieve government," and government as he saw it was "the art of formulating a policy and using the political techniques to attain so much of that policy as will receive general support; persuading, leading, sacrificing, teaching." Under such leadership politics became not merely what the politicians were engaged in, but everybody's business. In an editorial on "The Political Ferment" nearly a year before the 1936 election, the *New York Times* called attention to an unprecedented amount of political talk and interest. Nor was it confined to public men or newspapers. "In the streets, at chance encounters, in club corners, at private dinners, almost every topic of conversation is considered alien except politics. Women are as keen about it as men."[33] Senator Jonathan Dolliver would have been proud. "The democracy of England and America," he had said during an earlier period of progressive reform, "is no fierce mob, bewildered by the babble of tongues or the scribble of pens. It is an eager citizenship, anxious for the national welfare, having within it a tribunal of reason and conscience before which all causes are to be heard, and from which must emanate the final judgments that direct the progress of mankind."

ॐ 7 ॐ
THE CONTEMPORARY SCENE
Decline of Eloquence

> One of the interesting but troubling phenomena in our present-day life and art, particularly in America, is the decay and disrepute of oratory. The ancient statesmen — Themistocles and Pericles, the Scipios and the Catos, both Brutus and Caesar — were orators; and the orators — Demosthenes and Cicero — were statesmen. The same was true of England from the seventeenth century and even to the twentieth — from Pym, Vane, and Hampden, or the Pitts, Burke, Fox, and Sheridan, up to Mr. Churchill; and it was true of America at the time of Webster, Calhoun, and Clay, of Douglas and Lincoln. But what orators have we in public life at present?
> ELMER EDGAR STOLL

At the beginning of Franklin Roosevelt's fourth and final presidential campaign, public opinion pollster Elmo Roper expressed serious doubts about the efficacy of political campaign oratory. His experience in sampling public opinion had led him to believe that the winner's percentage of victory in an election was apt to be about the same as the percentage of preference given in polls at the beginning of the campaign. "Between the opening of the campaign and the actual voting," said Roper, "each candidate has his minor ups and downs. But in the end you have plenty of evidence that the actual hullabaloo and oratory of the campaign sway very few votes away from the decision the voter has made at the beginning of the campaign." Two years after Roosevelt's death, another public opinion expert, George H. Gallup, spoke with even greater confidence: "People are influenced to a far greater extent by actions and events than by words. Virtually all elections are won or lost before a single word has been uttered in a campaign . . . . Nine times in ten, election results would be no different if the candidates stayed home, saved their money, their time, their voices and their self respect."[1] But a year later Harry Truman gave Roper and Gallup reason for some second thoughts.

In May 1948 it seemed doubtful if Truman could even receive the Democratic presidential nomination, let alone win an election. Henry Wallace and his supporters were outspoken critics of his foreign policy; Southerners were furious at his stand on civil rights. On May 10, one thousand Dixiecrats gathered in the civic auditorium in Jackson, Mississippi, cheered Governor Strom Thurmond of South Carolina when he declared, "Harry Truman never has been elected President of the United States and never will be." Dixiecrats warned that they would be willing to help elect a Republican if necessary to defeat Truman. It was widely felt among Democratic leaders that the only hope for their divided party was to persuade General Dwight Eisenhower to accept the nomination.

In June President Truman made a 10,000 mile "nonpolitical" tour of the West to state his case and attack the "do-nothing" Eightieth Congress. Abandoning his manuscript and addressing his audiences in his own colloquial idiom, he discovered a formula for crowd-pleasing which was to serve him well during the campaign. But despite a generally favorable reception during this preconvention tour, criticism of his leadership continued. *Newsweek* conducted a poll of "fifty of the nation's leading political writers," all fifty of whom predicted a Republican victory and cited administration bungling and lack of confidence in Truman himself as major factors in their prediciton. Just before the Democratic convention, columnist Ernest K. Lindley reported that few Democrats really wanted Truman to run. Since his chances of election were hopeless, Lindley suggested that the best service Truman could render to his party would be to step aside. But the president, exuding confidence and pugnacity, made it clear that he had no intention of withdrawing. In late July, all overtures to General Eisenhower having failed, a divided and strife-ridden convention reluctantly offered its nomination to Harry Truman.

In his acceptance speech, delivered at two o'clock in the morning, Truman achieved the impossible by bringing the despondent delegates to their feet with a stirring denunciation of the Eightieth Congress and a pledge of ultimate victory: "Senator [Alben] Barkley and I will win this election and make these Republicans like it, and don't you forget that . . . . Victory has become a habit of our party. It's been elected four times in succession and I'm convinced it will be elected a fifth time next November."

Despite this optimistic prediction, the Democratic plight appeared hopeless, even to Democrats. The Dixiecrats seemed certain to capture some southern votes, and Henry Wallace's Progressive party was a threat in the big cities of the East. The disorganized Democrats lacked adequate funds and confidence in their candidate. Truman, left virtually alone to carry the burden of campaigning, made a series of whistle-stop campaign tours which ultimately took him 22,000 miles. Driving himself mercilessly, he made as many as sixteen speeches in one day, a total of 275 speeches after Labor Day. Many were brief off-the-cuff harangues to local audiences, but some major addresses reached millions through radio. In the closing weeks of the campaign the president drew larger and far more demonstrative crowds than Governor Dewey, but it was generally believed that he was attracting sightseers rather than votes. By September the Roper, Gallup, and Crossley polls — all with established reputations for accuracy — had written him off. A Dewey victory was certain; further campaigning was futile; there was simply nothing Truman could do to affect the outcome. With victory a certainty, Dewey, as someone observed, was not running but coasting. He treated the campaign as a mere formality and sought to avoid alienating anyone by delivering bland addresses on the desirability of national unity and world peace.

In October *Newsweek's* fifty political experts were again polled, and again unanimously predicted a Republican triumph, with Dewey winning 376 electoral votes to Truman's 116. On the first day of November they acknowledged a small Democratic advance by changing the prediction to 366 for Dewey and 126 for Truman but remained unanimous in their belief that Dewey would win, primarily because of an overwhelming voter desire for a change in administration and a conviction that Truman was inadequate. The *New York Times,* in a more conservative estimate, gave Dewey 305 electoral votes — almost precisely the number (303) which Truman actually received on election day.

It is impossible not to conclude that campaign oratory played a decisive part in Harry Truman's stunning defeat of Thomas Dewey. But this is not to say that the 1948 campaign was an oratorical battle in which the more eloquent candidate emerged victorious. The campaign produced no utterance memorable for its verbal felicity or argumentative cogency or its contribution to public understanding of vital issues. It is likely that the average American of either party if asked to pick the better speaker would unhesitatingly have named the Republican candidate. Dewey looked and sounded like a statesman. He spoke *ex cathedra;* he had dignity, magnificent confidence; his voice was a rich, well-modulated baritone, his articulation flawless. Truman had no polish, no grace. A writer for *Newsweek* described his campaigning style as "a blend of Will Rogers and a fighting cock." He was given to unsuppressed bursts of anger; he had no graces of voice, action, or phraseology. His inelegant language made judicious listeners wince. GOP, he said, meant "Grand Old Platitudes." The "do-nothing" Eightieth Congress, whose committee chairmen were "a bunch of old mossbacks," had, he said "stuck a pitchfork in the farmer's back." He proposed to "give 'em hell." He was not above saying of a retiring Republican senator that he "was never any good anyway." Still, audiences saw in this jaunty, irreverent figure a courageous fighter against almost hopeless odds, and millions of Americans comparing him with the suave, condescending Dewey, made up their minds late in the campaign to cast their votes for a continuation of Roosevelt's New Deal under Truman's leadership.

But the embarrassed pollsters who had confidently asserted that campaign oratory makes no difference at all in the outcome of elections were not altogether discredited. From the vantage point of the late 1970s there seems to have been no subsequent presidential campaign (with the possible exception of 1960) in which the public speaking of either major candidate could be said to have been a decisive factor in bringing about either victory or defeat. The national election campaign of 1952 brought to the platform some of the most eloquent and artistic political oratory since Woodrow Wilson. Adlai Stevenson became a world figure chiefly as the result of his ability to "talk sense to the American people," but General Eisenhower won the election, and another one four years later, for reasons that had nothing to do with comparative oratorical skill.

The campaign of 1960 was a hard-fought affair with the ultimate margin of victory less than 120,000 votes out of a total of nearly sixty-nine million votes cast. Richard Nixon stumped all fifty states; John F. Kennedy, forty-four. The candidates traveled far and fast, but their immense activity and a welter of words revealed little significant difference between the two men on the issues. It was essentially a battle of personalities. The outstanding event of the campaign was a series of "Great Debates" carried by radio and television to an audience of millions. These debates were considered by many to have constituted a decisive factor in Kennedy's narrow victory, not because the Democratic candidate displayed greater forensic skill or a more commanding grasp of issues but because he projected a more attractive image to a majority of viewers. The debates, despite a general assumption at the time that they would henceforth become part of all presidential election campaigns, were not repeated in 1964. The decision to omit them, whether or not it was in the national interest, was certainly in the interest of the incumbent president, Lyndon B. Johnson, since such national exposure would clearly have benefited his lesser-known challenger, Barry Goldwater.

In 1968 and 1972 the steady encroachment of Madison Avenue personnel and methods upon political campaigns (first evident in the Eisenhower campaign of 1952) became a virtual takeover. Television, which had rendered the old-time political rally practically obsolete, now changed the political speech into a snappy commerical. Use of this new medium was presumably too expensive, too technical, to be entrusted to mere politicians and their candidates. Political campaigning having become a process of "selling" a candidate, it could best be managed by merchandisers, professionals skilled in packaging and marketing products. Full-length speeches, these professionals were convinced, were boring; they had no entertainment value. What was being sold was "image," and image was best merchandised in small, attractive packages. Sales of candidates could be stimulated by sixty-second spot announcements, barely distinguishable from other paid advertisements for soap, beer, and deodorants, or by staged "pseudo-events" which would be reported free of charge on the news broadcasts. During the 1972 campaign, James Reston described a typically engineered welcome for candidate Richard Nixon. While hired jazz bands played and huge paper shredders showered the crowd with instant confetti, Atlanta, Georgia, was transformed into a glamorous stage setting for national television. "But the President didn't address the people. That is old-fashioned stuff. He spoke to a meeting of Republican Party leaders from the South and piped his remarks down to the reporters in the basement." While acknowledging that political contrivances were not exactly new to the American scene, Reston found the mechanization of deception by computer and television commercial especially offensive. Modern political techniques, he charged, are being used "in more devilish ways, not to spread the truth, but to suppress it, not to strengthen the democratic process but to distort it, not to inform the people on the basic questions of the election, but to use the people as actors in a play."[2]

In 1976, except for the acceptance speeches in the nominating conventions, few complete addresses were carried to the national audience via the mass media. Though they strove mightily, even the image-makers were unable to stir up much enthusiasm among the voters. The high point of the campaign was a revival (for the first time since 1960) of the "Great Debates," three television encounters between the nominees of both major parties. Afterward, there was the predictable speculation as to who had "won," with answers usually reflecting party affiliations. There was much dissatisfaction with the format, the absence of direct exchange between the participants, the mechanical and often unresponsive answers to reporters' questions; and there was general agreement that this great event had not measured up to expectations — though precisely what those expectations may have been was never quite clear. Not only did the "debates" fail to provide much insight into the specific policies of either candidate, or what decisions might be expected if either were elected, they did not even provide (as everyone including the debaters hoped they would) a vivid contrast of "images." Since neither man approached in color or flair the contestants of 1960, there was not much for their supporters to discuss beyond which of the two seemed the more "sincere" or the more "presidential."

The closing weeks of the campaign brought a blitzkrieg of spending by both major parties. Radio and television were blanketed — not by speeches setting forth policies or soliciting votes but by political advertisements. The candidates appeared almost hourly on the television screen in brief "commericals," appended whenever possible to entertainment programs with large audiences. The press reported extraordinary expenditures during the final week: Carter was said to have spent two million dollars on a hard-hitting series of commercials, and the Republicans "emptied a $12 million treasury on the most expensive barrage of TV and radio ads in the history of American Presidential campaigns."[3] As the campaign neared its close these advertisements became increasingly negative, each side attempting to discredit the other. Democratic commercials attacked the weak leadership of President Ford; Republicans paraded Georgians before the camera to testify that Carter was not highly regarded in his own state. Eventually what had come to be called "the longest campaign" was over. Despite gloomy predictions of voter apathy, the turnout at the polls was about the same as in 1972. But the vote was close, and many citizens, feeling themselves uninformed and confused by utterances which failed to make clear the positions of the candidates, were unable to make a decision until the last moment and then they voted more on impulse or out of desperation than from conviction.

This hasty chronology of presidential campaigning since the end of World War II is, of course, highly selective and scarcely does justice to the political oratory of this politically eventful period; an attempt will be made shortly to compensate for some obvious omissions. But in even the most complete account, it would be difficult to escape the conclusion that the quality of campaign oratory as well as public perception of its influence and importance have been decidedly on the wane. Nearly every presidential canvass has brought in its wake lugubrious commentaries on the state of the art. Raymond Moley, who had collaborated in the production of that remarkable series of campaign speeches delivered in 1932 by Franklin Roosevelt, commented in 1961 on the "mediocrity of the public discourse of our political leaders and statesmen." To Moley this discourse consisted largely of "flagrant appeals to the stomach and pocket-book . . . irrelevant lint-picking, and canned, ghost-written speeches — all clothed in jargon which only partially covers the stark nakedness of thought." Calling attention to the great increase in college-educated citizens, he expressed the opinion that, even allowing for the shortcomings of the educational system, "there is an audience waiting for higher quality in all media of communication." Curiously enough, Moley did not mention President John Kennedy's inaugural address, delivered only a few months earlier, but the excitement aroused by this speech might be taken as evidence of audience appreciation of "higher quality." The inaugural was commercially rerecorded, widely quoted and commented upon. For a time articles on oratory in general and Kennedy's oratory in particular appeared in the national journals. Representative of this brief flurry of interest in vividly persuasive speech was a major piece by Tom Wicker in the *New York Times Magazine* on "Kennedy as a Public Speakah." Recalling the eloquence of Presidents Jefferson, Lincoln, Wilson, Theodore and Franklin Roosevelt, and Kennedy, Wicker observed that "eloquence and greatness are by no means the same, but in politics the former is almost always the indispensable tool of the latter."[4]

The tragic death of the young president put an end to such speculations concerning a possible link between eloquence and political success. Neither Lyndon Johnson nor Barry Goldwater, principals in the 1964 presidential contest, managed to rise above the mediocrity described by Moley. One writer, deploring the "oratory" of the campaign, spoke of "the stark, stripped-down style of the utterance," the ideas "oversimplified to all but the vanishing point." The speakers sounded, he thought, like schoolboys reading aloud in the third grade. Dean Burch, Republican National Committee chairman during the Goldwater campaign, suggested an explanation. Presidential campaigns, said Burch, are a sham. Candidates, in an orgy of sheer motion, are forced to travel constantly, go without sleep, endure incredible fatigue, and then are expected several times a day "to communicate to us their deepest thoughts on issues of great complexity." And then, having done their best to overcome such obstacles, "their words are filtered and condensed by the rewrite men — or snipped to a 60-second film clip on TV news."[5]

A book published after the 1968 campaign did much to intensify public skepticism and to confirm the suspicion that "you can't believe a thing a politician says." In *The Selling of the President*, Joe McGinniss presented the Nixon campaign as an exercise in callous manipulation of the voters by cynical salesmen. Introducing the jargon of the trade (target group, ethnic specialist, image saturation, reaction shots, etc.) and reproducing excerpts from memoranda written by the sellers of a president, this book provided striking illustration of Marshall McLuhan's observation that "the shaping of a candidate's integral image has taken the place of discussing conflicting points of view." "We have to be very clear on this point," wrote Ray Price, a member of Nixon's staff, "the response is to the image, not the man. . . . It's not what's *there* that counts, it's what's projected — and, carrying it one step further, it's not what *he* projects but rather what the voter receives. It's not the man we have to change, but rather the *received impression*. And this impression often depends more on the medium and its use than it does on the candidate himself."[6] In this projection of a candidate's image public speeches are to play no part. Television politicians must not make speeches; they must converse with individuals. To create the desired illusion of intimacy and spontaneity, the best device is the closeup shot (preferably very close) in a thirty-second spot, all features of which can be carefully controlled.

But if full-length speeches were not frequently carried on television, politicans continued to address constituents on the hustings. The quality and effectiveness of such speaking, however, were open to question. At the end of the 1970 congressional elections, James Reston noted that the long campaign had produced not a single speech that had been published in full by all major newspapers of the country. Even the most partisan Republican papers, he said, had not published President Nixon's speeches, though he had delivered many. The editor of an annual volume of representative American speeches who each year examined hundreds of speeches before selecting fifteen or twenty for publication, found them for the most part commonplace, uninspiring, impersonal, lacking in artistic merit, revealing little concern for or adaptation to listeners. "If 1970-1971 is a weathervane," he wrote, "it may be that significant deliberative speaking in the public forum and in Congress is on the wane." Though it was apparent to most observers that slogans and image fabrication were being increasingly substituted for reasoned discourse, there was evidence that the public still wanted to think of themselves as being influenced primarily by reason. In a poll of voter opinion conducted in 1970 by CBS News the question was asked: "In thinking about which candidate you'd like to see elected, what has been most important for you . . . his own personal qualities, his stand on issues, or his political party affiliation?" A surprising 54 percent of those questioned named "his stand on issues" as most important; only 22 percent believed they had been most influenced by personal qualities. Yet further questioning revealed that 78 percent of those polled were unable to name a single issue that had been important in helping them choose among candidates.[7]

The denigration of political campaign speaking has continued undiminished to the present day. The *Christian Science Monitor* editorialized in 1972: "No one can say that the speeches made during the American presidential campaign of 1972 have added substantially to public understanding of national problems, national issues, or national means. There has been more obscuring than identifying, more vilifying than enlightening. The appeal has been to emotion rather than to reason." The *New Yorker* lamented that the mechanization of speechmaking had resulted in destroying the whole point of making speeches: taping and repetition destroy all sense of occasion; the electronic media intervene between speaker and audience; speechwriters come between the speaker and his own thoughts. "Political speeches are neither elevating nor demogogic; they are dead." There was no shortage of public talk in the "longest campaign" of 1976, but neither candidate went out of his way to clarify his stand on vital issues. There was undoubtedly truth to the charge that the press helped trivialize the campaign by dwelling upon sensational and unimportant details, but as one correspondent pointed out in rebuttal, the candidates themselves were largely responsible for setting the tone. "Where," he asked, "were the major policy speeches comparable to those by Franklin Roosevelt in 1932, or even to the sheaves of 'position papers' on every subject that Nixon put out in 1968?" "The campaign has been, in a word, banal," said commentator Howard K. Smith in an ABC newscast. "The public has the feeling of being nibbled to death by ducks, not addressed by titans as should be the case in a contest to choose not only our President but the *ex officio* leader of a troubled Western civilization." A Vermont farmer who said that he might not vote in 1976 for the first time in his life spoke for more than a few of his fellow-citizens when he complained: "Nobody stands for anything any more. Ford and Carter say what they think people want to hear. I say the hell with them both."[8]

The emphasis thus far has been upon political oratory, particularly campaign speaking, since this is the genre which in a democracy has the greatest mass appeal and of which the ordinary citizen is most likely to be aware. But what of the other types of speaking whose fortunes we have traced earlier in these pages? What has been the fate of congressional oratory, the ceremonial address, and the public lecture in the years since World War II?

The period of the "cold war" brought a resurgence of public interest in the activities of Congress. A series of vitally important debates on the containment of Communism, aid to Greece and Turkey, the Marshall Plan, China policy, the Korean war, and McCarthyism were reported in the press and followed with interest throughout the country. During the national agony of the Vietnam War and the disgrace of Watergate, public attention was again focused on Congress, and committee hearings were telecast hour after hour and day after day. But in recent years, except for such moments of crisis, congressional speaking has gone largely unreported in the media and unheeded by most Americans. This is partly the result of the low esteem in which congressmen are held and partly because of a widespread conviction that speaking on the floor of Congress has little or no effect upon legislation.

It is fashionable now as in years past to ridicule the quality of congressional speaking and to denigrate its importance. But such criticism has not gone unchallenged. Historian Charles Beard, describing himself as "a more than casual student of the *Congressional Record*," ventured the opinion that speeches could be found in the current *Record* which for breadth of knowledge, technical skill, analytical acumen, close reasoning and dignified presentation" would compare favorably with similar utterances by "great orators" of the nineteenth Century. Considering the complexity of contemporary problems, Beard regarded the quality of serious speeches in Congress as "amazingly high." Another student of Congress, acknowledging that the elaborate set speech has become pretty much of a museum piece, especially in the House, maintains that congressional debate continues to be the essence of the parliamentary system. The level is not always high; in fact, mediocrity is probably the rule. But it is not always so, and the occasional debate, carried on by the most competent and articulate members, is still capable of eliciting the pride of the House and of influencing the course of legislation.[9] Whatever the truth may be concerning the comparative quality of congressional oratory or its influence upon legislation, it is obvious that the subject engages the attention of the ordinary citizen not at all. In contrast to the pre-Civil War days when the debates of Congress were extensively reported, analyzed, and commented upon, today's communication media show little interest in Congress beyond reporting the news of personal scandal, official corruption, or flagrant demagogy. As a consequence, it is not entirely inaccurate to say, as did a prominent newspaper columnist, that "people don't give a damn what the average Senator or Congressman says."

Whereas congressional oratory and campaign speaking have undergone great changes in both quality and influence, the ceremonial address, the speech for special occasions — once an American institution and the ornament of the public platform — has practically disappeared. I have noted earlier some of the great occasional addresses which stirred the national pride and became part of the national literature: Daniel Webster, spokesman for the Constitution and the Union, dedicating a monument at Bunker Hill, laying a cornerstone at the Capitol, celebrating the Landing of the Pilgrims; Edward Everett, orator-at-large to the nation, eulogizing the father of our country in his oft-repeated oration on "The Character of Washington"; and perhaps the greatest of them all, Abraham Lincoln consecrating a burial ground at Gettysburg and coining an immortal definition of democracy. Modern America has apparently not felt the need for such public celebration of past heroes and events, for affirmation of national ideals — or if felt, it has seldom been fulfilled. Perhaps the closest we have come to the spirit of those earlier times was that day in August 1963 when Martin Luther King stood on the steps of the Lincoln Memorial and voiced the aspirations of millions of black Americans in his affecting "I Have a Dream" address.

It seems at the present moment in our history that the ceremonial address has become just that — merely ceremonial — incapable of evoking pride in the past, inspiration in the present, or resolve for the future. The Fourth of July oration, once honored, then ridiculed, is now simply ignored. The speech of tribute to great figures of the past — Webster on Adams and Jefferson, Everett on Washington, Phillips on Toussaint L'Ouverture — have long been out of fashion, though the tragic events of the 1960s forced a brief revival of the eulogy as prominent spokesmen engaged in outpourings of outrage and grief at the violent deaths of John Kennedy, Robert Kennedy, and Martin Luther King. The

Commencement Address, perhaps fortunately, seems headed for extinction. Commencement, for decades attended by only a fraction of graduates, was ferociously sabotaged by activists during the unhappy years of the Vietnam War. Many colleges at the students' request eliminated the usual speeches from the ceremony. Why is it necessary to have speeches? wrote one young graduate in *Seventeen*. Young people today are action-oriented; they find it difficult to sit through formal ceremonies. Why not, she asked, transform the artificial ceremony into a presentation of talent and creativity? In some colleges there has been talk of abandoning formal ceremonies altogether.

The public lecture, despite the surfeit of information created by the mass media, continues to be an immensely profitable business, estimated in the mid-1970s at 100 million dollars per year. Recent years have brought marked changes in audiences, lecturers, and subjects. At the beginning of the 1960s John Mason Brown, one of the most popular lecturers of the day, described the typical lecture audience as composed of "young or middle-aged wives, college-trained, very busy with their children or their jobs, who have managed to take an hour and a half off to come listen." They came to listen to men like Brown, Norman Cousins, Bennett Cerf, Harry Golden — critics, intellectuals, men of letters. But soon the typical lecture audience was no longer a women's club, with its bands of Helen Hokinson matrons wearing large hats covered with flowers and fruit, but a crowd of college students assembled to hear Al Capp, Dick Gregory, Julian Bond, or Gloria Steinem.

At times both before and after the Civil War the lecture platform became a veritable branch of the stump as advocates of all manner of reform — abolition, temperance, woman suffrage, and the like — crowded the exponents of "culture" from the podium. A similar development was seen in the late 1960s, when political activists were in great demand, particularly on college campuses. Lecturers were available to discuss whatever was most fashionable at the moment: women's liberation, water pollution, black power, abortion, homosexuality, psychedelic drugs. For a time the principal (sometimes the only) criterion was a disposition on the part of the speaker to buck the system, to attack the "establishment." The more radical the lecturer, the better. College audiences were transported by the iconoclasm of Timothy Leary, Andy Warhol, Abbie

Hoffman, and Mark Rudd. According to one student leader at Berkeley, the most desirable speakers, if available, would be Ho Chi Minh and Che Guevera. Television, which might have been expected to prove a competitor to the lecture business, was instead its most effective advertiser. People wanted to meet those who were making the news, to see them "in the flesh."

A striking development of the last decade has been the invasion of the lecture platform by members of Congress, who have discovered that they can attract more attention by speaking outside the Capitol Building than in it. In December 1971 Senator Margaret Chase Smith, noting the shocking absenteeism in the Senate, complained that "too many Senators have chronic absences because they are on lecture tours piling up annual lecture incomes that even exceed their Senate salaries." The Senate, she said, had become "a mere springboard to those who would use it — even abuse it — for their selfish interests," either through collecting exorbitant lecture fees or running for president. Mike Mansfield, Senate majority leader, also expressed his displeasure. The Senate, he observed, is degenerating into "a three-day-a-week body." In 1973 senators reported a total of over one million dollars in lecture fees. Among those lecturing for well over one thousand dollars a performance were George McGovern, Hubert Humphrey, Barry Goldwater, Henry Jackson, William Proxmire, Walter Mondale, Edmund Muskie, and Howard Baker.

Today college campuses still provide the most lucrative platforms for lecturers. There are some 2,500 colleges and universities, each booking ten or more speakers a year. Since these audiences turn over every four years, they can be booked again and again. Subjects change as fashions and enthusiasms change: women's liberation, consumer protection, gay liberation, control of nuclear power, affirmative action, pornography, sexual freedom, the rights of Indians, Chicanos, and other minorities. Since funds for special events are usually in the hands of student body leaders, high fees offer no obstacle. Undergraduate managers are not at all reluctant to lay out from one thousand to three thousand dollars for a Ralph Nader, an Art Buchwald, or a Dick Gregory.

Quite clearly, lecturing has become big business. Agency commissions, commonly 30 percent, sometimes exceed 50 percent. A book on *Lecturing for Profit* has sold very well. The quality of "lectures" (often rambling, unstructured, rap sessions) is usually incredibly low and with no trace of artistry, but no one seems to mind. Audiences come not to hear good speaking but to see celebrities in person, and whenever possible to hear an assault on the "power structure." The lecture is too often merely a branch of show biz — a showcase for television personalities.

REASONS FOR THE DECLINE

Having surveyed some of the evidence pointing to a decline in the influence of the public speaker as well as radical changes in the state of his art, one is impelled to speculate upon the reasons for these changes. Why, it seems relevant to ask, has political oratory fallen into such disrepute? Why, with vastly improved means of mass communication should carefully prepared discourses on public affairs, both in and outside of Congress be less frequently heard and heeded? How may the virtual disappearance of genuinely eloquent ceremonial addresses be accounted for? Why, with the increasing number and complexity of social problems, should there be so few effective attempts from the public platform to provide thoughtful analyses, persuasive arguments, assertions of national ideals, or stirring exhortations to concerted action?

Paradoxically, one reason for the decline in the quality and influence of public speaking is the dramatic development of the most influential of all media of mass communication, television. Newsman Robert MacNeil highlights the paradox in his observation that "no other medium has brought the ideal of an informed electorate so close to reality, yet poses so serious a threat of reducing our politics to triviality."[10]

We have seen how radio extended the range of the speaker's voice, brought public affairs into private homes all across the land, making it possible for Everyman to hear public addresses by eminent statesmen without moving from his easy chair. Radio during the thirties and forties created a virtual American town meeting of the air. For a time, television had a similar effect, and it seemed that the new medium would accomplish more efficiently and completely what radio had begun by communicating sights as well as sounds. In 1952, the first complete application of the new medium to a presidential campaign, television brought the pageantry of both national conventions into millions of homes. It also made possible the introduction of an unknown state governor, Adlai Stevenson, to a national audience, and it greatly enhanced the personal appeal of Richard Nixon's "Checkers Speech," in which he sought vindication from charges of improper financial influence. As a result of this single telecast, Nixon was transformed from a suspected politican to a political asset, a national hero who had "come clean as a hound's tooth." Later, television proved to be the perfect medium to project the fresh, vigorous image of a new political personality, John F. Kennedy. Television did for Kennedy's political career what radio had done for Franklin Roosevelt's.

But though television soon came to be used more widely as a political tool than even radio had been, it was seldom employed to carry speeches. It was used rather primarily as a marketing device. The advertising men who moved into political campaigning in 1952, and completely dominated it by the mid-sixties, were convinced that such a "crude device" as a full-length speech bored and alienated listeners. Television, they insisted, is an intimate medium; its effectiveness depends upon instantaneous impressions. It is best fitted to project images rather than reasoned argument. Whether this is indeed an intrinsic characteristic of the medium, or merely a reflection of the personal preference of the advertisers, there can be no question that this view of television's particular forte has prevailed and that it has drastically altered the manner in which political candidates approach and seek to influence their audiences via television. "Speeches" are out, replaced by thirty- or sixty-second spots, cunningly manipulated to convey a message about the candidate without antagonizing anyone by revealing a firm position on anything controversial. Some experts specializing in mass communication research come close to concluding that the "image" is everything, that the television viewer recalls little or nothing of the content of a message. Says one, "A candidate's appearance and demeanor appear to provide viewers with the most substantial clues to his character. The rational import of what the candidate says on television, as long as it is not blatantly offensive to the great central cluster of the electorate, appears to have very little influence on viewers' perception of image."[11]

On the face of it, there would not seem to be any good reason why substance as well as image cannot be communicated to voters

via television. Substance is very successfully transmitted in pro-
gramming other than political broadcasts — in scientific and historical documentaries, for example. But it is likely that the preponder-
ance of entertainment on television has created an attitudinal set,
an expectation that entertainment, activity, drama must inevitably
follow the flicking of a switch and the turning of a dial. Viewers are
quick to register their resentment with the station or the network
when popular entertainment programs are interrupted for political
speeches. When one of Adlai Stevenson's speeches preempted an
entertainment program during the 1952 campaign, he received this
telegram from an irate citizen: "I like Ike and I love Lucy. Drop
dead."

A striking illustration of the impact of television upon public-
speaking events is its influence in modifying the form and content
of the "Great Debates" of 1960. It is easy to see why the idea of a
series of debates was attractive to the communications industry.
Debates, because of the elements of conflict, drama, and general
entertainment value, have great drawing power. They also have a
unique potential for attracting huge audiences since they bring
together for the same program the followers of both major candidates. In 1960, the networks, having agreed to donate the time,
reserved the right to participate in determining the format, and the
details were worked out in twelve meetings between a committee
of television news executives and representatives of Vice President
Nixon and Senator Kennedy.

It became immediately apparent that this was to be a television
"show," with principal attention devoted to the mechanics of production. Nor can the blame be placed entirely on the television
experts. When Sig Mickelson, president of CBS News, proposed
the "Oregon Plan" of debate, in which debaters after opening
statements of their positions proceed to cross-question one
another, his suggestion was rejected by representatives of both
candidates. With few exceptions, neither television executives nor
political advisers, it appeared, had any enthusiasm for a genuine
debate. For one thing, there was no single clear-cut issue on which
the candidates could take definite positions pro and con. It was
feared that if they were drawn into tedious hair-splitting over differing methods of approach viewer interest would wane. A modified "Meet the Press" type of program was ultimately agreed upon.

The candidates would make opening and closing statements and would respond to questions by a panel of newsmen. Answers were to be limited to two and one half minutes, followed by comments of one and one-half minutes from the other candidate. Both Republican and Democratic representatives preferred questioning by reporters to direct cross-questioning by the "debaters" themselves. The panel format, they held, was familiar to the public and would enhance viewer interest. A Nixon aide feared the candidates would feel the necessity to be "too polite" if they were required to question one another. A Kennedy aide, explaining that no speaker wishes to be perceived as an unpleasant "public-attorney type," thought it better to let the press play this role. Both sides were obviously more preoccupied with image than argument.[12]

The minute attention paid to the details of "production" would have amused and astonished Lincoln and Douglas, the participants in those earlier "Great Debates of 1858." CBS was reported to have spent $633,000 on the first production at Chicago; the fourth program in New York required eight hours of rehearsal using stand-ins for the principal actors. According to one observer, the debates were "as much a duel between make-up artists and technical directors as contests for the Presidency of the United States."[13] After the first debate, in which Nixon had appeared pale and haggard, one newspaper story speculated that he might have been sabotaged by a makeup artist. Dozens of experts attended to the minutest details — the design of the set, the position of the moderator, the placement of lecterns, lights, and cameras, the color of shirts, suits, and backdrop. Each side jockeyed for advantage. Nixon (who tended to perspire profusely) wanted the studio temperature lowered and a pledge from the producer that he not be on camera when mopping his face. His aides requested that there be no left profile shots and saw to it that extra lighting was directed to Nixon's face. Kennedy representatives asked for more frequent "reaction shots" (showing one person's reaction while another is speaking), in the belief that this device favored their candidate more than his opponent. In the face of such jealous concern for the protection of image, the production staff took extreme measures to assure equal technical treatment. When in the third debate Nixon spoke from Los Angeles and Kennedy from New York City, the furnished "cottages" which served as dressing rooms for the debaters were identical in every detail. Identical too were the sets, the lighting, and the lenses in the cameras. The background cloths for the studios in Los Angeles and New York were bought from the same mill; the paint for both sets was mixed in New York and flown immediately to Los Angeles.

That the Kennedy-Nixon show was an outstanding theatrical success there can be no doubt; it attracted an audience variously estimated at from eighty million to over one hundred million citizens. It was the high point of the campaign; it quite certainly influenced the outcome of the election. It was hailed as a bold experiment which would be continued in all future presidential election campaigns. But these encounters, as discriminating observers were quick to point out, were not debates in any accurate definition of the term. A genuine debate is a clash of ideas, opinion, arguments, regarding a specific proposition. The participants confront each other directly, putting questions and evoking responses. Each side presents its case, and the audience judges which has argued most congently, presented the most substantial evidence in support of a position, rebutted most effectively the arguments of the other. The Kennedy-Nixon debates were joint appearances, parallel press conferences. There was no real confrontation; the participants did not question each other (as did Lincoln and Douglas a century earlier) but were questioned by news reporters. Instead of an agreed-upon proposition, affirmed by one side and denied by the other, there was a barrage of questions covering an enormous range of subjects. The two and one-half minute limitation allowed no time for reflection but put a premium on the rapid spewing out of facts and figures. Hesitation, according to students of the electronic media, is taken as a sign of weakness; television "abhors silence." Questions from the panel served only as convenient points of departure for a series of well-rehearsed snippets from endlessly repeated campaign speeches.

Consequently there could be no possibility of a decision, no meaningful speculation as to who "won" or "lost" the debate. "Winning," in this context, could only mean winning allegiance to one or the other personality. Which speaker was the more facile in snapping out two-minute responses; which appeared "cooler," more confident, least hesitant or fearful? An unintentional acknowledgment that what should have been a search for truth was actually a display of virtuosity came when Nixon protested that his opponent had at one point cheated by referring to notes before him on the lectern. The "Great Debates" of 1960 were, in short, essentially a clash of images rather than of arguments, policies, or basic positions. The question was not who was the more nearly "right," but who was the dominant personality.

Sixteen years later, each major candidate being convinced that it would be to his personal advantage, the presidential campaign debates were resumed. Gerald Ford, the incumbent (though unelected) president, trailing badly in the polls, was confident that he could triumph over his less-experienced opponent. Jimmy Carter, relatively unknown outside his own region, welcomed the opportunity for national exposure. Once again, as in 1960, the event was dominated by all the embellishments of show business. President Ford staged three dress rehearsals in the White House; Carter rehearsed with question and answer drills. Both enlisted the aid of coaching teams including project managers, experts on cosmetics and technical details, speech experts, and advisers who prepared elaborate briefing books. The Ford people wanted a dark blue background which supposedly deemphasized the president's receding hairline. The Carter people favored having the speakers sit during the debates, lest a standing position emphasize Ford's greater height. There were disputes about light and camera positions, about whether the audience should be photographed, and whether the presidential seal should be emblazoned on Ford's lectern. No detail was too trivial to escape attention; it was even decided to drill holes in the lecterns for water glass and pitcher to avoid spilling.

Again, as in 1960, a modified "Meet the Press" format was decided upon, with reporters posing questions which elicited heavily statistical set speeches redolent of briefing books and old campaign addresses — sometimes on the topics raised by the questioners, sometimes not. Both men struggled to maintain a stony, expressionless exterior, as if determined to avoid any show of emotion which might be caught by a closeup shot and interpreted as nervousness, weakness, inappropriate levity, or pugnacity. In this grim competition to appear presidential there were no flashes of wit, no spontaneity, few traces of good humor or human warmth. The air of unreality was intensified toward the end of the first debate when the failure of a twenty-five-cent electrolytic capacitor cut off the sound (but not the picture) from the podium. During the twenty-seven minutes of silence which followed, the two men stood impassively, unwilling to talk to each other, even to look at one another — actors uneasily awaiting the resumption of the play. After it was all over, TV newsman Sander Vanocur described the debates as "an unnatural act between two consenting candidates in public."

It is not difficult to find fault with the format of the Great Debates, to pronounce them "boring," to ridicule their preoccupation with appearances rather than substance. And in the atmosphere of public cynicism and skepticism following the disillusioning experiences of Vietnam and Watergate there was much ridicule and not a little apathy. But this "bold experiment" had very substantial values, values which make it important that it become an integral part of future campaigns, though modified so as to achieve its greatest potential.

Estimates of the size of the audiences drawn to the debates vary widely, but the number who listened to one or more of the 1960 confrontations was probably in excess of 100 million, and the 85 million or more who witnessed the first debate of 1976 continued to tune in on those that followed; there was apparently little audience "tail-off." Any event which can attract that many people to listen to candidates for political office is not without significance. Moreover, whatever their shortcomings as genuine debate, these joint appearances forced partisan members of the electorate, who might otherwise have listened only to their favorite, to see and hear both candidates at the same time. And though the debates may have aroused more interest in personalities than in issues, personalities are not altogether irrelevant. There is value in the opportunity to size up two aspirants to high office simultaneously performing in situations of great stress and to arrive at subjective judgments about their relative competence for leadership. Still another constructive contribution of the debates has been suggested by public-opinion analyst Samuel Lubell. Lubell's inquiries in 1960 led him to believe that "they made both candidates and the election result more acceptable to the electorate." Voters who had felt that neither Nixon nor Kennedy was big enough for the job were satisfied after the debates that the country would probably be safe with either man. It was Lubell's opinion that "if the TV debates had not been held, the razor-thin election outcome would probably have left much more rancor and ill-feeling in the country."[14] In 1976 also, the debates may have made the election results more acceptable by convincing many that both candidates were good, decent men, and that the victory of either one would not necessarily mean catastrophe for the nation.

We have charged television with being partially responsible for the decline in the influence and quality of public speeches. It must be added in fairness that television, by providng alternative means of information and persuasion, has helped bring about a situation in which formal public speeches are less necessary than they once were. Attention was called earlier to the fact that up to the middle of the nineteenth century the orator was the chief source of public information and inspiration. Today television, aided by newspapers, popular journals, and books, has created a glut of information. The public is saturated with knowledge of things about which orators formerly spoke. There is consequently less need for extended expository addresses or fireside chats relating what is going on in Washington or abroad. Furthermore, television enables us actually to see the news being made and hear it commented upon immediately afterward. Instant news reports keep us informed; documentaries after the fact provide in-depth analysis; a host of commentators introduce a variety of interpretations. Thus, while there is no diminution in the amount of talk, there is less dependence upon the formal public address. Television has been skillful in introducing alternate opportunities for the expression of opinion as well as means of conveying information. It is likely that a well-executed interview program like "Meet the Press," "Face the Nation," or "Issues and Answers" can reveal positions on issues as well as, perhaps better than, a public speech. Effective also are the unrehearsed conversations, sometimes lasting an hour or more, in which a public figure and a prominent newsman simply talk in an unstructured fashion about background, personal experiences, opinions, and concerns. An interesting indication of the shift away from dependence on the formal speech is seen in the fact that *Representative American Speeches,* issued annually since 1937 as part of the H. W. Wilson Company's Reference Shelf series, has in recent years included, in addition to the usual texts of public speeches, excerpts from presidential press conferences and transcripts of interviews on television.

While the peculiar characteristics and requirements of television have been at least partially responsible for modifying the speaking of political campaigns, we must look elsewhere for explanations for the decline of the ceremonial address. The speech for special occasions (the "epideictic oratory" of classical times) has as its primary aim neither persuasion nor the imparting of information but the affirmation of shared values. Through the commemoration of men or events in a nation's past, or at college commencement exercises, inaugurations, dedications, anniversaries, and celebrations of various kinds, speakers seek to build social cohesion by appeals to cherished symbols and attempts to energize or give new significance to established values. An influential nineteenth-century rhetorician described this oratorical genre as marked by "a general impulsion toward noble, patriotic, and honorable sentiments, and toward a large and worthy life." Its function, he thought, was a raising of public consciousness: "The people, in whose hands is the government, need just and lofty ideas on great issues, need continually to be lifted to a higher plane of public opinion."[15] This was the function performed by the great demonstrative speakers of the Golden Age, as they celebrated the events at Bunker Hill and Plymouth Rock, or held up the lives of Washington, Adams, and Jefferson as models worthy of emulation. "A true lover of the virtue of patriotism," Daniel Webster said on one of these occasions, "delights to contemplate its purest models."

But Americans of the 1970s (despite their recent celebration of a national bicentennial year) manifest little interest in contemplating the purest models of patriotism. Affirmation is not in style, having been replaced by cynicism and iconoclasm. Heroes are recalled primarily to reveal that they were not very heroic after all. Glowing tributes to American liberties are met, and not only among the young, with hoots of derision. Liberties indeed! What about the black man? What about women? What about the poor? In 1970, when college commencement audiences were shouting down speakers whose sentiments they did not share and ostentatiously turning their backs on such representatives of the establishment as Henry Kissinger and Nelson Rockefeller, Senator Margaret Chase Smith observed at Adelphi University that the old saying "see no evil, hear no evil, speak no evil" had apparently been replaced with a new creed of "see no good, hear no good, speak no good." Indeed, it seemed at the time that any affirmation of national ideals or principles was inevitably countered with examples of failure to measure up to the ideal. Obviously, a climate of skepticism, iconoclasm, and negativism is not one in which great speeches of affirmation are likely to prosper. Nor is it entirely clear precisely what it is that speakers might affirm. Most successful epideictic oratory has dealt with widely accepted ideologies; the speaker has been able to articulate what members of his audience already believed. But to what body of accepted values can today's speaker appeal? In our pluralistic society various ethnic groups proclaim separate identities. There are divisions of interest between economic and regional groups, between the generations, between the sexes. As a consequence, it becomes increasingly difficult to discern a common tradition or culture, a body of shared values to which a speaker can appeal to establish a greatly needed social cohesion. The difficulty is illustrated in General Douglas MacArthur's "Farewell to the Cadets," delivered at West Point in 1962. The eighty-two-year-old general took as his theme the motto of the academy, "Duty, honor, country." It would seem that these three words would represent values shared by a majority of his countrymen — and indeed many were moved and inspired by the speech. But, as the old soldier himself anticipated ("Every pedant, every demagogue, every cynic, every hypocrite, every troublemaker . . . will try to downgrade them even to the point of mockery and ridicule."), many were not. Nor was the negative reaction limited to pedants, troublemakers, and other objectionable types. Symbols that for some were evocative of the noblest sentiments were interpreted by others as code words for chauvinism and aggressive exploitation.

In continuing our attempt to account for the decline of oratory in our times, mention must be made of two contemporary phenomena which I shall designate the cult of informality and the cult of antirationalism.

The rule of conduct in both public and private life is informality, casualness, even intimacy. The implications for public speaking are obvious. No one wishes to be thought of as making a speech or delivering an address; instead he "gives a talk" or "shares his thoughts" with his listeners. Informality is manifested in dress, in posture, in relationship with audience, in manner of expression. The speaker sits at, or on, a table, or lounges on a lectern. In an attempt to avoid appearing "better" than anyone else, he affects a colloquial folksiness. The result is often banality, utterance devoid of any trace of artistry or distinctiveness. Today's speaker is a far cry from the stereotype of the orator of the Golden Age, with his frock coat, his mellifluous voice, and his stately periods. No one, of course, wishes to bring back that picturesque figure from a day long past, but despite his obvious excesses, he did on occasion manage to achieve an elevation of thought and of tone, an excellence of expression, and a moral grandeur, which are all too seldom encountered today. Great thoughts and profound emotions may be simply and succinctly expressed, as Lincoln demonstrated at Gettysburg, but great thoughts seldom appear in tawdry dress. And those who settle for mediocrity or less in manner of expression seldom achieve superiority in thought content or emotional impact. In striving for "eloquence" the orators of our nation's youthful days often missed the mark and succeeded only in making themselves ridiculous. But their aim was high; they aspired to excellence. Such aspiration, even when unfulfilled, is perhaps to be preferred to a present-day tendency to aim at mediocrity — and invariably to hit it.

The cult of antirationalism is one of the chief obstructions to the development of responsible public address. According to its adherents, since "logic" and "reason" have failed — indeed, are largely responsible for the mess we are in — we would be better off depending upon "gut feelings" as a guide to action. The political hucksters have been quick to perceive this proclivity and to exploit it to the full. "Reason pushes the viewer back, it assaults him," said one of the sellers of the president in 1968. "The emotions are more easily roused, closer to the surface, more malleable." But for more than two thousand years the essence of the rhetorician's task has been understood to be the finding and effective presentation of compelling reasons for belief and action. When audiences feel no necessity for good reasons, when they are content to do what "feels good," there can be no responsible rhetoric. Senator Alben Barkley, eloquent spokesman for Roosevelt's New Deal, used to tell the story of a minister who had been discharged by his board of deacons. "Don't I argufy?" he protested. "Don't I magnify? Don't I glorify?" "Yes," was the reply. "You argufy, magnify, and glorify, but you don't tell us wherein. We want a preacher who will tell us wherein." The story, said Barkley, illustrates what people expect from preachers, teachers, legislators, and others who speak to them from the platform.

Either public expectations have changed since then, or speakers are acting as if they have. No longer are audiences told wherein or wherefore. Instead of being provided with "good reasons," they are presented with a statement of conclusions. The evaluation of public expectations by Robert Goodman, political adviser to Spiro Agnew in 1972, is revealing: "People mostly want to know if he's for or against it. They don't want a bible of reasons pro and con. Does he believe we can have a black Vice President, or does he believe we can't have a black Vice President?" To the charge of not giving the substance of issues, of not explaining, Goodman responds, "Damned right we don't explain. We don't educate, we motivate. That's our job. We're not teachers, we're political managers. We're trying to win."[16] Since winning is supposedly the result of "the way people feel," Goodman sees nothing wrong in trying to create "an emotional feeling about a candidate." The thirty-second spot is the perfect medium for implementing such a philosophy. It projects an image; at best it makes an assertion, unaccompanied by a rationale. The slogan, the catch phrase, enforced by endless repetition, is substituted for good reasons. Its purpose, as John Gardner has pointed out, is not to make people think but to sell them an illusion, to make them act without thinking. Even on those rare occasions when a speaker takes the trouble to present carefully reasoned support for a position or a policy, it is seldom made available to the national audience via television. Preparers of the evening news reports, presumably acting on the assumption that "people mostly want to know if he's for or against it," and "don't want a bible of reasons," report as dramatically as possible the position taken and omit the rationale. And for many viewers, this is apparently enough.

Much of what has been said thus far suggests a final explanation for the present state of public address. It lies in the incapacity (or in some cases the unwillingness) of the audience to respond. Eloquence, as Daniel Webster declared, is in the assembly; great speeches require great audiences. William E. Gladstone observed: "[It is not] possible that in any age there should be in a few a capacity for making . . . [great] speeches, without a capacity in many for receiving, feeling, and comprehending them." Clearly, what it is that the many are able to receive, feel, and comprehend differs from age to age. In Gladstone's day, for example, orators could assume the existence of a common literary culture. Consequently, orations were studded with quotations from Virgil, Horace, Homer, Shakespeare, and the Bible. Such an option for illustration and embellishment is not available to today's orator. Few allusions beyond references to current movies, television programs, or sports personalities are recognizable by more than a small fraction of any general listening audience. Moreover, the idea that oratory might yield aesthetic satisfaction — or that it is an art to be cultivated by labor and training — seems to have occurred to few. The speaker who cultivates the skills of oral communication, whose voice, diction, and demeanor on the platform are allowed to rise above the level of the most commonplace conversational manner, is as likely to be suspected as admired. The passing of the old "oratorical style" of Everett, Choate, and Beveridge, or of Alben Barkley and Everett Dirksen, is not a cause for mourning. It is to the credit of modern audiences that they no longer take pleasure in being "dazzled," "enchanted," or "mesmerized." But if the time comes when American audiences can no longer feel admiration for distinctive utterance, if speakers discern no advantage in striving for excellence, or sense no favorable response to their impulse to give felicitous expression to worthy ideas and sentiments, then we shall surely have lost something of value.

But in discussing the capacity of audiences to respond to public address we are concerned with more than appreciation of the graces of style and delivery. Audiences must be able also to evaluate ideas, to assess the validity of arguments, to distinguish between mere assertion and logical demonstration, to recognize irrelevancies and distortions. Today's television audiences receive daily illustration of the advertiser's corruption of the concept of proof. It usually begins with the announcement, "Here's Proof!" followed by the presentation of a gaudy illusion of proof. Charts and graphs reveal that a pain killer contains one-third more than the "leading brand" of a mysterious ingredient recommended by doctors; all but one tablespoonful of oil is poured back into the can after the "grease-free" frying of chicken; a mop obliterates the words "Dirt" and "Grime" from a floor, proving that Scritch is an effective cleanser. As advertising methods are extended into politics, and comparable devices are employed to sell candidates and ideas as well as products, it becomes increasingly likely that we shall lose what John Morley once called the first quality of an educated person, namely, knowing what evidence is, and when a thing is proved and when it is not proved. If, as the hucksters assert, people really have no interest in "reasons pro and con," we should not be surprised if speakers fail to expend the enormous effort necessary to produce reasoned discourse.

Throughout our history speakers have manifested a tendency to provide what audiences appear to value. If much of the speaking heard today from the public platform is commonplace and unimaginative, inept and undistinguished in style and delivery, the fault may lie in part in the cultural limitations of the audience, or in a disposition to identify skill in speech with deceit and intellectual shallowness. If public speaking is lacking in substance, it may be because audiences do not "have the time," or lack the ability or inclination to attend to the sustained development of an idea. If speeches lack idealism and inspiration, the explanation may be found in a pervasive cynicism and iconoclasm, a widespread distrust of all ideologies and dogmas. There is more than a little truth in the mordant commentary of the New Yorker cartoon which has one hard hat say to another in a bar: "Nixon's no dope. If the people really *wanted* moral leadership, he'd give them moral leadership."

In 1968, after President Lyndon Johnson's announcement that he would not run again, a Chicago columnist wrote this poignant valedictory: "Goodbye LBJ. You weren't the best President a people ever had. But then, we weren't the best people a President ever had." Perhaps we should have the grace to temper our criticism of contemporary speakers and speaking by acknowledging that we are not the best audience a speaker ever had.

BRIEF MOMENTS OF GLORY

Fortunately, it is possible to conclude this discussion of the decline in public favor of the public speaker and his art on a more optimistic note. It is well to remember that the death of oratory has been proclaimed at intervals for hundreds of years, and for many of the same reasons — competing means of communication, unresponsive audiences, the trivialization of politics, the impossibility of persuasion. It is well to remember also that even in the days of the giants, all oratory was not of high quality. Demosthenes, Cicero, Pitt, Gladstone, Webster, Wilson, Churchill, Roosevelt were hardly typical of their times; all are remembered because they stood out from the crowd. Despite the waning influence of the platform speaker, despite the indisputable fact that the orator is not, as he once was, foremost among national heroes, there are still traces of that appetite for eloquence which once was confidently asserted as a national trait. "Oratory," the manifestation of a now-discredited speaking style, may indeed be dead, but eloquence — speech that is vivid, fluent, vigorous, graceful, appropriate, persuasive — is still recognized and appreciated in those rare moments in which it appears. At times when speechmaking has risen above mediocrity, enthusiastic public response has seemed to give credence to Raymond Moley's claim that "there is an audience waiting for higher quality." Recollection of a few of these moments may serve to modify our bleak characterization of American public speaking since World War II.

One thinks first of the strong, carefully wrought inaugural address of President John F. Kennedy in January 1961. This speech was a vivid demonstration (to many for the first time in their lives) of the immense potentialities of political oratory. Members of the crowd before him in Capitol Plaza and the national and world television audience were stirred by the spectacle of a vigorous young chief executive, hatless and coatless on a frosty winter day, sounding the trumpet in a "call to bear the burden of a long twilight struggle . . . against the common enemies of man: tyranny, poverty, disease and war itself," accepting, nay welcoming, the responsibility to lead in "defending freedom in its hour of maximum danger." Like everything Kennedy did, the speech had style. It invigorated the national spirit and set the tone for a new administration. Not since 1933 had a presidential inaugural address had such an impact. Its ringing phrases were quoted everywhere. Professors of english and speech analyzed its rhetorical devices in college classrooms and professional journals. Even the sophisticated

New Yorker, not noted for its admiration of political orators and oratory, offered a detailed rhetorical analysis of the speech, noting its clear, precise diction, its richness of figurative language and appropriately dignified rhythms, and venturing the opinion that both Aristotle and Cicero would have approved. Noting the high praise it had received, the writer expressed a hope that the address would revive a taste for good oratory, "a taste that has been alternately frustrated by inarticulateness and dulled by bombast," and would reestablish the tradition of political eloquence. Later in the year, the Nobel Prize winning writer André Maurois contributed a piece to the *New York Times Magazine* in which he pronounced Kennedy's inaugural a classic reminiscent of the Gettysburg Address. There are times, wrote Maurois, when the old platitudes are tolerated. But the time inevitably comes when the nation welcomes a leader with distinction of style, "for it seems to feel that the worth of a statesman's character is often equivalent to the excellence of his prose."

Kennedy's hour on the national stage was destined to be brief, but his distinctive prose survives, a manifestation of his passionate devotion to excellence in everything he undertook, a shining example of the power of human speech. Less than a month after his death in November 1963, seven memorial record albums containing speeches and excerpts from speeches had sold a combined total of five million copies. On December 22, 1963, the *New York Times* announced a new printing of a prayer card with Kennedy's picture and selections from his inaugural address. The first printing of 10,000 had been distributed during and shortly after his funeral. Earlier that month the National Symphony Orchestra and the combined choirs of Catholic University and Howard University presented the world premiere of a musical composition by Howard Hansen in which portions of the inaugural were sung. The premiere a memorial to Kennedy, marked the fifteenth anniversary of the United Nations' universal declaration of human rights. The opening words of Hansen's "A Song for Human Rights" were these: "Let the word go forth from this time and place, to friend and foe alike, that the torch has been passed to a new generation of Americans."

Almost equal to President Kennedy's inaugural address in its immediate impact was the speech of a southern minister before the

Lincoln Memorial on August 28, 1963. More than 200,000 people, about one quarter of them white, had converged on the nation's capital in an orderly, well-planned March on Washington to protest discrimination and unemployment and to hasten the passage of pending civil rights legislation. The formal program, which included ten major addresses interspersed with freedom songs, continued for hours. By late afternoon the immense crowd, packed together in the humid August heat, had become weary and restless. Revived momentarily by Mahalia Jackson's singing of "I've Been 'Buked and I've been Scorned," they awaited the final speech of the day. The climactic position on the program had been assigned to the Reverend Martin Luther King, president of the Southern Christian Leadership Conference — to provide the "rousements," as Roy Wilkins had put it.

The rousements were duly provided. Introduced as "the moral leader of the nation," King used the occasion to deliver the sermon of an aroused southern Baptist preacher — rhythmic, repetitive, biblical in flavor, rich in the imagery of patriotism and religion. America, he said, has defaulted on its promissory note in the Declaration of Independence; Negroes have come to Washington to cash a check. As he proceeded, his listeners began to participate. His repetition of the phrase "Now is the time" brought echoing shouts of "now," "now," from the audience. When he spoke of transforming "this sweltering summer of the Negro's legitimate discontent" into "an invigorating autumn of freedom and equality," they cried "yes, yes." And later as the now-famous "I have a dream" peroration moved steadily toward a climax, his listeners punctuated its successive images with "Dream on," "Keep dreamin'," and "I see it!" In the tumult that followed his final sentence, "Thank God almight, we're free at last!" Mrs. King, seated on the platform, felt that "for that brief moment the Kingdom of God seemed to have come on earth."

It is doubtful that the speech changed the minds or votes of congressmen opposed to civil-rights legislation or placated activists who favored blunter talk, but it had other effects. That speech, in that setting, the ecstatic crowd response, the speaker's emphasis upon dignity and discipline gave national impetus to the civil-rights movement and aroused sympathy among whites for King's cause of nonviolence. The speech raised the morale of black citizens, and its approval by whites persuaded them that they did not walk alone. Of all the speeches given that day its manner of delivery, its musical cadences and memorable phrases, its power to evoke audience participation made it a symbol of the 1963 Negro civil-rights revolution. To James Reston it seemed "an anguished echo from all the old American reformers" — Roger Williams, Samuel Adams, Thoreau, Garrison, Debs. Another columnist observed that King's speech "proved that the art of oratory is not yet dead in America, the evidence in Congress to the contrary notwithstanding."

The addresses of Kennedy and King stand out as perhaps the most extraordinary single utterances of recent years, but there have been numerous other occasions which have revealed that Americans, though accustomed to banality, have not become insensitive to genuine eloquence. One such occasion came on a day in February 1947, when for a moment a calm voice of reason was heard above the hysterical anti-Communist clamor of the postwar era. The Joint Congressional Committee on Atomic Energy was meeting to consider the confirmation of David E. Lilienthal as chairman of the Atomic Energy Commission. Senator Kenneth McKellar of Tennessee, bitter critic of the Tennessee Valley Authority, had used the hearings to attack Lilienthal, who had headed that agency, and to portray him as a Communist. On one occasion, McKellar had asked for some figures on TVA's production costs and had received the reply that althouth the figures would be supplied, he did not carry them in his head. The senator made several subsequent references to this response, representing it as evidence of the nominee's incompetence. Later, goaded beyond endurance by McKellar's insistence that he discuss Communist doctrine, Lilienthal faced his tormentor and with the words, "This I *do* carry in my head, Senator," launched into a fervent declaration of his personal democratic credo. Quietly, but with deep feeling, Lilienthal affirmed his belief in a system based upon "the fundamental proposition of the integrity of the individual," contrasting it with the communistic tenet that the state is an end in itself. "It is very easy simply to say that one is not a Communist. . . . It is very easy to talk about being against communism. It is equally important to believe those things which provide a satisfying and effective alternative. Democracy is that satisfying, affirmative alternative." Warning that imprudent attempts to ferret out subversion could lead to "innuendo and smears, and other unfortuante tactics" which divide and generate hatred, he stressed the need for adherence to procedures which would protect the individual against irresponsible charges of witnesses not subject to cross-examination and strict rules of credibility. When such precautions are not taken, he warned, "we have failed in carrying forward our ideals in respect to democracy. This I deeply believe."

This brief impromptu statement made in the course of a routine congressional hearing was nationally lauded in editorials and radio commentary. The *New York Times* carried the story on page one under the banner "Lilienthal Rejects Red Aims in a Moving Credo at Hearing" and printed the statement in full on page three. Alfred Friendly's article on the incident in the *Washington Post* was widely read and commented upon. *Commonweal* quoted the credo nearly in full, calling it "a declaration which has been read throughout the nation." Other magazines of opinion printed excerpts and comments. *Scholastic* committed its entire editorial page: "It is so important as an expression of genuine Americanism that we turn over our editorial platform to Mr. Lilienthal this week." Some years later Houston Peterson included the statement in his *Treasury of the World's Greatest Speeches*.

Another memorable moment of eloquence was William Faulkner's acceptance of the Nobel Prize for Literature in Stockholm, Sweden, in 1950. It was a time of worldwide despondence and gloom. A thermonuclear bomb had recently been exploded by Russia, and people were fearful of the possibility of atomic destruction. Acknowledging this "general and universal physical fear," Faulkner proclaimed: "I do not believe in the end of man. . . . I believe man will not merely endure, he will prevail. He is immortal . . . because he has a soul, a spirit, capable of compassion and sacrifice and endurance." This welcome affirmation of faith, reprinted in newspapers, magazines, and anthologies, was quoted and admired by many who had never read a Faulkner novel.

The list of such moments is too long to be recounted here. One thinks, for example, of Eugene McCarthy's impassioned but illtimed plea for the nomination of Adlai Stevenson in 1960 ("Do not reject this man who made us all proud to be called Democrats"), which elicited a demonstration longer and more enthusiastic than that for the successful candidate, John F. Kennedy. Or of President

Lyndon Johnson's finest hour, his televised address on the voting-rights bill to a Joint Session of Congress ("I speak tonight for the dignity of man and the destiny of democracy"), when this southern president, not renowned as an effective speaker, moved the nation with a poignant account of his early days as a schoolteacher in rural Texas and challenged his listeners to eliminate bigotry and hatred, repeating the words of a civil-rights marching song, "We Shall Overcome." Or of the eloquence of Congresswoman Barbara Jordan during the televised hearings on the articles of impeachment against Richard Nixon, or later in her fervent address to the 1976 Democratic National Convention.

Even more noteworthy, perhaps, than these moments of elo-quence — single occasions which as often as not created temporary excitement and then receded into history — was an extended period of national absorption with superb political oratory in the early 1950s. Responsible for this oratorical renaissance was a little-known Illinois politician whom events thrust suddenly and against his will into the center of a campaign for the presidency of the United States. From the moment when as governor of Illinois he welcomed the Democratic National Convention to Chicago in July 1952, transforming a commonplace ritual into an inspiring experience, to his affecting little speech conceding defeat in which he repeated a story of Abraham Lincoln's about a small boy who had stubbed his toe in the dark (He was "too old to cry, but it hurt too much to laugh"), Adlai Stevenson caught and held the attention of millions of Americans by using the language of public speech as it had not been used by a presidential candidate since Woodrow Wilson. His speeches were marked not only by unusual felicity of expression but by substance and candor. "This is not a time for superficial solutions and endless elocution, for frantic boast and foolish word," he said in his welcoming address to the convention. "Where we have erred, let there be no denial; where we have wronged the public trust, let there be no excuses. Self-criticism is the secret weapon of democracy, and candor and confession are good for the political soul. . . . What counts now is not just what we are *against,* but what we are *for. Who* leads us is less important than *what* leads us — what convictions, what courage, what faith — win or lose." It had been a long time since anyone had addressed a partisan crowd in words like these. In doing so, Stevenson established himself as an exceedingly uncommon politician. Some passages of his acceptance speech must have raised eyebrows among seasoned politicians of both parties and caused the political hucksters to conclude that he had lost his sanity. Never in living memory had a candidate for the presidency led his forces into battle with a slogan like this: "Better we lose the election than mislead the people; and better we lose than misgovern the people." His greatest concern, he said, was "not just winning the election, but how it is won, how well we can take advantage of this great quadrennial opportunity to debate issues sensibly and soberly." Then, striking the keynote for the kind of campaign he intended to wage, he said, "Let's talk sense to the American people. Let's tell them the truth, that there are no gains without pains, that we are now on the eve of great decisions, not easy decisions . . . but a long, patient, costly struggle which alone can assure triumph over the great enemies of man — war, poverty and tyranny — and the assaults upon human dignity which are the most grievous consequences of each."[17]

Throughout the campaign Stevenson continued to assume an audience that was intelligent and literate, listeners who were worthy of his best. A candidate for partisan office, he displayed a preference for what William O. Douglas called "the hard, unpartisan thought." Representatives of the press, rendered cynical by years of reporting the inanities of politics, could not conceal their admiration for this rarity on the political scene, a man who could speak with wit and charm while uttering hard truths. The foreign press, also, was favorably impressed by this unusally articulate American politican. Howard K. Smith, chief European correspondent for CBS, reported from London that the Democratic candidate's speeches were receiving high praise in English papers. The English, Smith explained, cherish words in much the same way as the French cherish food. Language to them is something which must be treated with respect and finesse. Americans, on the other hand, characteristically behave toward words as the English do toward food: words are something used for the ordinary purposes of keeping the system alive, no more. Perhaps so, but there was evidence in 1952 that even Americans could reveal an appreciation of verbal finesse when given the opportunity. It was inevitable, of course, that Stevenson should become the darling of the intellectuals — men and women who are interested in ideas and in the way ideas are expressed. Members of the academic community who usually remained aloof found themselves caught up in this campaign. A full-page, individually signed endorsement of Stevenson by the Columbia University faculty in the *New York Times* was subsequently reproduced and endorsed by professional men and women in newspapers elsewhere in the nation. Such support led some Democratic leaders to wonder if intellectualism was good politics. True, the "eggheads" were solidly for Stevenson, but how many eggheads were there?

In the end, Stevenson lost the election, but not because he spoke well or, as some charged, because he talked over the heads of the American people. It does not seem likely that he would have done better had he adopted the usual course, had he avoided taking positions and used words "calculated to catch everyone." The long Democratic reign, the scandals of the Truman administration, the Korean war, the security felt by many in elevating to leadership in a time of international crisis a popular General of the Armies — all were factors affecting the outcome. But the Democratic candidate, in being himself, had won the fierce loyalty of millions who would have resented being classed as "intellectuals." In defeat he polled 27.3 million votes — more than Truman in 1948, more than any previous winning presidential candidate except Roosevelt in 1932 and 1936. And there was triumph even in defeat. He had elevated the level of public discourse, a fact that had not escaped even those who voted for his opponent. For the rest of his life, as candidate for public office, as private citizen, and as ambassador to the United Nations, he continued to address America's better self, holding up in luminous phrases a vision of what the future might be. He once said, "I would like most to be remembered as having contributed to a higher level of political dialogue in the United States." Most of his countrymen would agree that Adlai Stevenson is so remembered.

During the years under review here, there have been many other occasions on which speeches have attracted national attention and interest and stimulated widespread public discussion. Some, like Nixon's "Checkers" speech, General Douglas MacArthur's "Old Soldiers Never Die" address to the Congress, and the presidential "debates" of 1960 and 1976, were made noteworthy by the dramatic situations out of which they grew. Others, and there have been many, were of historical, rather than rhetorical significance — General Marshall's Commencement Address at Harvard announcing the Marshall Plan; Truman's message to Congress proposing aid to Greece and Turkey, and his inaugural address in which he outlined the Point IV program to provide technical and scientific aid to economically underdeveloped nations; Kennedy's addresses on the Cuban missile crisis and the crisis in Berlin. But the examples included here have been selected because they possess a quality found in all great oratory of whatever age or style, a quality that is possibly best designated "eloquence." Whether described, as it once was, as "logic on fire," or "heightening the impressions of reason by the colouring of imagination," or simply as an appropriate blend of thought and feeling, it refers to the power to persuade, to move, often to lift and ennoble, by vivid, artistic human speech. It has been my purpose in recalling the popular response to these selected utterances to suggest that even during a period in which the powers of expression are not assiduously cultivated, in which the general level of public discourse is acknowledged to be deplorably low, there is still evident an appreciation of genuine eloquence and an admiration of speakers who pay their audiences the compliment of giving them their very best.

EPILOGUE

Sometime in the future there will appear again
strong leaders who will also be strong orators, —
men imbued with a sense of history, an abiding respect for the perennial creativity of their language,
and a capacity to use the spoken word to convey the
deepest commitments of their minds and hearts. In
that future, the ancient art of speechcraft — what
Plato called 'the universal art of enchanting the mind
by arguments' — will be exemplified and dignified
by speeches not of faltering virtuosity but of genuine
political eloquence.

RICHARD M. HUNT (1962)

THIS inquiry into the role of the platform speaker during the two
hundred years of our national development has served to illustrate
the truth of Gladstone's assertion that "his choice is to be what his
age will have him, what it requires in order to be moved by him."
When audiences have delighted in ornate rhetorical flourishes and
platform histrionics, there have been orators eager to oblige. When
the public has followed with interest the clash of ideas in genuine
congressional debate, other Great Debates have followed. When
the national attention has been centered on the acquisition of material wealth, political speakers have willingly cooperated by obscuring the real issues (as in the 1870s and 1880s) or by fatuous lauda-
tion of things-as-they-are (as in the 1920s). Managers of the lecture
platform have been perceptive in ministering to public demand —
providing information and "culture" when there was a felt need,
entertainment when that need was no longer manifest, and when
other media were available for both information and entertainment, presenting "live and in-person" the celebrities of the moment.
In times of crisis, when feelings of impotence and despair have
engulfed the citizenry, strong leaders have appeared (most of them
gifted speakers), some to reassert once-cherished values and keep
the nation on course, others merely to wield personal power or to
propose beguiling but perilous panaceas.

There is good reason to believe that the public address of the late twentieth century will be what this age will have it be. Clearly, the oratory of our earlier days will not serve present or future needs. There should be no desire, nor is there any need, to recapitulate our Golden Age. We are no longer as in Patrick Henry's day a small cluster of colonies struggling to throw off foreign domination and achieve a national existence, nor as in Daniel Webster's time a new nation needing to define itself and formulate its ideals and goals. As external conditions have changed, so have styles, tastes, and expectations. The oratory of personal ascendancy, of striking individual triumphs over audiences, is no longer admired — or (one would hope) even possible. No longer do we ask of those who speak to and for us from the platform that they "subdue" or "mesmerize" or "hold in thrall" those who listen. We have no wish to yield ourselves to the fascination of verbal virtuosos; such conduct we rightly regard as the very antithesis of democracy. Oratory is no longer cultivated as a fine art, a purely aesthetic experience to be admired and enjoyed like music, drama, or painting. The tempo of modern life is such that never again can a public figure allow himself the luxury of devoting three months' preparation (as did George William Curtis) to a single address, nor will ever an audience again sit still to listen to such a speech. Oratory, insofar as it is regarded as an art at all, is considered a useful or instrumental art, serving a specific purpose — preferably as quickly and efficiently as possible. The simplifying, streamlining influences observed during the 1920s have become established — permanently, one would suppose.

In the future, as in the past, changes will undoubtedly occur — changes in the role of the speaker, in his manner of expression, in public evaluation of his value and importance. It seems likely that formal addresses will be less frequently heard. The set speech in Congress has already become a rarity. The speech to inform is less necessary than it once was, since information concerning public issues can be more attractively presented in the press, through televised press conferences, panel discussions, interviews, and documentaries. In speechmaking, emphasis will continue to be placed upon communicativeness, probably upon informality — though it is not likely that speakers will (or can) move further in the direction of the commonplace or the colloquial. It is possible that the immense popularity of books calling attention to the sad state of our public language may presage a reaction leading to more precision in utterance and an elimination of some of the dreadful jargon which renders speech unintelligible. A preference for simplicity or directness in speech does not necessarily result in a diminution of excellence, nor does it signal the death of eloquence. Eloquence does not imply the Grand Style; eloquence is a quality, an attribute, and it speaks through many styles. We sense it in the unschooled Bartolomeo Vanzetti's final halting speech of self-justification, as well as in polished academic addresses of the learned Woodrow Wilson. It may be premeditated, as in Lincoln's beautifully crafted sentences at Gettysburg, or spontaneous, as in Lilienthal's impassioned response to Senator McKellar. It is a fusion of thought and feeling, usually arising out of a great moment. It speaks most often to the heart, but there is a kind of eloquence too in an elegant argument, a masterful statement of a case. It is, in short, the power to move men and women through speech. And since one of its principal ingredients is appropriateness to audience and occasion, our conception of eloquence will change with changing times. It may be that audiences incapable of responding to the oratory of an Everett or a Webster can be reached by the earnest, low-keyed colloquy of a Jimmy Carter or a Walter Mondale. Perhaps our best hope for the future is that expressed by the commentator of the twenties quoted in an earlier chapter, namely, that to this intensely practical art (public speaking) may be added something of the beauty and inspiration of the fine art (oratory) so that once again "it will not be an insult to a man to call him an orator."

As has been displayed amply in these pages, there have always been disparagers of oratory. Even in the days when the orator stood high among national heroes there were those who, like Carlyle, regarded public speech as a substitute for thought or action and preached that skill in speaking is inevitably accompanied by a lack of competence in anything really worthwhile. That similar disparagement is heard today need not be a matter of great concern. What is a matter for concern, however, is what appears to be an increasing tendency to regard public address as outmoded and superfluous. "Speeches are out," the political hucksters of television have decreed, and their proscription may extend beyond television. Where Gladstone once asked what an age required in order to be moved by the speaker, the question now seems to be whether we will choose to be moved by him at all. Much has been written of late concerning our lack of commitment, individually and as a nation, to a body of shared values and beliefs. We do not like to hear talk about values. We tend to regard "facts" as somehow antithetic to "values," and in our passion for facts we tend to disparage "value judgments." We choose to avoid whatever commitments are avoidable. We are amused or embarrassed by the expression of deep feelings about social or political issues, unless those feelings are totally negative. We prefer to be "cool." When to this complex of attitudes are added a general disregard for and distrust of authority and a resistance to persuasion of all kinds, the implications for public address, which at its best deals with feelings, beliefs, and values and which frequently aims at persuasion, are not propitious.

But it is impossible to conceive of a truly democratic government that is not, in Macaulay's words, a government by speaking. We shall always need men and women who can articulate a mood, an attitude, a hope, a concern which others are experiencing but are unable to express. This function is not, of course, performed exclusively by the speaker. But there seems to be an advantage when common sentiments are expressed orally by a personality with whom listeners can identify. Since government through public discussion is the only alternative to government by fiat, an articulate opposition, able to speak freely, is as important as spokesmen for the party in power. A wise student of representative government has expressed the deep conviction that self-government is government by orators. "A vast nation," said Woodrow Wilson, "must govern itself by proxy, by delegation, and it will be safe and content under such representative government only so long as that government is conducted openly by the nation's representatives, that is, only so long as it is conducted by candid and unrestricted discussion. *Self-government must be managed through the instrumentality of public speech.* There is no other safe, no other possible, method. And government by public speech is government by orators — a style of government accepted by all students of history and politics as the freest and best the world has yet seen."[1] Government by speaking, as Wilson was quick to point out, is not government by *mere* speaking; words are not substitutes for action. But there is evidence in our own time and in times past that the greatest statesmen have been able to combine words and action. And we know that words can provide the impulse to action — can explain and justify, can focus and canalize determination, and thus make action possible.

If we accept the proposition that public speech is an ingredient indispensable to representative government, it is greatly to our advantage to try to insure that the speaking we attend to is of the highest quality possible. We need not expect "eloquence" in the daily conduct of public business, though we may justifiably demand clear, direct, unadorned good sense. But it would be a tragedy indeed if in times of crisis, or when decisions must be made which affect the public welfare, we should not be able to look forward to hearing as our countrymen have heard in the past speeches affirming enduring values, interpreting complex situations, urging effort and commitment, in language designed to reach both head and heart. And it would be a greater tragedy still if drugged by apathy or cynicism or mindless iconoclasm we should be unable or unwilling to respond. For, as Denis Brogan, a distinguished commentator upon America and her institutions, reminds us: "Oratory, phrases, the evocative power of verbal symbols must not be despised, for these are and have been one of the chief means of uniting the United States and keeping it united."

NOTES

INTRODUCTION

1. *Congressional Record* 97:10336 (1951).
2. "Ancient and Modern Eloquence," *Littell's Living Age* 29 (May 3, 1851):193.
3. *The Genius of American Politics* (Chicago: University of Chicago Press, 1953), p. 156.
4. William Ewart Gladstone, *Studies on Homer and the Homeric Age* (Oxford: Oxford University Press, 1858), 3:107. Italics mine.
5. (New York: Macmillan, 1892), 2 vols.

CHAPTER 1

1. Rufus Choate, *Addresses and Orations*, 6th ed. (Boston: Little, Brown, 1891), p. 198; Hezekiah Niles, *Principles and Acts of the Revolution in America*, Centennial ed. (New York: A. S. Barnes & Co., 1876). p. 12.
2. *The Literary History of the American Revolution: 1763-1783*, 2 vols. in one (New York: Putnam's, 1905), 1:9.
3. William V. Wells, *Life and Public Services of Samuel Adams* (Boston: Little, Brown, 1865), 2:61.
4. Frank Moore, *Diary of the American Revolution* (New York: Privately Printed, 1865), 1:315.
5. Carl Bridenbaugh, *Seat of Empire* (Williamsburg: Colonial Williamsburg, 1958), p. 62.
6. *Orations Delivered at the Request of the Inhabitants of the Town of Boston* (Boston: Peter Edes, 1785).
7. *The Works of John Adams*, ed. Charles Francis Adams (Boston: Little, Brown, 1856), 2:332.
8. Adams, *Works*, 10:203-4.
9. Ibid., 2:287.
10. John W. Thornton, *The Pulpit of the American Revolution* (Boston: Gould and Lincoln, 1860), p. xxix; quoted in Adams, *Works*, 4:55 n.
11. Alice M. Baldwin, *The New England Clergy and the American Revolution* (Durham, N.C.: Duke University Press, 1928), p. 123.
12. Ibid., pp. 117-19.
13. Charles Francis Adams, *Familiar Letters of John Adams and His Wife Abigail Adams during the Revolution* (Boston: Houghton, Mifflin, 1875), p. 76; *The Deane Papers, 1774-1777, Collections of the New York Historical Society for the Year 1886* (New York: 1887), 1:77.
14. Moore, *Diary of the American Revolution*, p. 44; Baldwin, p. 113 n; Tyler, *Literary History of the American Revolution*, 1:138-39.

15. *Old South Leaflets* (Boston: Directors of the Old South Work, n.d.), Vol. 8, No. 183.

16. John P. Kennedy, *Memoirs of the Life of William Wirt* (Philadelphia: Lea and Blanchard, 1849), 1:122.

17. Kennedy, 1:129.

18. Kennedy, 1:279; 2:21, 11.

19. Kennedy, 1:387, 396, 352-55.

20. Moses Coit Tyler, *Patrick Henry* (Boston: Houghton, Mifflin, 1887), pp. 149-51.

21. Adams, *Works*, 10:271-72.

22. William Tudor, *The Life of James Otis* (Boston: Wells and Libby, 1823), p. 488.

23. Adams, *Works*, 2:124 n.; 10:248-49.

24. Charles Botta, *History of the War of Independence of the United States of America*, 8th ed., 2 vols. (New Haven, Conn.: Nathan Whiting, [1834]).

25. "Otis was a flame of fire! — with a promptitude of classical allusions, a depth of research, a rapid summary of historical events and dates, a profusion of legal authorities, a prophetic glance of his eye into futurity, and a torrent of impetuous eloquence, he hurried away every thing before him. American independence was then and there born; the seeds of patriots and heroes were then and there sown . . . . Every man of a crowded audience appeared to me to go away, as I did, ready to take arms against writs of assistance. Then and there was the first scene of the first act of opposition to the arbitrary claims of Great Britain. Then and there the child Independence was born. In fifteen years, namely in 1776, he grew up to manhood, and declared himself free" (Adams, *Works*, 10:247-48).

26. Tudor, *Life of James Otis*, p. 57; Adams, *Works*, 10:251.

27. Adams, *Works*, 10:283.

28. *Deane Papers*, 1:20.

29. John Trumbull, "An Elegy on the Times," *Poetical Works of John Trumbull* (Hartford: Goodrich, 1820), 2:212-13.

CHAPTER 2

1. Edward G. Parker, *The Golden Age of American Oratory* (Boston: Whittemore, Niles and Hall, 1857), pp. 274, 291.

2. *The Complete Works of Ralph Waldo Emerson,* Concord ed. (Boston: Houghton, Mifflin, 1870), 7:63.

3. Charles H. Peck, *The Jacksonian Epoch* (New York: Harper & Bros., 1899), p. 17.

4. *Memoirs of John Quincy Adams,* ed. Charles F. Adams (Philadelphia: Lippincott, 1874-1877), 7:138.

5. Edward Everett, *Orations and Speeches on Various Occasions* (Boston: Little, Brown, 1870-1872), 1:103-30.

6. Quoted in Daniel J. Boorstin, *The Americans: The National Experience* (New York: Random House, 1965), p. 383.

7. *The Works of Daniel Webster* (Boston: Little, Brown, 1872), 1:220-21.

8. Edward T. Channing, *Lectures on Rhetoric and Oratory* (Boston: Ticknor and Fields, 1856), p. 65

9. *Life, Letters, and Journals of George Ticknor* (Boston: James R. Osgood, 1876), 1:330.

10. Parker, *Golden Age of American Oratory,* pp. 84-85.

11. Emerson, *Works,* 10:315.

12. *Memoirs of John Quincy Adams,* 9:305.

13. Quoted in Frances Lea McCurdy, *Stump, Bar and Pulpit* (Columbia: University of Missouri Press, 1969), p. 24.

14. *The Americans: The National Experience* (New York: Random House, 1965), pp. 308, 311.

15. Everett, *Orations and Speeches,* 4:50-51, 77-78; Webster, *Works,* 1:78, 2:619.

16. Edward L. Pierce, *Memoir and Letters of Charles Sumner* (Boston: Roberts Brothers, 1893), 3:307, 301.

17. *The Works of Charles Sumner* (Boston: Lee and Shepard, 1870), 4:182-83.

18. Ibid., 4:276-77.

19. Pierce, *Memoir,* 3:456-57.

20. These and a number of other reactions to the speech are reproduced in Sumner, *Works,* 4:129-36, 249-50.

21. Pierce, *Memoir,* 3:559.

22. Peter Harvey, *Reminiscences and Anecdotes of Daniel Webster* (Boston: Little, Brown, 1877), p. 156.

23. Quoted in Webster, *Works,* 1:xcii-xcvii; March's full account is given in his *Reminiscences of Congress* (New York: Baker and Scribner, 1850), pp. 129-51.

24. Webster, *Works,* 1:xcix.

25. *North American Review* 31 (October 1830): 462; Webster, *Works,* 1:194.

26. *Memoirs of John Quincy Adams,* 10:274, 402-3, 405-6, 273.

27. Ibid., 9:118, 11:216.

28. *Congressional Globe,* 35th Cong., 1st sess., 27:603. Mr. Keitt was no stranger to violence; he had stood by to prevent interference when Brooks beat Sumner into unconsciousness.

29. In an article on "Rows in Congress," written many years later, Speaker Thomas B. Reed gives a dramatic account of this affair. According to Reed, Grow went to the Democratic side of the House to confer with a colleague and was ordered by Keitt to return to his own side. When he refused, Keitt seized him by the throat and called him "a black Republican puppy." Grow replied, "No negro-driver shall crack his whip over me," and struck his hand aside. Keitt seized him again, and Grow knocked him down. A general melee ensued in which "Barksdale of Mississippi rushed at Mr. Cavode, who uplifted a spittoon, but Barksdale's wig came off and

Cavode had not the heart to smite his unprotected skull." *Saturday Evening Post* 172 (December 9, 1899): 474-75.

30. *Annals of Congress,* 14th Cong., 1st sess., pp. 695-718.

31. *Congressional Debates,* 20th Cong., 1st sess., 4:1755.

32. "Speeches in Congress," *North American Review* 26 (January 1828): 159.

33. *North American Review* 52 (January 1841): 109-48.

34. Ibid., p. 117. In further illustration of his point, the author of this article relates an anecdote: "The Versatile General Alexander Smyth, of Virginia, — now legislator, now soldier, now commentator on the Apocalypse, — in the course of a two days' speech upon nothing in Committee of the Whole, was called to order by Arthur Livermore of New Hampshire, for irrelevancy of matter. 'Mr. Chairman,' said Smyth, 'I am not speaking for the member from New Hampshire, but to posterity.' 'The gentleman,' rejoined Livermore, 'is in a fair way, before he finishes, to have his audience before him'" (pp. 110-11).

35. Webster, *Works,* 5:358.

36. Henry Steele Commager, *American in Perspective* (New York: Random House, 1947), pp. 146-47.

37. *The Western World* (Philadelphia: Lea and Blanchard, 1849), 1:185-87.

38. 52 (January 1841): 113-14.

39. *The Complete Works of Charles Dickens* (New York: Harper & Bros., n.d.), 22:330.

40. "Congressional Eloquence," *North American Review* 52 (January 1841): 115.

41. *The Western World,* 1:184.

42. *Democracy in America* (New York: Colonial Press, [1900]), 2:94-95.

43. *Memoirs of John Quincy Adams,* 10:352-53, 355-56.

44. Nathan Sargent, *Public Men and Events* (Philadelphia: Lippincott, 1875), 2:105.

45. *Congressional Globe,* 26 Cong., 1st sess., 8 Appendix, p. 814.

46. Quoted in Robert G. Gunderson, *The Log-Cabin Campaign* (Lexington: University of Kentucky Press, 1957), p. 107. I have drawn freely upon this sprightly account of the campaign of 1840. See also Arthur M. Schlesinger, Jr., *The Age of Jackson* (Boston: Little, Brown, 1946), Chapt. 23.

47. Sargent, *Public Men and Events,* 2:105, 108.

48. Quoted in Gunderson, *The Log-Cabin Campaign,* p. 218.

49. John G. Nicolay and John Hay, eds., *Complete Works of Abraham Lincoln* (New York: F. D. Tandy, [1905]), 1:137-38.

50. *Perley's Reminiscences* (Philadelphia: Hubbard Bros., 1886), 1:209.

51. Horace White in *The Lincoln Reader,* ed. Paul M. Angle (New Brunswick, N. J.: Rutgers University Press, 1947), p. 233; Paul M. Angle, *Created Equal?* (Chicago: University of Chicago Press, 1958), p. 284.

52. For an attack on "the myth of the southern orator," see Waldo Braden, *Oratory in the Old South, 1828-1860* (Baton Rouge: Louisiana State University Press, 1970); see also Braden's "The Emergence of the Concept of Southern Oratory," *Southern Speech Journal* 26 (Spring 1961): 173-83, and *The Lower South in American History* (New York: Macmillan, 1902), p. 125.

53. Edward W. Emerson, *Emerson in Concord* (Boston: Houghton, Mifflin, 1889), pp. 15-16.

54. This explanation is suggested, but not developed, in Francis P. Gaines, *Southern Oratory: A Study in Idealism* (University: University of Alabama Press, 1946), Preface.

55. *The Mind of the South* (New York: Alfred A. Knopf, 1941), p. 52; Brown, *The Lower South in American History*, pp. 127-28.

56. Clement Eaton, *The Mind of the Old South* (Baton Rouge: Louisiana State University Press, 1964), pp. 210-11.

57. *The Memories of Fifty Years* (Philadelphia: Claxton, Remsen & Haffelfinger, 1870), pp. 353-54.

58. A. G. Beach, "An Example of Political Oratory in 1855," *Ohio Archaeological and Historical Quarterly* 39 (October 1930): 673-82.

59. Ibid., p. 678.

60. Braden, *Oratory in the Old South*, pp. 5, 21; *The Mind of the South*, p. 79.

61. Parker, *Golden Age of American Oratory*, p. 83; *North American Review* 75 (October 1852): 338; 23 (October 1826): 453; *Characteristics of Literature*, 2d ser. (Philadelphia: Lindsay and Blakiston, 1851), pp. 244-45.

62. Pierce, *Memoir*, 4:370; *Recollections of Eminent Men* (Boston: Houghton, Mifflin, 1893), p. 242.

63. *North American Review* 71 (October 1850): 446.

64. "A power which has dotted over the surface of the whole globe with her possessions and military posts; whose morning drum-beat, following the sun, and keeping company with the hours, circles the earth with one continuous and unbroken strain of the martial airs of England." "The Presidential Protest," in *Works*, 4:110; *North American Review* 75 (July 1852): 101.

65. *Characteristics of Literature*, p. 254.

66. Allan Nevins, ed., *The Diary of Philip Hone, 1828-1851* (New York: Dodd, Mead, 1936), p. 525.

67. *Orators of the American Revolution* (New York: Baker & Scribner, 1848), p. 91.

68. *Golden Age of American Oratory*, pp. 118-21.

CHAPTER 3

1. Chauncey M. Depew, *My Memories of Eighty Years* (New York: Chas. Scribner's Sons, 1924), p. 15.

2. "Educated Men in Centennial Politics," *Nation* 23 (July 6, 1876): 5-6; *Theodore Roosevelt: An Autobiography* (New York: Macmillan, 1919), p. 56.

3. "Rhetorical Training," *Nation* 20 (March 4, 1875): 145.

4. "The Gift of the Gab," *Nation* 3 (July 26, 1866): 75.

5. *Discourse on Edward Everett* (Boston: Rand & Avery, 1865), p. 10; "The President on the Stump," *North American Review* 102 (April 1866): 533; "The Eloquence of Congress: Historical Notes," *Records of the Columbia Historical Society* 9:177.

6. "Less favorable conditions for oratory cannot be imagined," observed James Bryce. Woodrow Wilson, in his *Congressional Government* (1885), also commented on the difficulty of speaking amidst the "disorderly noises that buzz and rattle" through the vast House of Representatives chamber.

7. *The American Commonwealth,* 3rd ed. (New York: Macmillan, 1899), 2: 799-807.

8. Mayo W. Hazeltine, ed., *Orations* (New York: P. F. Collier, 1902), 21:9127-46.

9. "Great Speeches," *Nation* 44 (April 14, 1887): 311; "The Nominating System," *Unforeseen Tendencies of Democracy* (Boston: Houghton, Mifflin, 1898).

10. *Masks in a Pageant* (New York: Macmillan, 1928), pp. 63-75.

11. One historian of public address has declared that professional lecturing is to public speaking as commercial art is to painting. Though some illustrators may approach greatness, and some painters are incompetent, "the two groups remain in separate spheres." Robert T. Oliver, *History of Public Speaking in America* (Boston: Allyn & Bacon, 1965), p. 434.

12. "The Popular Lecture," *Atlantic Monthly* 15 (March 1865): 362.

13. "The Celebration," *Nation* 23 (July 13, 1876): 20-21.

14. He was later to enjoy the best of both worlds, serving for twelve years as United States Senator from the state of New York while serving as chairman of the Board of Directors of the New York Railroad.

15. *The Library of Oratory* (New York: A. W. Fowle, 1902), 12:322-23.

16. *North American Review* 71 (October 1850): 455-56.

17. *My Memories of Eighty Years,* p. 319; *Literary Digest* 48 (June 17, 1914): 133.

18. Epitaph quoted in obituary notice, *Nation* 126 (April 18, 1928): 421; *Cosmopolitan* 40 (March 1906): 487-502; *My Memories of Eighty Years,* pp. 396-97.

19. "Great Speeches," *Nation* 44 (April 14, 1887): 311.

20. George William Curtis, *Orations and Addresses* (New York: Harper, 1894), 1:243.

21. *Southern Oratory: A Study in Idealism* (University: University of Alabama Press, 1946), p. 70 n.

CHAPTER 4

1. In the following discussion I have drawn illustrations from my "Principal Themes of Nineteenth-Century Critics of Oratory," *Speech Monographs* 19 (March 1952): 18-26.

2. *The Works of Thomas Carlyle*, Edinburgh Ed., 30 vols. (New York: Chas. Scribner's Sons, 1903-1904), 20:172-213.

3. Ibid., pp. 175-76, 212-13.

4. *The Complete Writings of Nathaniel Hawthorne*, Old Manse Ed., (Boston: Houghton-Miffin, [1870]), 22:160; *Autumn Leaves* (New York: Hurd and Houghton, 1865), pp. 259, 168-69.

5. *Atlantic Monthly* 6 (December 1860): 740-45.

6. For a detailed treatment of this subject see my "Nineteenth-Century Burlesque of Oratory," *American Quarterly* 20 (Winter 1968): 726-43. *Bill Nye's Sparks* (New York: Hurst & Co., [1901]), p. 15; *Fables in Slang* (Chicago: H. S. Stone, [1899]), pp. 115-21.

7. R. H. Newell, *The Orpheus C. Kerr Papers* (New York: G. W. Carleton & Co., 1871), pp. 29-30.

8. Finley P. Dunne, "Oratory," in *Dissertations by Mr. Dooley* (New York: Harper and Bros., 1906), pp. 22-23.

9. "Memories of a Hundred Years," *Outlook* 71 (June 7, 1902): 405; "Is Congressional Oratory a Lost Art?" *Century* 81 (December 1910): 307.

10. *North American Review* 71 (October 1850): 446; "Ancient and Modern Eloquence," *Littell's Living Age* 29 (May 3, 1851): 193-208; *Lectures Read to the Seniors in Harvard College* (Boston: Ticknor & Fields, 1856), p. 12.

11. Dorsey Gardner, "Oratory and Journalism," 114 (January 1872): 86-87.

12. "Some Notes on Political Oratory," *Bookman* 4 (December 1896): 332.

13. *Colliers'* 32 (January 2, 1904): 4; Theodore P. Greene, *America's Heroes* (New York: Oxford University Press, 1970), pp. 275-76.

14. *The American Commonwealth* (New York: Macmillan, 1923), 2:75.

15. "Congress Again Debating," *Nation* 74 (April 24, 1902): 320-21.

16. *Twenty Years of the Republic, 1885-1905* (New York: Dodd, Mead & Co., 1929), p. 500.

17. *The American Political Tradition* (New York: Alfred A. Knopf, 1949), p. 183.

18. Quoted in Henry F. Pringle, *Theodore Roosevelt* (New York: Harcourt, Brace & Co., 1931), p. 520.

19. R. N. Matson, "The 'Speak-Out' Age," *New England Magazine* 33 (September 1905): 87-96.

20. *Nation* 47 (August 30, 1888): 162-63.

21. *New York Tribune*, November 4, 1888.

22. John D. Champlin, ed., *Orations, Addresses, and Speeches of Chauncey M. Depew*, 8 vols. (New York: Privately Printed, 1910), 2:306-11. Italics mine.

23. See, especially, Forrest Crissey, "Spellbinders and Straw Votes," *Reader* 4 (November 1904): 635-42; C. F. Bacon, "Itinerant Speechmaking in the Last Campaign," *Arena* 25 (April 1901): 410-18; L. B. Little, "Campaign Orators," *Muncey's Magazine* 24 (November 1900): 281-85; William D. Foulke, "The Spellbinders," *Forum* 30 (February 1901): 658-72; Curtis Guild, Jr., "The Spellbinder," *Scribner's Magazine* 32 (November 1902): 561-75.

24. W. D. Foulke, "Campaigning in the West," *North American Review* 156 (January 1893): 126; James Bryce, *The American Commonwealth*, 2 vols. Rev. Ed. (New York: Macmillan, 1927), 2:866.

25. C. F. Bacon, "Itinerant Speechmaking in the Last Campaign," p. 418.

26. Lorenzo Sears, *The History of Oratory* (Chicago: Scott, Foresman & Co., 1896); Henry Hardwicke, *The History of Oratory and Orators* (New York: G. P. Putnam's Sons, 1896). Of the two histories, Sears's is unquestionably the better, though neither is of much critical significance.

27. Curtis Guild, Jr., "The Spellbinder," p. 562; "Oratory of the Stump," in *Modern Eloquence,* ed. Thomas B. Reed (Philadelphia: John D. Morris & Co., [1900]), 10:xxi-xxiii, xxviii.

CHAPTER 5

1. Albert E. Winship, "Comparing the Oratory of Twenty Years Ago with the Public Speaking of Today," *Emerson Quarterly* 3 (June 1923): 4.

2. "The Disappearing Orator," *Commonweal* 9 (March 13, 1929): 531; "Winged and Unwinged Words," in *Essays* (New York: Harcourt, Brace, 1927), p. 115.

3. "Which Knew Not Joseph," in *Modern Speeches*, ed. Homer D. Lindgren (New York: Crofts, 1926), pp. 406-12.

4. *Modern Eloquence,* ed. Ashley H. Thorndike, 12 vols. (New York: Modern Eloquence Corp., 1923).

5. See, for example, Homer D. Lindgren, ed., *Modern Speeches* (New York: Crofts, 1926); Basil G. Byron and Frederic R. Coudert, eds., *America Speaks* (New York: Modern Eloquence Corp., 1928); and William P. Sanford and Willard H. Yeager, eds., *Business Speeches by Business Men* (New York: McGraw Hill, 1930). The editors of one anthology claim to have examined 2,000 business speeches, from which they selected seventy-five.

6. *Miscellaneous Addresses* (Cambridge: Harvard University Press, 1917), pp. 249-58.

7. Sanford and Yeager, *Business Speeches by Business Men,* pp. 3, 165.

8. G. R. Collins, "Public Speaking in Colleges of Business Administration and United YMCA Schools," *Quarterly Journal of Speech Education* 10 (November 1924): 374-79.

9. *Public Speaking and Influencing Men in Business* (New York: Association Press, 1936), pp. ix-x.

10. Freeland Hall, "Talking One's Way," *Saturday Evening Post* 200 (November 19, 1927): 151; Charles E. Carpenter, "What You in the Audience Have Taught Me about Yourselves," *American Magazine* 96 (September 1923): 69.

11. *American Magazine* 96 (October 1923): 54-55; H. J. Fenton, "After-Dinner Speaking," *Educational Review* 69 (May 1925): 249-52.

12. Roe Fulkerson, "Dollar Chasing," in *Modern Speeches,* ed. Homer D. Lindgren, pp. 365-66.

13. "The Future Lecture Deluge," *Literary Digest* 61 (May 31, 1919): 33-34.

14. Gregory Mason, "Quenching America's Mental Thirst," *Scribner's* 75 (May 1924): 557.

15. "The Parliament of the People," *Century* 98 (July 1919): 401-16.

16. Ibid, p. 416.

17. "The Presidents We Deserve," *Harper's Monthly Magazine* 149 (November 1924): 756; *Our Business Civilization* (New York: A. and C. Boni, 1929), p. 16.

18. Montaville Flowers, "What Young America Is Thinking," *World's Work* 54 (August 1927): 446; Robert S. Lynd and Helen Lynd, *Middletown* (New York: Harcourt, Brace, 1929), p. 419.

19. Elmer Murphy, "The Decline of Oratory," *Bookman* 57 (April 1923): 129-32.

20. *Emerson Quarterly* 3 (February 1923): 10; *Outlook* 136 (March 19, 1924): 465-67; "The Spellbinders and the Radio," *Saturday Evening Post* 197 (August 23, 1924): 20.

21. H. I. Phillips, "We Have with Us Tonight —," *American Magazine* 101 (June 1926): 58-59.

22. *Middletown,* p. 271.

23. *Up to Now* (New York: Viking Press, 1929), pp. 391-92.

24. "Electioneering, Old and New," *Saturday Evening Post* 203 (August 30, 1930): 66; *Saturday Evening Post* 202 (May 24, 1930): 3-5.

25. *A Puritan in Babylon* (New York: Macmillan, 1938), p. 315 n.

26. W. P. Sandford, review of *Foundations of the Republic, Quarterly Journal of Speech Education,* 13 (April 1927): 199.

27. Donald Day, *Will Rogers* (New York: David McKay, 1962). This book, from which these quotations are taken, contains many examples of Rogers's social criticism.

28. *American Mercury* 5 (May 1925): 95; *A Carnival of Buncombe* (Baltimore: Johns Hopkins Press, 1956), pp. 38-39.

29. *Babbitt* (New York: Harcourt, Brace, 1922), pp. 180-88.

30. P. W. Wilson, "The Great God Gab," *North American Review* 229 (March 1930): 274; *The Babbitt Warren* (New York: Harper and Bros., 1927), pp. 101-4, 106.

31. *Men Who Are Making America* (New York: B. C. Forbes Pub. Co., 1922), p. x.

32. "Why College Oratory?" *Emerson Quarterly* 10 (November 1929): 3.

33. Joseph E. Connor, "Trimming the Sails of Oratory to the New Wind," *Emerson Quarterly* 9 (November 1928): 17-18.
34. "The Image of Salesmanship in Public Speaking," *Quarterly Journal of Speech* 16 (April 1930): 164-71.
35. *History of American Oratory* (Indianapolis: Bobbs- Merrill, 1928).

CHAPTER 6

1. Rexford G. Tugwell, *The Democratic Roosevelt* (Garden City, N.Y.: Doubleday, 1957), p. 273.
2. James A. Farley, *Behind the Ballots* (New York: Harcourt, Brace, 1938), pp. 163-64.
3. Raymond Moley, *After Seven Years* (New York: Harper & Bros., 1939), p. 62.
4. *Interpretations: 1933-1935* (New York: Macmillan, 1936), p. 249.
5. Samuel I. Rosenman, *Working with Roosevelt* (New York: Harper & Bros., 1952), and Robert E. Sherwood, *Roosevelt and Hopkins* (New York: Harper & Bros., 1948).
6. *Roosevelt and Hopkins*, pp. 214-19.
7. Frances Perkins, *The Roosevelt I Knew* (New York: Viking Press, 1946), p. 72.
8. *Experiment in Autobiography* (New York: Macmillan, 1934), p. 683.
9. Sherwood, *Roosevelt and Hopkins*, pp. 228, 503.
10. For these and other facts concerning the White House mail, see Ira R. T. Smith, *Dear Mr. President* (New York: Julian Messner, 1949), and Louis M. Howe, "The President's Mail Bag," *American Magazine* 117 (June 1934): 22-23, 118-20.
11. Leila Sussmann, *Dear FDR: A Study of Political Letter-Writing* (Totowa, N.J.: Bedminster Press, 1963), pp. 107-17.
12. December 17, 1933, Sect. 4, p. 5.
13. It is interesting to speculate upon the possible effect on the League of Nations debate in the Senate if Wilson had been able to address the whole nation by radio rather than breaking his health and his spirit in an arduous speaking tour through which he reached personally only a few thousand listeners.
14. Orrin E. Dunlap, Jr., "Talking to the People," *New York Times,* March 19, 1933, Sect. 9, p. 8.
15. Ibid.
16. Quoted by Leila A. Sussmann, "FDR and the White House Mail," *Public Opinion Quarterly* 20 (Spring 1956): 16.
17. Arthur M. Schlesinger, Jr., *The Coming of the New Deal* (Boston: Houghton Mifflin, 1959), p. 573.
18. H. G. Wells, *The New America: The New World* (New York: Macmillan, 1935), pp. 19-26.
19. *Vital Speeches* 1 (March 11, 1935): 354-60.
20. *Vital Speeches* 1 (March 25, 1935): 391-97.
21. Ibid., pp. 386-91.

22. "Is the New Deal Socialism?" *New York Times,* February 3, 1936, p. 6.

23. *Behind the Ballots,* p. 316.

24. October 24, 1936, p. 13.

25. On at least one occasion, however, the *New York Times* seemed to give grudging acknowledgment that a speech might be both sensible and well delivered. After Roosevelt's Chicago Speech of October 14, that paper observed editorially, "His address was sagacious in conception and most telling in delivery." It quelled old apprehensions and roused fresh hopes. "A political speech which does that must be reckoned a great success."

26. *New York Times,* August 22, 1938, p. 3. In the 1940 campaign, after Wendell Willkie had roared himself hoarse, a friend urged lessons in voice placement. Willkie contemptuously dismissed the suggestion; the public had become distrustful of a smooth voice. Roosevelt, who continued to address the public in his smooth voice, won a third term by five million votes.

27. Harry A. Overstreet and Bonaro W. Overstreet, *Town Meeting Comes to Town* (New York: Harper & Bros., 1938), p. 3.

28. *Christian Science Monitor,* August 5, 1936, Magazine Section, p. 6.

29. Quoted by Marquis W. Childs, *They Hate Roosevelt* (New York: Harper & Bros., 1936), p. 24.

30. Perkins, *The Roosevelt I Knew,* p. 385.

31. *Interpretations: 1933-1935,* p. 305.

32. Jay Franklin, *What This Country Needs* (New York: Covici, Friede, 1931), pp. 29-30, 36.

33. February 2, 1936, 4:8.

CHAPTER 7

1. Elmo Roper and Walter Davenport, "Can the G.O.P. Win?" *Collier's* 114 (July 1, 1944): 68; "They Want to Be Good Citizens," *National Municipal Review* 36 (January 1947): 29.

2. "How Nixon Took Atlanta," *Seattle Post Intelligencer,* October 18, 1972.

3. *Newsweek,* 88 (November 8, 1976): 19.

4. "Raise the Sights," *Newsweek* 58 (July 31, 1961): 84; *New York Times Magazine* (February 25, 1962), p. 71.

5. Charles W. Morton, " 'I Am a Vegetarian' (cheers),"*Atlantic* 214 (December 1964): 118; *Saturday Evening Post* 238 (March 27, 1965): 12-14.

6. Joe McGinniss, *The Selling of the President 1968* (New York: Trident Press, 1969), pp. 193-94.

7. James Reston, *New York Times,* November 1, 1970, Sect. 4, p. 14; *Representative American Speeches: 1970-1971,* ed. Waldo W. Braden (New York: H. W. Wilson Co., 1971), p. 4; Robert Chandler, *Public Opinion* (New York: Bowker, 1972), p. 146.

8. *Christian Science Monitor,* November 1, 1972; "Talk of the Town," *New Yorker* 47 (January 15, 1972): 19; Thomas Griffith, "The Press as Minefield," *Time* 108 (November 15, 1976): 87; *U.S. News* 81 (November 1, 1976): 16-17.

9. "In Defense of Congress," *American Mercury* 55 (November 1942): 531; Neil MacNeil, *Forge of Democracy: The House of Representatives* (New York: David McKay Co., 1963), pp. 324-29.

10. *The People Machine* (New York: Harper & Row, [1968]), p. xii.

11. Gene Wyckoff, *The Image Candidates: American Politics in the Age of Television* (New York: Macmillan, [1968]), p. 217.

12. Herbert A. Seltz and Richard D. Yoakam, "Production Diary of the Debates," in *The Great Debates,* ed. Sidney Kraus (Bloomington: Indiana University Press, [1962]), p. 77. I have drawn upon this informative account, as well as from other essays in this book. Douglas Cater, "Notes from Backstage," in Kraus, *The Great Debates,* p. 129.

13. Earl Mazo, et al., *The Great Debates* (Santa Barbara: Center for the Study of Democratic Institutions, [1962]), p. 3.

14. "Personalities vs. Issues," in Kraus, *The Great Debates,* p. 151.

15. John F. Genung, *The Practical Elements of Rhetoric* (Boston: Ginn & Co., 1891), pp. 473-74.

16. Lewis W. Wolfson, "The Media Masters," *Washington Post,* February 20, 1972.

17. In preparing his Inaugural Address, John Kennedy had asked his aide Theodore Sorenson to examine all former inaugurals. He seems also to have examined this speech of Stevenson's (see p. 227, above).

EPILOGUE

1. "Government by Debate," *Papers of Woodrow Wilson,* ed. Arthur S. Link (Princeton: Princeton University Press, 1967), 2:270. Italics mine.

INDEX